Russia's Life-Saver

Russia's Life-Saver

Lend-Lease Aid to the U.S.S.R. in World War II

Albert L. Weeks

LEXINGTON BOOKS
Lanham • Boulder • New York • Toronto • Plymouth, UK

LEXINGTON BOOKS

A division of Rowman & Littlefield Publishers, Inc.
A wholly owned subsidiary of The Rowman & Littlefield Publishing Group, Inc.
4501 Forbes Boulevard, Suite 200, Lanham, Maryland 20706
http://www.lexingtonbooks.com

Estover Road
Plymouth PL6 7PY
United Kingdom

Copyright © 2004 by Lexington Books
First paperback edition 2010

All rights reserved. No part of this publication may be reproduced, stored in a retrieval system, or transmitted in any form or by any means, electronic, mechanical, photocopying, recording, or otherwise, without the prior permission of the publisher.

British Library Cataloguing in Publication Information Available

Library of Congress Cataloging-in-Publication Data

Weeks, Albert Loren, 1923–
  Russia's life-saver : lend-lease aid to the U.S.S.R. in World War II / Albert L. Weeks.
    p. cm.
  1. Lend-lease operations (1941–1945) 2. World War, 1939–1945—Equipment and supplies. 3. United States—Foreign relations—Soviet Union. 4. Soviet Union—Foreign relations—United States. 5. United States—Military relations—Soviet Union. 6. Soviet Union—Military relations—United States. I. Title.
D753.2.R9W44 2004
940.53'2273—dc22

2003020274

978-0-7391-0736-2 (cloth alk. paper)
978-0-7391-4563-0 (pbk. alk. paper)
978-0-7391-6054-1 (electronic)

Printed in the United States of America

∞™ The paper used in this publication meets the minimum requirements of American National Standard for Information Sciences—Permanence of Paper for Printed Library Materials, ANSI/NISO Z39.48-1992.

Contents

Preface		ix
1	Introduction	1
	Assistance to Communist U.S.S.R.	4
	Role of Soviet "Agents of Influence"	7
	Today's Assessments	7
2	The "Arsenal of Democracy"	11
	America Edges toward War	12
	The American Factor	14
	Stalin Zigzags	15
	Two-Pronged Approach	18
	The "American Colossus"	20
	The Birth of Lend-Lease	22
	Lend-Lease Underway	25
	Soviet Propaganda on Lend-Lease	28
3	Stalin and America	31
	Dealing with the Man in Charge, Stalin	32
	Stalin's Weapon of Diplomacy	38
	Stalin and FDR	39
	Spies and Agents of Influence	41
	Armand Hammer's Role	49
4	Historical Roots of Lend-Lease—I	52
	Traditional Russian-American Ties	54
	Earliest Phase of Friendship	55

	Russia in the American Northwest	58
	Russia and the American Civil War	59
	"Seward's Folly"	63
5	Historical Roots of Lend-Lease—II	65
	Russian-American Economic Ties	65
	Earliest Period of U.S. Technological Assistance	68
	Assistance in the Nineteenth and Twentieth Centuries	71
	Railroad Building	72
	Agricultural Machinery	74
	U.S. Railroad Commission in Russia, 1917	76
	Miscellaneous Technological Assistance	78
	U.S. Technological Aid during the Soviet Period	80
6	Western-Soviet Relations before "Barbarossa"	86
	Ambivalence toward Germany	87
	America at a Distance	89
	Perishable Nazi-Soviet Alliance	90
	Warming toward the U.S.?	92
	New Tensions with Germany	93
	Shift toward the West	94
	Preinvasion Détente Trend	96
	"Ignoring" Warnings of Attack	98
	The Welles-Umansky Talks	99
	Demarche	103
7	The "Strange Alliance" Is Born	107
	The Great Patriotic War Begins	108
	Onwards to Aid	110
	The First U.S.-Soviet Lend-Lease Talks	111
	Planning the Main Routes	112
	"The Russians Are Coming"	114
	Lend-Lease Details	115
	Trusting and Verifying	121
	Vital Food Aid	122
	Spasibo . . . But . . .	124
8	Summation: Will the Debt Be Repaid?	128
	Silver Bullion to Stalin	129
	Settling the Debt Issue	133
	The "Gratitude Factor"	135
	APPENDIX Mutual Aid Agreement between the United States and the Union of Soviet Socialist Republics: June 11, 1942	137

TABLES

Table I Lend-Lease Shipments to the Soviet Union
by Time Period, etc.   141

Table II Aircraft Deliveries to the Soviet Union (by Route) 144

Table III Aircraft Deliveries to the Soviet Union
(by Type and Route)   145

Table IV Vehicles Delivered to the Soviet Union
under the Lend-Lease Program   146

Table V Random Exports to the Soviet Union
under the Lend-Lease Program   147

Table VI Distribution of Tonnage by Ship Registry
(Vessels Involved in the Transfer of Lend-Lease to the
Soviet Union)   152

Table VII Cargo Shipped from the Western Hemisphere
to the Soviet Union   152

Bibliography   153

Index   165

About the Author   175

Preface

The present study of Lend-Lease was inspired by significant new research, findings, and analysis published in Russia by native historians. During the last two years these histories about the wartime aid have turned up new evidence from previously closed Russian archives.

On the successive sixtieth anniversaries of various phases of this crucial aid to the U.S.S.R. that began in late 1941 and continued through 1945, it is an appropriate time to update the most comprehensive study of Lend-Lease to Soviet Russia written over thirty years ago by an American scholar working on the topic at the time of Brezhnev's tightly closed regime. A second remaining major study on Lend-Lease is over fifteen years old. Like the first, it is lacking in new data.[1]

Two courageous, assiduous Russian historians, Boris V. Sokolov and Alla Paperno, joined by a few other, younger native scholars, have broken through what they call the enforced silence surrounding the true extent and effect of the assistance given the Soviets by the estimated $12.5 billion worth of U.S. Lend-Lease during World War II. Their book-length works were published in the late 1990s and in 2001.[2] Articles by them continue to appear in Russian scholarly journals. One such piece of research, by Russian historian Aleksandr Vislykh appeared in the November 12, 2001 edition of the Russian publication, *Independent Military Observer* (*Nezavisimoye voyennoye obozreniye*), bearing the title "Lifesaver Lend-Lease: It Is Not Necessary to Minimize Its Importance in Our Victory in the Great Patriotic War" ("*Spasitel'nii Lend-Liz Ne nado preumenshivat' ego zacheniye v nashei pobede v Velikoi Otechestvennoi Voine, in Nezavisimoye obozreniy*" [*Independent Observer*]).

The several new Russian historians reveal, for instance, that the "Soviet Eisenhower," Marshal Georgi K. Zhukov, himself stressed the importance of this aid in the Russian victory over Wehrmacht. In an interview with the popular wartime correspondent and novelist Konstantin Simonov in 1963, Zhukov frankly and confidentially lamented the fact that Soviet propaganda had systematically demeaned the importance of this American aid to the Soviet war effort. He noted that the rationale for this Soviet propaganda line was to counter what the Soviet authorities considered to be—unwarrantedly—a detraction from the heroism of Soviet soldiers and civilians in the war.

Our study will update the story of Lend-Lease based on new, post-1995 information. Tables of corrected statistics by types of aid are reproduced in the main text and in the tables in the appendices. Such data should be helpful to those readers who are interested in the fullest available panoply of facts about this historic four-year assistance, data in some cases that have never before been readily available to them.

NOTES

1. Robert Huhn Jones, *The Roads to Russia: United States Lend-Lease to the Soviet Union*, Norman, University of Oklahoma Press, 1969; Mark Harrison, *Soviet Planning in Peace and War 1938–1945*, Cambridge, Cambridge University Press, 1985. Both books are out of print.

2. A. Paperno, *Lend-Liz Tikhii Okean* (Lend-Lease the Pacific Ocean), Moscow, Terra, 1998; Boris V. Sokolov, *Tainy Vtoroi Mirovoi* (Secrets of the Second World War), Moscow, Veche, 2001.

1

Introduction

"How to get the United States involved in the war against Germany in Western Europe, and in the Western Pacific against Japan, and how to quickly generate sympathy for the communist state inside the halls of capitalism, the United States. *The task is to influence.*"

—Peter B. Niblo, former U.S. intelligence officer, in *Influence The Soviet "Task" Leading to Pearl Harbor, the Iron Curtain, and the Cold War,* Elderberry Press, 2002

* * *

"When we entered the war, we were still a backward country in the industrial sense as compared to Germany . . . Today [in 1963] some say the Allies really didn't help us . . . But, listen, one cannot deny that the Americans shipped over to us materièl without which we could not have equipped our armies held in reserve or been able to continue the war . . . We did not have enough munitions, [and] how would we have been able to turn out all those tanks without the rolled steel sent to us by the Americans? To believe what they say [in the U.S.S.R.] today, you'd think we had all this in abundance!"

—Marshal G. K. Zhukov[1]

In fall 2001, historic Lend-Lease got a new lease on life in Alaska. That's the place where it all started back in 1941. In November 2001, sixty years to the month after the event, a local organization in Fairbanks, known as the Alaska-Siberia Lend-Lease Program (ASLLP), thought it was time to commemorate this important historical event.

In that critical year of 1941, the Northern Pacific route leading from Alaska to Vladivostok, Russia—a sea lane then known as Alsib—was chosen as one of four main routes to be used for shipping millions of tons of invaluable Lend-Lease aid in arms and other supplies to Russia. Beginning modestly late that year, then in earnest by early 1942 and lasting through 1945, the Alsib North Pacific route was the first of the four sea lanes ('SLOCs') so used. During World War II it became the one that carried twice the amount of tonnage in Lend-Lease shipments reaching the Soviet Union than by any other route. Thus, this far exceeded the tonnage carried via that second most important, yet more dangerous and famous SLOC—the Nazi sub–infested North Atlantic route terminating at Murmansk, Russia.

To commemorate the launching of the first Lend-Lease shipments out of Fairbanks, Alaska, in 1941, the state capital of Juneau became the site of an historic meeting that was attended on November 19, 2001, by the Russian Ambassador to Washington, Yuri Ushakov, and by the director of ASLLP, Alexander Dolitsky, plus U.S. government and Alaska officials.

On April 4, 2002, Russian President Vladimir V. Putin thanked Alaskan officials for the commemorative Lend-Lease medal that had been sent to him in Moscow. In letters to the Governor of Alaska Tony Knowles and to ASLLP, Russian President Putin wrote: "I value your personal contribution to the development of Russian-American relations . . . The Lend-Lease Program . . . noticeably contributed to our common victory in World War II [and] is a good example of [Russian-American] interaction."

Putin added that the Lend-Lease tradition of such interaction has been continued in the form of collaboration between the United States and the R.F. in fighting terrorism following the 9/11 attacks in America.

It is chilling to think that Lend-Lease aid might not have materialized in mid-1941 if the Japanese attack on Pearl Harbor on December 7 had occurred earlier than it did. For by that date, America itself was thrown into war—both in the Far East and Europe. Hitler had declared war on the United States December 8. America's means of defense were being severely challenged in two huge theaters of operations. By that critical time, the United States needed all the weapons it had. The Japanese enemy had all but decimated the U.S. Navy's Pacific Fleet (without, fortunately, destroying its aircraft carriers). The Empire of Japan had set about capturing one Pacific island outpost after another.

Lest it be forgotten, the United States had sharply scaled back defense expenditures, weapons production, and military readiness in the interwar period after 1918. A combination of American isolationism and traditional neglect of military defense in peacetime had led to a dangerous vulnerability in the external security of the United States. In 1940–1941, "military preparedness," although bandied about, was an almost meaningless phrase as applied to this country in any realistic way.

Yet, thankfully, rather robust defense-related research and development had continued after World War I. By the 1930s significant strides were made in air force and naval development. Robert Goddard was even testing rockets. Still, the nation remained critically pinched as combat began on a big scale for the United States after Pearl Harbor.

Nevertheless, Lend-Lease aid to embattled Russia was signed, sealed, and delivered over five months before Pearl Harbor. Preparing this assistance had proceeded apace, as agreed in Moscow and Washington, D.C., as far back as July 1941—i.e., just days after the German invasion of June 22nd.

As it turned out, a stunning acceleration of U.S. arms production at the end of 1941 and into 1942 made it possible for America not only able to meet its own defense needs in the war against the Axis. It was also able punctually and fully to make good, with very few exceptions, on its Lend-Lease shipments to Russia as well as to England during all four wartime years.

Here is some background on Lend-Lease as a whole. The first Canadian assistance to the Mother Country began on September 16, 1939, just two weeks after World War I started. The first convoy departed Halifax, Nova Scotia, for the United Kingdom. The first loss to German submarines did not occur until February 14, 1940. The availability of French bases after the fall of French greatly increased German submarine warfare capabilities, and this advantage, coupled with Admiral Karl Doenitz's "wolf-pack" technique, caused losses to mount steadily. Relieved in part by the transfer of destroyers to Britain in 1940, by the end of that year some 70 percent of the British destroyer fleet was laid up for repairs.

By March 1941 the U.S. Navy was able to report to President Roosevelt that it would soon be capable of convoying to merchant shipping and Lend-Lease cargoes across the North Atlantic. The next major U.S. step to aid the British was taken on April 11, 1941 when President Roosevelt notified Prime Minister Churchill that the neutrality patrol was to be extended to 26 deg. W. longitude. He proposed notfying British convoys so that warnings of enemy submarines in the area might be transmitted to them.

The Battle of the Atlantic was well underway. Despite these and other steps taken by the United States, however, British losses continued to mount. In May a convoy lost nine ships well within the patrolled zone. In consequence of such losses, which reached 590,000 tons in June 1941 alone, Great Britain decided to provide convoy escort for the full length of the crossing. The British Admiralty on 23 May asked Canada to assume the responsibility for protecting convoys in the western zone and to establish the base for its escort force at St. John's in Newfoundland from there to a meeting point south of Iceland, where British convoys took over.

The first transatlantic convoy to be escorted by the U.S. Navy sailed from Halifax on September 16, 1941. It was accompanied by a Royal Canadian Navy escort group acting under overall U.S. direction. The next day, escort of the convoy was taken over by a U.S. Navy group at the "Westomp" (for "Western Ocean Meeting Place"), a designated point south of Argentina. The fifty merchant ships, which sailed under a variety of flags and types of ships from a 1,500-ton cargo ship to the 17,000-ton *Empress of Asia,* were met at the "Momp" ("Mid-Ocean Meeting Place") by a British escort group. Here part of the convoy split off and steamed for Iceland under U.S. escort. The rest proceeded to the United Kingdom under Royal Navy escort. On June 6, 1941, FDR seized eighty foreign merchant ships in U.S. ports to serve in Lend-Lease convoys. By now, on both the East and West Coasts industrialist Henry Kaiser was turning out Liberty Ships like sausages, or rather like the postwar prefab houses.

By the time the Lend-Lease convoys were steaming to Murmansk, the Germans had developed torpedoes, wire-guided bombs, and similar munitions that allowed the He-111 and Do-17 to be effective against naval targets. Actually these munitions were developed in large part in response to the convoys—technology that simply did not exist in 1940.

From 1941 to early 1942, convoys in the North Atlantic suffered a number of tragic losses from the "wolf packs." However, new Allied equipment, including airborne radar, soon saved the convoys from the kinds of losses in tonnage endured in the earlier years. Thus, while the shipments to Britain had seen some major losses, by the time the lifeline to Murmansk, U.S.S.R., was operating, such losses became less frequent. That part of the Battle of the Atlantic had been won.

ASSISTANCE TO THE COMMUNIST U.S.S.R.

The story is immensely intriguing as to how the Roosevelt administration, elected in 1940 on the President's promise that American troops would *not* fight wars on foreign shores, was able to mount such huge aid programs to the combatants Great Britain and later the Soviet Union in ways that certainly moved the United States nearer to war. To convince the American public and Congress—as early as mid-1941—to give aid to Communist Russia required virtual political sleight-of-hand and Ciceronian oratory on the part of the Roosevelt administration.

Recall that FDR had first proposed such assistance to Stalin's dictatorship fully nine months before Pearl Harbor—that is, at the time of the German invasion of the U.S.S.R., June 22, 1941. Even before that fatal Sunday morning—when Hitler put Operation Barbarossa into effect along Soviet Russia's long 1,500-mile-plus border—Roosevelt, like the British Prime Minister, had pondered the consequences for the Allies of Soviet Russia's becoming embroiled in the same war.

The initiative for actually fashioning a radically new approach to totalitarian Russia as a potential ally, as far as we know, originated with Winston Churchill. According to some scholars, Churchill regarded Stalin as more of a nationalist than as a Marxist-Leninist ideologue, meaning that the Soviet dictator should be regarded as a traditional, -defense-minded head of state rather than a revolutionary bent on overturning the world order. On this, President Roosevelt did not need much convincing. This, despite the fact that one of the leading senators in FDR's own party, Harry S. Truman, Democrat of Missouri and future Vice President (then President following Roosevelt's death in April 1945), had declared publicly that he hoped as many Germans and Soviets would kill each other as possible in the war being fought in the East between Nazi Germany and Soviet Russia.[2] FDR, on the other hand, had a certain softness of heart when it came to the man he was later to call in messages to the British Prime Minister, "U.J.," "Uncle Joe." This became apparent after the President's first meeting with Stalin in Teheran, November–December 1943.

In contrast to FDR himself and his closest aides, a number of others within the Roosevelt administration and the Congress concurred with the sanguine view toward the Soviets as expressed by Truman. Moreover, they held the opinion that the U.S.S.R. would probably not survive the Nazi blitzkrieg. Such skeptics not only included noted senators and congressmen but even some top officials in the War and State Departments. Similar notions were held by top officials in White Hall in London. They, too, reckoned that the Soviet Union would fall like a house of cards in the Nazi onslaught of late June 1941.

Indeed, one Soviet town and major city after another did fall to the Wehrmacht as the German juggernaut drove at an amazing clip eastward deeply into Soviet territory in summer 1941. Russia was fast losing almost half of its principal industrial base located in Ukraine. Shifting defense factories to a safer location in the Ural Mountains region had only just got underway.

However, what was most significant was that a minority of key administration officials close to FDR along with the President himself took an entirely different view. Like Winston Churchill and his foreign secretary, Anthony Eden and a few others, the President viewed the Soviet Red Army that would be engaged on the Eastern front at Hitler's rear as a golden opportunity to weaken Nazi Germany. These strategists saw the East as a potentially crucial front that would ultimately drain Hitler's strength if only the U.S.S.R. could withstand the onslaught. To their minds—recall that they were in a distinct minority among their colleagues—it was worth the gamble to help the Soviets. They reasoned that the gigantic U.S.S.R., a country stretching eleven time zones with a backup military manpower of millions of reservists, far outnumbered the forces Hitler could possibly maintain in a lengthy war. With its burgeoning arms buildup underway, Stalin's Russia was bound to present a serious problem to Hitler. In this, the strategists calculated correctly.

Moreover, U.S. and British intelligence was aware of the fact that the already fragile German economy had become more vulnerable by two years of grueling war against Poland and the several West European countries that became part of Hitler's *Festung Europa*. This "fortress" itself required the presence of many German Army divisions (Hitler even discarded the term "*Festung*" by late 1940 since it suggested internal problems of security for Germany). Allied bombing of industrial targets in Germany had a deleterious effect on the German economy.

Having failed to defeat England in 1939–1941, Hitler by mid-1941 faced a rebounding England that was now receiving significant Lend-Lease aid from the overseas colossus, America. In fact, one of the main reasons Hitler had attacked the U.S.S.R. was precisely because he and his top aides reasoned that sooner or later the powerful United States would enter the war. It was better for Germany that the Americans entered the fray later rather than sooner.

After conquering Russia, the Führer reasoned, America would then be cornered. The Japanese would lend a helping hand against both Britain and the United States by seizing valuable Allied assets in the southwest Pacific. The whole of Eurasia, the world's "heartland," would fall to the Axis, which included Japan.

The methods used by Roosevelt actually to get this aid in the pipeline to Britain by early 1941 were shrewd and well-timed. The politics of it had to be carefully calibrated given an American public that was anti-war at that time. After all, the United States had long been shackled to a policy of isolationism, shying away from foreign involvements. This posture was upheld not only by tradition but by such laws at the Neutrality Act of 1937. To railroad through aid not only to Britain but also especially to Soviet Russia (after June 22, 1941), presented what appeared to be an all but insurmountable political challenge to the administration.

ROLE OF SOVIET "AGENTS OF INFLUENCE"

Enter Soviet espionage as an abetter to the Lend-Lease program. Hundreds of Soviet "agents of influence" and outright spies operating in the United States were in the employ and under the guidance of Stalin's NKVD, NKGB, and GRU (military intelligence) in Moscow and its branching network of nests, or "*rezidentury*." The story of pre–Pearl Harbor Soviet espionage in America is a record that is well known to spy buffs. What is not so obvious to the authors of such books and their readers was *the effect of this Soviet underground activity upon the politics of the Roosevelt administration and, ultimately, on the consciousness of the American public.*

As one of the subplots told about Lend-Lease in succeeding chapters, the very conception and eventual administration of Lend-Lease was in large part made possible by officials under the influence—directly as spies or tangentially in their respective administrative agencies—of such Soviet underground activity by spy "illegals."

Indeed, the inspiration for Lend-Lease, the initial fuzzed-over method of payment for rendering such assistance to Stalin's Russia together with the actual administration of the Lend-Lease program, were all in large measure in the hands of "softened" American officials. Several of these men were those who were duly targeted successfully by Soviet agents of influence. Among these were key personnel close to Roosevelt—inside the White House, in fact. The officials included, above all in importance, the first deputy secretary of the Treasury Department—that is, the bureaucrat who administered all but singlehandedly that division in the Treasury that was specifically in charge of proposing and overseeing foreign monetary aid, including Lend-Lease.

Another side to Lend-Lease history concerns the assessment of the importance of the many-sided assistance in contributing to the eventual Soviet victory in the east over Nazi Germany. This highly controversial subject likewise is canvassed in this book. The discussion is based on the latest available archive material out of post-Soviet Russia. The analysis also relies on the findings of Russian historians. Some of these native Russian researchers courageously broke with the pre-1991, boilerplated Soviet view, often echoed in Western books as well, that Lend-Lease was merely a subsidiary, hardly a crucial factor at all in the victory in the east.

TODAY'S ASSESSMENTS

Today, however, some Russian historians claim that Lend-Lease was a virtual "life-saver," a term actually used by a Russian historian. They show that without this aid, Soviet Russia would have been fatally delayed in achieving victory, or at very least it would not have been able to overcome the Nazi onslaught by 1943–1944. *This delay in turn might have allowed Hitler time, which ran out on him, to perfect several new lethal weapons that were on the Nazis' drawing board—such as atomic bombs and long-range rocket-propelled missiles.*

Of particular note in getting the record straight on the importance of Lend-Lease aid to Russia is the new work by a zealous post-Soviet historian, Boris Vadimovich Sokolov. He devotes a whole chapter to Lend-Lease in his book, *Pravda o Velikoi Otechestvennoi Voine* (*The Truth About the Great Patriotic War*), published in St. Petersburg, R.F., in 1998.[3]

He writes: "In contrast to both Soviet and American histories of the war, the role of Lend-Lease always had a telling effect as the decisive factor in the Soviets' ability to continue the war. Although one American historian, Robert H. Jones, sketched in the fundamentals of the military role played by American and British shipments of certain types of vitally needed goods, the author lacked the statistics on Soviet production of the same goods." The same shortcoming, Sokolov continued, is true of other books, British or American, on Lend-Lease.

Upon examining newly available Russian data, Sokolov found that an egregious error had been made by Soviet propagandists—a distortion that unfortunately has been repeated in Western books to date on Lend-Lease. Soviet historians had always maintained that Lend-Lease military-related goods made up a mere 4 percent of what the Soviets themselves produced in military hardware during the war.[4]

Sokolov corrects this figure by pointing out that heretofore these official Soviet statisticians had failed to adequately reproduce the actual Soviet production figures. *When this calculation is made, Lend-Lease shipments make up anywhere from 15 percent to 25 percent and in some cases upwards to 50 percent of various types of military goods as a percentage of what the Soviets themselves were able to produce.*

Sokolov's findings show these contrasts with the old Soviet distortions:

Military aircraft: Instead of the Soviet claim that Lend-Lease aircraft composed 15 percent of such domestic production, Sokolov found that it was 30 percent.

High-octane aviation fuel: The true percentage is 57.8 percent, not the much lower figure of a fraction of this proffered by Soviet texts. Sokolov notes that just before June 22, 1941, Soviet domestic production of this fuel contributed only 4 percent of total stocks.

Wheeled vehicles (trucks, jeeps, motorcycles, etc.): By the end of the war, 32.8 percent of the Soviet "park" of such vehicles were Lend-Lease vehicles. Sokolov notes that "clearly without these shipments

Introduction 9

of Lend-Lease vehicles, the Red Army would have lacked the mobility it had achieved by 1943."
- **Railroad equipment (rails and ties, freight cars, locomotives, etc.):** Soviet production of such goods made up only 5.4 percent of such equipment, Lend-Lease supplying most of the rest, or 92.7 percent, as shown by the Russian production statistics reproduced in Sokolov's study.
- **Ordnance (ammunition, artillery shells, mines, assorted explosives):** Sokolov found that 53 percent of such materials used in the war by Soviet forces had been contributed by Lend-Lease. Soviet propaganda always reduced the figure to a small fraction of this.
- **Metal goods (aluminum, rolled steel, lead, cable, etc.):** The shares of these Lend-Lease goods as percentages of Soviet production varied anywhere from 50 percent to more than 80 percent. For instance, aluminum, used, for example, in the powerful Soviet T-34 tank, was 80.3 percent derived from Lend-Lease shipments of that metal. Sokolov notes that by supplying aluminum, Soviet tank production could continue to grow without waiting for additional supplies of the metal from domestic production, which was frequently disrupted by German occupation, bombing, etc. This, in turn, saved on labor manpower, which was drawn thin.
- **Production-line machinery:** The Soviet researcher strongly emphasizes the importance of Lend-Lease shipments of these goods. They greatly expedited Soviet arms mass production. If Soviet statisticians had once put this factor at 12–24 percent of increased Soviet military aircraft production, Sokolov finds, by carefully recomputing the statistics, that the true figure is nearly 30 percent.
- **Garages:** Protecting the Soviet park of vehicles were garages, 43.1 percent of which were from Lend-Lease shipments of building materials, including blueprints, cement blocks, girders, roofs, etc.

Sokolov similarly reproduces new figures for the amounts of food contributed by Lend-Lease as a percentage of the total Soviet food supply as well as for other goods.

The Russian historian concludes:

> "On the whole the following conclusion can be drawn: that without these Western shipments under Lend-Lease the Soviet Union not only would not have been able to win the Great Patriotic War, it would not have been able even to oppose the German invaders, since it could not itself produce sufficient quantities of arms and military equipment or adequate supplies of fuel and ammunition. The Soviet authorities were well aware of this dependency on Lend-Lease. Thus, Stalin told Harry Hopkins [FDR's emissary to Moscow in July 1941] that the U.S.S.R. could not match Germany's might as an occupier of Europe and its resources."

NOTES

1. Albert L. Weeks, *The Other Side of Coexistence: An Analysis of Russian Foreign Policy*, New York, Pitman Publishing Corporation, 1970, 94.

2. B. V. Sokolov, *Pravda o Velikoi Otechestvennoi Voine* (The Truth About the Great Patriotic War), Sankt-Peterburg, Aleteiya, 1998, 160–190.

3. The 4 percent figure is reproduced in many Western books on the war, among them studies by U.S- and U.K.-based experts on the Soviet Army. Cf. Sokolov, Pravda, 161.

2

✛

The "Arsenal of Democracy"

> We must become the arsenal of democracy. [In lending aid] we shall be repaid within a reasonable time following the close of hostilities, or, at our option, in other goods of many kinds, which they can produce and which we need . . . If the United States extended these material loans, the democracies would win.
>
> —President Franklin D. Roosevelt (radio address, Dec. 29, 1940); address to Congress in support of Lend-Lease, Jan. 6, 1941

* * *

President Franklin Roosevelt made no mere rhetorical flourish when he proclaimed in 1940 that in the Franco-British war against Hitler's aggression, the United States would become the "arsenal of democracy." This was the first use of this term and it was made in the context of prospective Lend-Lease aid to Britain.

America's tooling-up for war from 1937–1939 and accelerating at the start of World War II became an awesome threat to Hitler. This fact has been acknowledged in Foreign Minister Joachim von Ribbentrop's memoirs. It was food for thought as well for the dictator of Soviet Russia, Joseph Stalin. He also acknowledged America's economic prowess and its defense capabilities.

Whereas the Germans hoped the United States would stay out of any European conflict as long as possible, Stalin reasoned that sooner or later America would enter the war. And from his point of view, the sooner, the better. His "agents of influence" worked assiduously in this direction as they attempted to manipulate public and official opinion in America.

Stalin had indicated his wishes in this direction by the time—late 1940—that the "Nazi-Soviet honeymoon," begun in August 1939, had run its course. This fact has been neglected in standard histories of the period. Such writers have failed to detect the early signs of Stalin's newfound wariness and disenchantment with his alliance with Hitler. The Soviet leader also showed signs of anticipating an alliance with the Western capitalist states in opposing Hitler with arms—a story likewise neglected in mainline histories of the period.

AMERICA EDGES TOWARD WAR

Even before World War II began in September 1939, the Roosevelt administration had been taking various steps "short of war," as the expression went at that time. This telltale sign, too, was observed by Stalin in some detail, in fact, by his several networks of spies operating in the United States, some even in high places within the Roosevelt administration.

Well before the Japanese attack on Pearl Harbor, December 7, 1941, these administration-initiated measures were leading by a red thread to U.S. involvement in the Second World War, this country's virulent isolationism to the contrary. The process of gradual American entry into the world-historical conflict was closely followed by the belligerents and potential belligerents of Europe, including, above all, the U.S.S.R.

The step-by-step process unwound as follows:

- FDR's "quarantine" speech of 1937 formally ending American isolationism (the sternness of which shocked the appeasement-minded Chamberlain cabinet in Britain);
- The Roosevelt administration's sharp increase in defense expenditures, January 1939;
- Its circumvention, then congressional amendment of the Neutrality Act (1939–1941);
- The President's restoration of the U.S. Advisory Commission for the Council of National Defense, May 1939;
- FDR's declaration of a "limited" national emergency and his establishment of the Liaison Committee to supervise assistance to the Allies, September–December 1939;
- His sale of surplus war materièl to Britain and the trade of U.S. warships for British bases in the Caribbean Sea and Newfoundland, June and September 1940, harbingers of Lend-Lease;
- The Roosevelt-backed, first peacetime draft in the nation's history passes by a single vote, September 1940;
- Introduction of the historic Lend-Lease bill to Congress, January 1941;

- Conducting secret U.S.-UK British army staff talks in Washington, January–March, 1941;
- Lifting of the "moral embargo" on trade with the U.S.S.R., January 1941;
- Lend-Lease Act is passed, signed by the president; it includes both Britain and Greece, March 1941;
- Establishing naval patrols for the purpose of reporting to British warships on locations of German submarines in the Atlantic Ocean, April, 1941;
- American Army occupation of Greenland and Iceland, April–July, 1941;
- Heavy Nazi U-boat damage to Lend-Lease convoys en route to Britain in the North Atlantic, April–June 1941;
- Following German invasion of the U.S.S.R., June 22, 1941, trip by close FDR aide Harry Hopkins to Britain and Russia, June–July 1941;
- Extension of the Lend-Lease Act of March 1941 to the Soviet Union, June 1941;
- Establishment of America's "first CIA," known as OSS (Office of Strategic Services), July 1941;
- Proclamation of the propitious Anglo-American Atlantic Charter by Roosevelt and Churchill, August 1941, with its tacit invitation to all nations victimized or to be victimized by aggression to join in an alliance in the name of collective security (this translated into the "Declaration of the United Nations," January 1942);
- Orders to American warships to shoot on sight at German submarines, September 1941;
- Beginning of the first U.S.-U.K.-Soviet Lend-Lease supply conference in Moscow, September 1941: "First Protocol" for aid signed, October 1941;
- Authorization to arm merchant ships and dispatch them into war zones, November 1941.

These and other moves by the Roosevelt administration—that is, especially the ones made well before December 7, 1941—surely must have made Stalin think twice about totally alienating the powerful "imperialist" republic overseas. There were indications, in fact, that a demarche toward the United States was precisely his intention, *in contrast to Hitler's tactic of writing off and alienating America altogether.*

In the first week of July 1941, that is, a week following the German invasion, the Soviet dictator had executed his abrupt turn toward the Western Allies. Before this reorientation, however, the long-held tactic of the Bolsheviks, and in particular of Stalin, had been to take advantage of, even provoke divisions within the "capitalist-imperialist" world. At times, the Soviets, said Stalin, must align themselves "with one section" of the bourgeois states through skillful diplomacy so as to avoid being overwhelmed by another coalition of bourgeois states.² Scrapping of this line "for the duration" was a major change in Stalin's formulation of Soviet foreign policy and grand strategy.

THE AMERICAN FACTOR

Throughout 1940–1941, Stalin had been kept informed by his ubiquitous GRU (military intelligence) and NKVD-NKGB (civilian intelligence) agents in Washington, D.C. He was well aware of FDR's various actions against the Axis. He knew of the sympathies that FDR and others in the Roosevelt "Brain Trust" so often voiced toward the U.S.S.R., and specifically toward Stalin. This, despite traditional American anti-Communism and the president's own, occasional anti-Communist statements (as at the time of the Nazi-Soviet pacts of August–September 1939 and the Soviet aggression against Finland in December of that year).

Not to be forgotten, either, was the significant U.S. economic aid rendered Soviet Russia in the recent past under Stalin's vast industrialization program during the 1930s (see chapters 3–4). The great Dnepropetrovsk hydroelectric station, for instance, was built with American equipment. American assistance was lent for the Gorky tractor plant that began to materialize in production of farm machines. Many other U.S.-assisted breakthroughs occurred during the Soviet industrialization program under the Five-Year Plans (see chapter 3). Stalin more than once referred to what he called the Americans' great "business acumen" (*delovitost'*).³

Did he perhaps not reckon that one day America must surely enter the war? Did he reason that when it did, it would tip the scales in ways that could favor Soviet national interests and security—that is, via a joint U.S.-Soviet coalition fighting the Nazi-Fascist-Japanese Axis?

The Soviet leader certainly had no doubts about the strength and durability of the American economy. He recognized this even during the Great Depression. In his conversation with H. G. Wells in Moscow, July 1934, Stalin—America's stalled economy and growing unemployment aside—expressed strong confidence in America's speedy recovery. He specifically praised President Roosevelt's efforts in helping to bring this about. The Soviet leader described FDR as a leader with "initiative (*initsiativa*), courage (*muzhestvo*), and decisiveness (*reshitel'nost'*). "There is no doubt," Stalin told Wells, "that of all the captains (*kapitany*) ruling in the contemporary capitalist world, Roosevelt is the strongest figure." Rare praise of a capitalist president by the leader of the "socialist citadel," the U.S.S.R.!

As much as Stalin admired the firm leadership of Hitler, or so he said (no doubt disingenuously) now and then during the Nazi-Soviet honeymoon beginning in August 1939, he never once rated the Führer as highly as he did Roosevelt.

During World War II Stalin made other flattering comments about America and FDR. The praise was obviously motivated by the service Washington was rendering Soviet state interests, of course. Yet, beyond that Stalin had a certain personal rapport with Roosevelt that he proceeded to exploit to the hilt in the two wartime summits with him and the British prime minister. Stalin realized that FDR had a similarly favorable attitude toward him. On Roosevelt's part, however, his admiration for Stalin seemed genuinely motivated by respect, even affection for "Uncle Joe," even grinding up some of his Chesterfield cigarette tobacco for Stalin to tamp into his pipe at one of the Big Three meetings.

In early 1939, nearly six months prior to the start of World War II, Stalin already appeared to have second thoughts about his obdurate anti-American stance and propaganda. The latter had been rigidly cast in traditional, simplistic Marxist-Leninist dogma. Official Soviet ideology had generally lumped the USA in with the other "imperialist" nation-states that included Nazi Germany and Fascist Italy together with, given some reservations in America's favor, Great Britain and France.

STALIN ZIGZAGS

One example of this phraseology turned up as early as March 10, 1939. The occasion was the watershed Eighteenth Party Congress. GenSek Stalin led off his main report—as customary, giving priority to international affairs—by making some telltale distinctions among the "imperialist powers."

First, Stalin bluntly stated that a "new imperialist war has already become a fact."[4] Then in a lengthy passage he proceeded to strike a contrast between what he called the "openly-aggressive" capitalist states and the "nonaggressive" ones. The latter, he said, included not only France and Britain but also the United States. Taken together, he said, these states "possess enormous resources"—a hint that this would become a major factor in the coming war against the Axis. Any weakness perceived in their "appeasement" policies toward Nazi Germany and fascist Italy, Stalin claimed, did not stem from the Western states' very considerable economic and military power. This strength, he said startlingly, makes them, in fact, "undeniably stronger [than all the Axis countries] combined." If Stalin could think this, could he not also imagine a "grand alliance" that would include these powerful states in opposing the Axis?

As to the democratic nations' appeasement policies culminating in the Munich Conference of 1938, Stalin alleged, perhaps disingenuously, that these policies merely reflected a "fear of revolution that would arise if they became involved in war and if the war became worldwide in scope." The implication here was that if their participation in the coming war turned out to be offensive instead of merely defensive, the Western powers would be depicted as traditional "imperialistic plunderers." Here was an offensive stigma, he hinted, that those countries would surely wish to avoid. It was also, by implication, a stigma that the U.S.S.R. itself would likewise seek to avoid in its quest for world revolution as a hoped-for by-product of a second world war. A stigma, in fact, it did attempt to avoid.

Here Stalin seemed to be revealing his own future strategy for the Soviets. Namely, that Soviet entry into the future, "inevitable" war—most likely against the aggressive Axis—would be, or be made to look, purely defensive. Indeed, during and after World War II, Stalin repeatedly emphasized the innocent "defensiveness" of the Soviet entry into that war.

Back in December 1939, this had been the "defensive" line unfurled under Stalin in the Soviet aggression against Finland. So was it in 1950, when Soviet propaganda claimed that South Korea had first attacked North Korea in the post-Stalin period. In 1968 under Brezhnev, the invasion of Czechoslovakia by the Soviet Army in August was depicted by Soviet propaganda as a defensive "retaliation" against an imminent imperialist attack. Again, in 1979 in the war against Afghanistan, the latter, a "hostile, anti-Soviet regime," said Soviet propaganda, was planning to attack the U.S.S.R. The Soviets, after all, "never waged aggressive war," as Soviet doctrinal statements always touted. The Red Army was a "deeply defensive" army.

After Hitler's armies attacked the U.S.S.R. on June 22, 1941, and in subsequent speeches and references to the invasion, Stalin always stressed that the Soviet Union, possessing a harmless, purely defensive strategy, had been deceived and victimized by the Nazi aggressor. The enemy had not even issued a declaration of war, he complained. Here Stalin conveniently overlooked the fact that the Soviets in the past had never issued such declarations whenever they themselves had opened aggressive military hostilities. If, therefore, Stalin had been planning to wage offensive war against Germany—say, by the next year, 1942—this claim would have been regarded as totally disingenuous. In such an event Stalin, as usual, would have invented a pretext for launching "*Groza*," the putative plan to preempt the German attack.[5]

Continuing in his March 1939 report, Stalin accused the Western democracies "of hoping," he said accusingly, "to foment aggression [and] not to interfere with the aggressors' plans to involve the Soviet Union in war . . . so as to ultimately dictate terms to those powers who would be weakened by war." This line had been enunciated in so many words by Stalin on several occasions in the past. It was a foregone conclusion, he claimed, that the Western powers' strategy was one of "active neutrality." Or better, exploitative neutrality at Soviet expense. Yet, this was an accurate enough description of Moscow's own strategy! How else to explain its acquisition of vast amounts of territory, 1939–1940, during its so-called "neutrality"?

Stalin proclaimed, furthermore, that the U.S.S.R. "would never pull chestnuts out of the fire," as he put it, for any other countries victimized by aggression and war. Indeed, the Soviets never lifted a finger when Hitler occupied Czechoslovakia in 1938 following the Munich Conference "of appeasement."

For its part, Stalin had indicated in an earlier analysis, the U.S.S.R. would enter the coming, "inevitable" war deliberately, at its own choosing, when the time was ripe for it to do so. When it did enter the war, the Soviets would be able, said Stalin, to "tip the scales" to their advantage. They would thereby reap the most benefit for themselves from the war. Part of that tipping-of-the-scales was the added "weight" of America, which Stalin sought to exploit to Soviet advantage.

Obviously, these candid statements of Stalin's had little to do with the innocent, defensive posture of Soviet propaganda. Here, instead of propaganda, Stalin was suggesting in no uncertain terms a Soviet policy of exploitative, opportunistic neutrality—the mirror image of the very policies he was attributing to the Western capitalist democracies.

In retrospect, what is significant about his report to the Eighteenth Party Congress of March 1939 was not Stalin's customary, semi-official knee-jerk "paranoia" about the imperialist powers or about their putative "fear" of revolution. The Western powers in reality were not ganging up on the U.S.S.R. or "encircling" it with the intent of overthrowing the socialist order. These powers were not, as Stalin claimed, biding their time in order eventually to divvy up the war booty among themselves to Soviet disadvantage.

Nor perhaps was Stalin's allusion to be taken seriously as to the likelihood of "revolution" in the Western capitalist countries should they become involved in war. That would obviously depend on the justness of the war from the democratic peoples' perspective. Stalin added disingenuously that such countries recalled well what had happened within their polities after World War I when Soviet-inspired revolution was on the rise in eastern and central Europe. All this had the ring of mere propagandistic invocations.

Rather, what was striking and not a little pregnant in terms of the immediate future was the fact that Stalin had made the distinction between "aggressive" and "nonaggressive" states in the capitalist West. Lenin had never made these distinctions whenever he had described the putatively solid, "imperialist bloc" of nations, including America, which latter state, in fact, claimed Lenin, was one of the principal "imperialist marauders" destined to play an even greater "plundering" role in the future. What Lenin sought was to rally peace forces *within* capitalist states in order to weaken them. He did not sort out capitalist states according to their nonaggressiveness. Yet Stalin seemed to be doing exactly that in the run-up to World War II.

Was this flexible, zigzagging line meant solely for propaganda? Perhaps, but how? At very least, on the other hand, was there not the palpable hint in Stalin's early 1939 report that the Western Allies-to-be were to be considered the lesser evil when it came to the imperialist camp? Or perhaps after the catastrophic German invasion of June 22, 1941, did Stalin simply choose to reach into his grab bag of tactics pulling out the one about he had unfurled in embryonic form in March 1939 as "different kinds" of capitalist states—relatively warmongering ones versus the relatively peaceful ones in the West?

Leaving aside the twenty-two-month-long, tinsel-like "Nazi-Soviet honeymoon" with its extravagant, mutual, Nazi-Soviet eulogies and its propagandized condemnations of the Anglo-French "*plutocrats*"—a Nazi epithet politely mimicked by Soviet propaganda, which had never used that term previously in its ideology—here was Stalin early on voicing an even more un-Bolshevik, revisionist view toward the United States as a potential ally in the struggle against "fascist" (that is Axis) aggression.

TWO-PRONGED APPROACH

At same time, Stalin's focus on America at that time was by no means benign. His attitude toward the United States showed a mixture of respect and an almost compulsive wish to see it weakened and defeated—that is, *in the long term*. Meanwhile, however, in the short term he sought to exploit American friendship as was indeed reflected in Lend-Lease and in the "strange alliance" of World War II with the capitalist West. Lend-Lease had the effect of not only crucially helping the Soviet Union drive the Germans out of that country, it also strengthened Stalin's regime, the unwanted but perhaps unavoidable by-product of this major assistance. Though such strengthening was never acknowledged, of course, by Stalin and Soviet propaganda.

In terms of his subversive plans vis-à-vis the United States, Stalin often showed that he personally resented the reluctance of American "progressive forces" to unite solidly around the Communist Party of the USA. Stalin's security forces had little faith in the CPUSA as a contributor of spies for the NKVD-NKGB or as a truly revolutionary party. The notorious political and personnel misfortunes of the CPUSA were assiduously followed by Stalin. He never ceased to interfere in that party's affairs. This took the form of purging leading party officials when they got out of line as viewed from Moscow or dictating the policies and tactics and strategy to be followed by the CPUSA. His interest in the American Communist Party was also conditioned by its recruitment of spies, one of the principal tasks, after all, of the Third Communist International (Comintern), or "general staff of world revolution," and of all the foreign CPs composing it.

The culmination of the unique Soviet attitude toward America as a strong, out-of-area power easily transitioned into a radically new line that Stalin unfurled by mid-1941. Just days after the German invasion of the U.S.S.R., June 22, 1941, Stalin had withdrawn from public view. He had "disappeared," but *only for two days after June 30*. He appears in this short period to have "retreated," so to speak, in order to think things over, to review the critical situation that had arisen dramatically after the German onslaught. In other words, the Soviet dictator was not "paralyzed," as per Khrushchevian and post-1956 and post-1964 anti-Stalin propaganda. This is an erroneous claim that continues to be made today in Russian as well as Western histories.

Once back in his Kremlin office, Stalin immediately went on the air to broadcast his first postinvasion speech to the nation on July 3. He also resumed holding his daily meetings with top officials. In his surprisingly "new course" speech, Stalin said he was now prepared to describe Moscow's newfound cooperative relations with Britain, France, and the U.S. as an "alliance"—"*soyuz*"—against the common enemy. He did not describe it merely as an "anti-fascist *coalition*" (*koalatsiya*), a moderate term that was used after the war. Stalin now pronounced the Soviet-Western relationship to be a fighting "democratic *alliance*" (*demokraticheskii soyuz*) of lasting importance. "Alliance"—"*soyuz*"—was an especially flattering term; it was used in the very name of the Union (*Soyuz*) of Soviet Socialist Republics. Significantly, this term was never applied to the "marriage of convenience" with Nazi Germany after the Molotov-Ribbentrop Non-Aggression and Friendship Pacts of autumn 1939.

In all this, it seems fitting to ask retrospectively: Why did Stalin choose not to join the Axis Powers in the proposed Quadpartite Alliance that was repeatedly proffered to him in 1940? Such an alliance, after all, would have placed the U.S.S.R. in the ranks of the powerful, wave-of-the-future group of Axis Powers of Italy, Germany, and Japan.

Discussion of this broadened alliance actually had been raised seriously in the 1940 Soviet-German talks in Berlin. It had arisen at other times during that year in messages exchanged between Moscow and Berlin. At first there had been tangible indications of Soviet interest in joining such an alliance. As late as April 1941, Stalin purportedly remarked to the Japanese Foreign Minister in Moscow that "he was a convinced adherent of the Axis and an opponent of England and America." This appears to have been a gratuitous comment, a piece of disinformation, proffered by the Soviet leader. The fact was that Stalin stubbornly refused to bring the U.S.S.R. into the Axis coalition.

That a Quadpartite Pact including the U.S.S.R. never materialized is profoundly significant. The subject of Stalin's reluctance in this respect is often neglected in histories of the period. Yet examining it might throw light on what Stalin's calculus was in ultimately refusing to join the Axis. This was an arrangement that, after all, could have offered the U.S.S.R. a number of benefits.

THE AMERICAN "COLOSSUS"

In his calculations, Stalin, no less than Hitler, obviously had taken into account what was then often known abroad in the interwar years as the "American colossus." The U.S. was like the "shotgun on the wall" that is bound go off by the last act of a three-act play.

After World War I, Europeans became accustomed to the flow into their countries of advanced American commodities—their stunning importation of the great variety of American consumer goods. Most of Europe's washing machines, refrigerators, sewing machines, factory equipment, radios, cars, finance capital, and so on, all bore the "Made-in-the-USA" label or the logos of American banks. The same was true of the flow of such American-made heavy-industrial producers' goods into Stalin's Russia in the 1930s.

A number of American consumer goods, too, Stalin likewise ordered to be copied and produced in Soviet factories—which they eventually were. For example, the first Soviet official limousine was a carbon copy of an American Packard. It was used by the upper Nomenklatura, or Party and State officialdom. Many other American designs, whether of Douglas civilian aircraft or the Singer sewing machine and other textile, et al., machinery were similarly adopted and imitated. As a result, the U.S. was universally regarded as the vanguard among the industrialized nations or those planning to be such, as was the U.S.S.R.

American economic dominance was particularly visible during the immediate post–World War I and interwar periods. At that time recovery from the extremely destructive, demoralizing Great War was followed in a decade by the Great Depression. The sharp downturn in the American economy seriously hobbled Europe's own economic performance and development. American capital by then had become a critical factor in the economic health, or ill health, of Europe.

The dynamism of the American economy, especially as it involved its military-industrial potential, and its recovery out of the Depression were as impressive as they were crucial. When viewed from abroad, U.S. economic prowess, above all its military-industrial potential, came to be seen as a factor that would come into play in a future war. Moreover, the country's economic success, the Depression (1933–1937) aside, was based significantly not on state-socialist command of the economy, as found in Soviet Russia, fascist Italy, and Nazi Germany. Recovery took off on the basis of private enterprise. Capitalism's grassroots energy could not be easily dismissed by the totalitarian powers, and, in fact, was duly recognized and appreciated by them as an engine of progress.

As viewed from Nazi Germany, America was a country that Hitler preferred to keep out of European affairs. He ordered his navy at all costs to avoid torpedoing American naval craft or any hostile acts that would precipitate war with the USA. For obvious reasons, Moscow, by contrast, seems to have had its eyes on America as a potential, wartime ally—pro tem Soviet propaganda to the contrary.

U.S. corporate and small business, organized labor, and able business management teams with their legally trained executives—who in some cases began to leave private business to head the newly established government agencies in Washington D.C. that were to supervise the U.S. military buildup—got the American economic juggernaut off to a roaring start. This was especially true of arms production even before Pearl Harbor, December 1941.

The American economy soon began to meet the country's military necessities amid the crescendo of war abroad. Stalin did not need his *"rezidentura"* spies in the United States to be cognizant of this fact. To use a Russian expression, "even sparrows were chirping about it."

Having by 1937–1938 already helped to tame the Depression, the Roosevelt administration and the New Deal Congress rose impressively to the new challenge of girding up the country's loins. This response was undeniably "world-historical" in its implications at that time. As the world grew more dangerous by the hour, the economic feats performed by the "American miracle" did not go unnoticed in the capitals of London, Berlin, and Moscow, if not in Tokyo, except for the fanatical war party there.

During the two years after war broke out in Europe in September 1939 and around the time of Pearl Harbor, the U.S. economy was already turning out a staggering $181 billion worth of military aircraft, ships, and munitions alone. By 1942, American defense production equaled the combined total of Germany, Italy, and Japan! Two years later even this figure doubled![6]

The Soviets, as did the Germans, watched closely as this upturn in American defense production took place, and most particularly as Lend-Lease began to flow to their main enemy, Britain. Hitler, in fact, had decided on his conquest of Soviet Russia when he did (i.e., even before defeating England) precisely because of his fear and loathing of eventual direct American involvement in the war. (This may be documented by referring to the memoirs and diaries of leading Nazi officials.)

THE BIRTH OF LEND-LEASE

It was after U.S. President Franklin D. Roosevelt's homey analogy of lending a neighbor a garden hose to put out a fire that Americans came around to the concept of Lend-Lease. Though some agreed with Senator Burton K. Wheeler of Montana that the Lend-Lease agreement would "plow under every fourth American boy," Congress nevertheless passed the Lend-Lease bill by a sizable majority in March 1941.

The Lend-Lease Act became law on March 11, 1941. Ironically, the signing by FDR took place on the very day that NKGB chief, V. N. Merkulov, issued a secret report stating that there was solid evidence from "many reliable diplomatic sources in Berlin [that] Germany is planning an attack on the Soviet Union that very likely will take place in summer of this year."[7]

Above all, Lend-Lease signified that the U.S. economic achievement would translate tangibly into many-sided aid to Britain. The legislation, which was by its scale all but unprecedented in United States or, in fact , the history of any country, authorized the president to send an initial $7 billion in war materièl wherever and to whatever nation was assigned by the White House to be the recipient (the Democrat-controlled Congress, in any case, seldom let FDR down). Britain and Russia were the principal recipients among the over two dozen eventual ones.

The law gave the president exclusive power to sell, transfer, lend, or lease such war materièl. The president was to set the terms for aid; repayment "in kind or property, or any other direct or indirect benefit which the president deemed satisfactory." Days after Lend-Lease was passed, Roosevelt appointed his close friend and adviser, Harry L. Hopkins, as the initial expediter of the war aid program. A few months later, in July, probably for reasons of poor health, Hopkins yielded his job to Edward R. Stettinius, Jr. This official, another of Roosevelt's reputed "pro-Soviet" braintrusters, headed the new Office of Lend-Lease Administration, organized on October 28, 1941.[8]

In its original form in spring 1941, the Lend-Lease program was intended for Great Britain, China, and countries of the British Empire. It was not until November 7, 1941, the twenty-fourth anniversary of the Bolshevik Revolution, that Soviet Russia was formally included under the program (although *de facto*, Lend-Lease aid had started to flow to the U.S.S.R. in September).

Total Lend-Lease aid exceeded $50 billion. The British Commonwealth received some $31 billion, the U.S.S.R. over $11 billion, or as later estimated, at $12.5 billion. Within fifteen years after the termination of Lend-Lease, settlements were made with most of the countries that had received aid, although a settlement with the U.S.S.R. was not reached until 1972. Smaller countries received more than $1 billion in Lend-Lease goods. Among these forces were Mexico, Central America, Iceland, South America, Africa, the Near East, countries in the Caribbean, and some of the smaller European countries.

Lend-Lease became what British Prime Minister Churchill referred to as "the most unsordid act in the history of any nation." In all, thirty-eight countries and nineteen American republics benefited from the program. It amounted to fourteen cents out of every dollar the United States spent to fight the war. An agreement at the end of the conflict called for the British Empire to repay $650 million out of its $31 billion debt.

Ironically, one of the main drafters of the administration's side of the Lend-Lease particulars, especially as Lend-Lease was to be extended later to the Russians, was Assistant Secretary of the Treasury Harry Dexter White. In well-documented testimony in a congressional hearing in 1948, White was identified by ex-Soviet spies as having acted as an agent for the NKGB. Only three days after these accusations were made against him amid his denials, White died of a "heart attack." The *Venona* documents establish beyond any doubt his treason in the Silvermaster spy ring (named for another Treasury official), and as an agent in the secret Soviet "Operation Snow."

Meantime, the warring powers observed how much-vaunted American neutrality and isolationism were fast becoming anachronisms. In any case the Neutrality Law of 1935 had contained many convenient loopholes. These were duly exploited by the administration. Here was a government that in the mid-to-late 1930s had already perceived the Axis as America's and the world's main enemy. Indeed, in his memoirs, Ribbentrop complained that the U.S. government, in taking the early, anti-German stand that it did, had exempted the U.S.S.R. from its list of a potential enemies, despite, complained Ribbentrop, the Soviets' communism and obvious aggressiveness.

Early on, it was perceived in Moscow that Roosevelt and many, if not all, of his closest aides perceived that the U.S. was far readier than the French or British (later, Churchill and Foreign Minister Anthony Eden being exceptions in London) to accept Stalin's Russia as a potential ally. This, despite misgivings among some top officials within FDR's administration itself. Some, for example, not only denounced the Communist regime of Stalin. They regarded it as a house of cards that would collapse with a German invasion. Some in the Roosevelt administration held out little hope for a Soviet victory in a war fought with Nazi Germany.

As to Soviet Russia as a civilized nation-state, FDR himself had once spoken some distinctly unflattering words about it. At the height of Soviet Russia's aggression against Finland, in February 1940, Roosevelt had said:

> The Soviet Union, as everybody who has the courage to face the fact knows, is run by a dictatorship as absolute as any of the dictatorships in the world. It has allied itself with with another dictatorship [*with the Nazi-Soviet pacts—A.L.W.*] and it has invaded a neighbor so infinitessimally small that it could do no conceivable possible harm to the Soviet Union, a neighbor which seeks only to live at peace as a democracy and a liberal, forward-looking democracy at that.[9]

Moreover, U.S. public opinion was much slower than the Roosevelt brain trust in accepting Russia in this friendly way—even after June 22, 1941. A poll taken on on June 24 showed 35 percent in favor of aid to Soviet Russia, 54 percent opposed. A month later, however, the Gallup Poll indicated that 70 percent of the sample favored the "sale of war supplies" to Russia. In September of that year a third poll showed that almost half the sample approved extension of credits to the U.S.S.R. to purchase American supplies. Even the American Federation of Labor, a strongly anti-Communist organization, expressed similar strong support for giving aid to the U.S.S.R.

On March 27, 1941, just after Lend-Lease became law, Roosevelt declared an unlimited national emergency. This unique action served to broaden the effect of the first, or "limited" emergency decreed in 1939. It served to provide further underpinning for the Lend-Lease policy. The President also broke off relations with Germany and Italy, freezing all their assets in America. He proceeded to make other quasi-military moves. These included dispatching U.S. troops to Iceland to help that country bolster its military defenses. In April, Lend-Lease aid was extended to China, a country Roosevelt had long favored in its war against Japan. Interestingly, Stalin later joined in a limited way in this U.S. pro-China policy, Japan being a threat as well to the Soviet East, or rear, despite the Soviet-Japanese neutrality agreement of April 1941.

Already by the end of 1941, just two months after the German invasion of June, the U.S.S.R. was receiving Lend-Lease aid.

LEND-LEASE UNDERWAY

Total Lend-Lease aid 1941–1945 (i.e., to Britain and the U.S.S.R.) was to amount to approximately $40.1 billion, or in current dollars, around $300 billion. The British share of this was $31 billion. The Soviet share of the total was over $12 billion, or about $80 billion at today's currency values. Thus, the U.S.S.R. got just less than one-third the total U.S. Lend-Lease aid extended abroad during the war. Lend-Lease tonnage (long tons at 1016 kg per ton) to Russia alone amounted to upwards to 17.5 million.

How was all this aid—in food, clothing including coats and boots, metals, chemicals, munitions, locomotives, and military equipment embracing everything from tanks, radars, and other communications equipment, trucks and jeeps to combat aircraft and especially high-octane aviation gasoline—to be delivered to far-off Russia? It would appear to have been a logistical impossibility. Especially since such supplies would have to be shipped through enemy-infested waters whether in the Atlantic, Pacific, or Indian Oceans, all of which were patrolled by German U-boats.

The North Atlantic was particularly forbidding. It was constantly prowled by Hitler's growing submarine fleet. The northwest Pacific was a Japanese "pond," at least in formal terms of Japanese Navy destroyers and other surface naval assets as well as aircraft and aircraft carriers. The Japanese also operated submarines in the northern Pacific. But the Pacific Ocean is very large. Moreover, these relatively few Japanese subs did not constitute much of a threat. The Japanese submarine fleet in the Pacific Ocean hardly equaled Germany's U-boats deployed in the Atlantic, Mediterranean, Indian Ocean, Arabian Sea, and elsewhere. Besides, Japanese submarine strategy was largely directed against warships, not merchantmen. Its subs were engaged in action mostly to the south where the Japanese were "island-hopping" against U.S. and British possessions.

These factors meant that American Lend-Lease shipments to Russia mostly went via the Pacific route (see chart, below). Yet this was a sea lane that was significantly longer than the North Atlantic route if the Pacific route is measured from continental U.S. ports, shorter if measured from Fairbanks, Alaska, to Vladivostok.

Liberty ships and other merchant vessels, mostly but not only under U.S. registry, used three main routes in order of tonnage of Lend-Lease matériel: 1) the Western Pacific to the Far East Soviet port of Vladivostok; 2) the North Atlantic to Murmansk in the extreme north of the U.S.S.R. bordering Norway; 3) the route over the South Atlantic, Indian Ocean, and then into the Persian Gulf, where Tehran (Iran) became the transshipment point into the southern Caucasus region of the U.S.S.R.; 4) and to a far lesser extent the Black Sea and even in the extreme north via the Arctic Ocean during the few summer weeks when the sea was not locked up in ice.

The distribution of shipments by routes was as follows (in tons):[10]

	Tonnage	Distance (est. mi)*
Vladivostok	8.2 million	4,500**
Persian Gulf	4.2 million	12,000
Murmansk	4 million	4,600
Black Sea	680,000	4,000
Arctic Ocean	452,000	over 4,500

*Note: Distances do not include overland routes to Soviet war fronts in the U.S.S.R. nor shipments within the U.S. to Alaskan and other ports.
**From continental U.S. West Coast.

As can be imagined, making these shipments by sea back in those early years was an enormous challenge. Yet 90 percent of the shipments nevertheless were completed.

Going by sea was the only way. There were, of course, no large transport planes like today's capacious C-5 Galaxies. Such modern aircraft can carry several main battle tanks, vehicles, assembled helicopters and disassembled aircraft, artillery pieces, tactical rockets and munitions, and other bulky military equipment. Their ranges today match the distances of war fronts as far away as 7,000–12,000 miles with refueling. For transport ships in the 1940s, the danger of submarine and bomber attack (mostly German), not to mention hazardous seas, especially in winter, were real and present.

A terrible toll, in fact, was taken in the lives of American—and British—merchant seamen. Russian seamen were also victims. One in twenty-six U.S. mariners (merchant seamen) on Lend-Lease ships and runs died in the line of duty (one of several memorials dedicated to this sacrifice is located in Battery Park, New York City and is marked with the names of soldiers, sailors, airmen, and mariners). This represents a greater proportion of war-related deaths than for any other single branch of the U.S. armed forces: *viz*, 7,300 mariners lost at sea; 12,000 wounded, of whom at least 1,100 died from their wounds; 663 men and women taken prisoner by the Axis enemy. The total American mariners killed is estimated at 8,380 men and women. These figures omit the number of lives of airmen and Navy personnel lost in combat incidents at sea related to defense of Lend-Lease convoys.

Material losses in ships and cargo tonnage could be at times staggering, especially in the opening phase of Lend-Lease, 1941–1942 but also in 1943–1944. In his diaries, Nazi Propaganda Minister Josef Goebbels tells of his fondness in reporting in the German media that "30,000 tons were sunk by our U-boats" in a single day, etc. In another entry he sneers, "In the press, [Roosevelt] is threatening us with war if we sink his arms convoys. He will soon come to see what we can do."[11]

Taken together, however, the loss in ships and their valuable cargoes mounted in the Atlantic, and to a lesser extent in the Pacific (the Japanese being much less effective at fighting the convoys than was their Axis partner in Atlantic), to less than 5 percent of the total shipments. Under the then-prevailing conditions this was an amazing accomplishment, to get through virtually all of the ships in the hundreds of convoys plying the four routes to the Soviet Union.

There is no doubt that British and American reading of the German military codes (via the Enigma decryps) was an important factor. So was radar on the Allies' side. In fact, throughout the war as Allied defensive measures in protecting the convoys improved, the percentage of ships lost on Lend-Lease runs, even along the North Atlantic sea lane, began to decline sharply after those worst years of 1941–1942. The British and Americans devised many types of countermeasures to overwhelm Admiral Doenitz's submarines. These included radar-bearing long-range aircraft flown out of bases in the U.K. and the United States; new types of sub-seeking depth bombs; scouting planes that carried sensors that were capable of detecting submerged U-boats. By 1944, the German U-boat menace had all but been defeated.

At its height in 1941–1942, the submarine menace surely could have been a good deal worse for the Allies—Britain and Russia. However, Hitler had chosen largely to ignore the pleas of his naval commanders. Admirals Doenitz and the German fleet commander in chief Admiral Raeder had urged the Füehrer—unsuccessfully—to build more U-boats to meet and defeat the challenge represented by the colossal U.S. enterprise with its long lines of Lend-Lease convoys. But Hitler, a ground-force zealot, was notorious in neglecting the German sea arm; he was only a bit more attentive to the needs of the Luftwaffe.

"The Soviet population and the Red Army carried the war to victory at great cost," writes one American specialist. "When the deliveries amounted to a little over 150,000 tons of cargo—it took time to organize the production, secure the SLOCs [sea lanes], and make the deliveries via Murmansk, the Middle East (Iran), and the Soviet Far East." However, he continues, during the second (November 1942–July 1943) and third (July 1943–August 1945) rounds (or "Protocols") of shipments, Lend-Lease "was making critical contributions to the civilian population, to Soviet war production and stocks, and in military equipment and weapons."

The designated "Fourth Protocol" deliveries for the final phase of the war in Europe in 1944–1945 were in excess of 6 million tons. (For positive Russian statements about the overall value of Lend-Lease aid for their war effort, see Appendix I.)

SOVIET PROPAGANDA ON LEND-LEASE

Lend-Lease aid became so significant and crucial for the Soviet war effort that Soviet propaganda, especially after the war, made every effort to diminish its importance. Such propaganda was used as a ploy to influence domestic and world public opinion about the Soviet Union's exclusive, great "single-handed" defeat of the Axis. The posture of minimizing the importance of Lend-Lease continued into the postwar period, even into the post-Soviet period after 1991.

Yet in the most recent years, there has been a turnabout in the way the Russians have come realistically to assess the importance of Lend-Lease in the Soviet military victories against Nazi Germany. By the end of the decade of the 1990s, closer approximations to the truth about Lend-Lease and its crucial contribution to the Soviet victory began to surface. Russian historians began to avail themselves of the several Russian archives on World War II events and statistics that heretofore had been closed to them. As one Russian historian, Boris V. Sokolov, went about correcting mistaken impressions about this aid as depicted in a number of earlier, classic Soviet as well as Western histories of World War II and Lend-Lease, he disclosed in his 2001 volume, *Secrets of the Second World War*:

> The role of Western aid during the years of the Great Patriotic War were traditionally cretanized by Soviet historians even before the advent of the "cold war" . . . In the 1980s, although Lend-Lease was given some degree of recognition, it continued to be demeaned by Soviet historians . . . The aid was described as "not having been significant and in no way made a decisive contribution to the course of the war. [American studies by Mark Harrison and Robert H. Jones respectively in 1985 and in 1969] were written under the biased influence [of Soviet economic theories and practices] which caused incorrect [lower] assessments [by the authors] of the contribution of Lend-Lease aid to the Soviet economy. Since then, we have been able to take into account the weight of this aid in the light of newly published statistics [in Russia] as well as from our [the author's] own calculations."[12]

NOTES

1. Zhukov quoted in B. V. Sokolov, *Tainy vtoroi mirovoi* (Secrets of the Second World War), Moscow, Veche, 2001, 199–200. Sokolov is a noted Russian scholar who has investigated Lend-Lease and its effect on the Soviet war effort. His research is based on the latest available Russian archive data (see preface).

2. Robert C. Tucker, *Stalin in Power: The Revolution from Above, 1928–1941*, New York, W. W. Norton & Company, 1990, 225.

3. Albert L. Weeks, *The Other Side of Coexistence: A Study of Russian Foreign Policy*, New York, Pitman, 1970, chapter 4.

4. J. V. Stalin, *Otchetnyi doklad na XVIII s"ezde partii o rabote TseK VKP(b)*, Moscow, Ogiz, 1948, 10.

5. Cf. discussion of Stalin's strategy in this connection in Albert L. Weeks, *Stalin's Other War: Soviet Grand Strategy 1939–1941*, Lanham, Rowman & Littlefield Publishers, 2002.

6. Michael Burleigh, *The Third Reich: A New History*, New York, Will and Wang, 2000, 734.

7. A. N. Yakovlev, ed., *1941 god Dokumenty (Documents)*, Moscow, Mezhdunarodniy Fond, 1998, Vol. 1, 740–41.

8. In Sept., 1943, Lend-Lease was incorporated into the Foreign Economic Administration under Leo T. Crowley. In Sept., 1945, it was transferred to the Dept. of State; by the end of the war practically all the allies of the United States had been declared eligible for Lend-Lease aid. Although not all requested or received it, Lend-Lease agreements were signed with numerous countries. In 1942, a reciprocal aid agreement of the United States with Great Britain, Australia, New Zealand, and and the Free French was announced. Under its terms a "reverse lend-lease" was effected, whereby goods, services, shipping, and military installations were given to American forces overseas. Other nations in which U.S. forces were stationed subsequently adhered to the agreement. On Aug. 21, 1945, President Truman announced the end of Lend-Lease aid. Arrangements were made—notably with Great Britain and China—to continue shipments, on a cash or credit basis, of goods earmarked for them under Lend-Lease appropriations. Robert Huhn Jones, *The Roads to Russia: United States Lend-Lease to the Soviet Union*, Norman, University of Oklahoma Press, 1969, 299.

9. Matthew B. Wills, *Wartime Missions of Harry L. Hopkins*, Raliegh, Pentland Press, Inc., 1996, 26.

10. Data is from the Russian State Archive (RGAE) as reproduced in A. Kh. Paperno, *Lend-liz Tikhiii Okean* (Lend-Lease the Pacific Ocean), Moscow, Terra, 1998, 5–6.

11. Josef Goebbels, *Diaries 1939–1941*, New York, G. P. Putnam's Sons, 1982, 267.

12. B. V. Sokolov, *Tainy Vtoroi Mirovoi Voiny* (Secrets of World War II), Moscow, Veche, 2001, 198, 200. The works by the authors cited by Sokolov above are: Mark Harrison, *Soviet Planning in Peace and War 1938–1945*, Cambridge, Harvard University Press, 1985; and particularly Jones, *Roads*.

3

Stalin and America

We are definitely in favor of economic deals with America, and with all countries but *particularly* with America . . . We will need American industrial commodities such as locomotives, automobiles, and so on more than the commodities from any other country.

—Lenin, in October 1919 and February 1920

* * *

Despite his being the leader of a capitalist nation, President Roosevelt is today one of the most popular men in the Soviet Union.

—J. V. Stalin

* * *

Stalin said he had good personal relations with Roosevelt.

—N. S. Khrushchev

* * *

In his own way, [Stalin] was an Americanophile. He considered the United States a determining factor in world politics at a time when Americans thought themselves . . . isolationists.

—William Taubman, *Stalin's American Policy*[1]

* * *

Stalin was a one-hundred-percent realist. [Moreover] even in his advanced years he possessed a phenomenal memory, never forgetting anything [or] anyone with whom he worked and respected. [As to Maxim

Litvinov] in the entirely new international situation confronting the U.S.S.R. after the German attack [June 22, 1941] Litvinov [who had been dismissed in favor of Molotov in 1939] was appointed Deputy Commissar of Foreign Affairs as well as Ambassador to the United States.

—Robert Ivanov, Russian historian[2]

During Stalin's long tenure, Soviet foreign policy zigzagged along a serpentine path. It swung "dialectically" between two poles. At one extreme was the traditional Soviet assertion of world revolution based on Marxist-Leninist ideology. It included the tactic of carrying out subversion in foreign lands. At the other pole was the pursuit of national interests employing the more traditional tools of diplomacy. In this kaleidoscope of tactics and strategy oscillating between the two poles, America always occupied a leading position in Stalin's calculus.

Often both aspects of Kremlin behavior were employed together in the international arena. As a result, Soviet relations with the U.S. became affected by this two-sided combination: On the one hand, this meant extension of the Soviet sphere of influence via diplomatic means. Or it meant advancing toward Lenin's—and Stalin's—avowed goal of territorial expansion and the eventual establishment of a global, "World Republic of Soviets." To achieve this, arms would be used where necessary and feasible.

The Roosevelt administration's price for recognition of the U.S.S.R. as a state in 1933 was based in large part on the Kremlin's promised renunciation of subversion in America in pursuit of world revolution. Which, of course, the Soviets would not and did not truly abandon. Nor did U.S.-Soviet friendship during World War II, sealed with Lend-Lease aid, deter Stalin's grand strategy of Soviet world domination.[3]

In a curious and ironic way, in fact, this formidable assistance actually abetted Soviet global strategy while also, during the war at least, being in America's national interest.

Given these contrasting parameters of Soviet behavior, how, then, did Lend-Lease aid ever materialize under such unfavorable conditions?

DEALING WITH THE MAN IN CHARGE, STALIN

It is impossible to study the process by which Lend-Lease came into being and the way it played out for over three years without understanding the outlook and methods of the powerful leader of the country to which this aid was to go, and who, in fact, had made it possible immediately after it was first suggested to him in person by American emissaries in July 1941.

When it came to foreign policy, Joseph Stalin was a past master at making the needed combinations. First, he would emphasize Soviet global designs. Then he would table this remote goal in favor of more immediate, attainable ones. Above all, Stalin knew how to exploit diplomacy alone to advance Soviet interests. He employed flexible and pragmatic means in a process in which the Soviet leader showed impressive skill.

Stalin was as cautious as he was deceptive. Perhaps the illegitimacy of the very regime he headed and its bad reputation abroad helped make him that way. He realized that revolutionary, expansionistic ambitions had to be tempered by the realities of space and time, and by the power of rival nation-states, most of whom despised communism. His ultimate, expansionistic goals had to be carefully concealed and/or camouflaged. Moreover, in his process the regime's basic, world-girdling, Leninist aims often had to be postponed. This prompted debate abroad as to how seriously Stalin really took Marxist-Leninist ideology.[4]

Stalin conducted foreign policy like chess, Russia's indoor sport. This brainy, multi-layered game was known to have been a favorite of Stalin's as well as of Lenin's. As in chess, Stalin would study his opponent and make his moves accordingly in order to better his rival. He would keep his eye on the overall strategy, his own and his opponent's. He would zero in on the other's big, backboard pieces. He especially kept in his sights the opponent's king, the paradigm of the ultimate "world-historical" goal of Marxism-Leninism. This goal the Soviet leader never slighted despite zigzag tacking.

In Stalin's way of conducting it, Soviet diplomacy, like chess, went by discretely phased stages. The moves resembled openings, middle- and end-games. As the overall game proceeded, plays had to be carefully calibrated in advance, crafted dynamically en route in accordance with the opponent's own dynamic strategy. Too, they had to be adjusted to the vagaries of unforeseeable events in the world arena. As in chess, the diplomatic game was bound to have twists and turns, advances and losses ("sacrifices") all in the hope of maneuvering Soviet power in the long run into a better, more commanding position on the board—that is, in the global arena.

For his part, Winston Churchill likened Stalin's methods to the quite un-chess-like tactics of a burglar. "[He] will try every door in the house, enter all rooms which are not locked and when they come to one that is barred, if [he is] unsuccessful in breaking through, [he] will withdraw and invite you to dine that evening."[5]

The burglar metaphor aside, the chess analogy is more useful in tracing Stalin's behavior toward the West, including the United States, through the 1920s, 1930s, and 1940s. The Soviet leader would maneuver in apparently baffling ways. Sometimes he was warmly ingratiating, other times brutally uncompromising. During the first talks in July 1941 leading up to the Lend-Lease shipments beginning in the autumn, Stalin would display this supposedly erratic, contradictory behavior within the space of twenty-four hours.

However, in the final analysis, using at times such baffling tactics, the Soviet dictator always attempted and often succeeded in putting the Soviets into a better position "on the board." This in turn helped them more closely approach their ultimate goal. Even joining the League of Nations, as the Soviets did belatedly in 1934, after disowning it bitterly for fifteen years, was one of those pregnant, if apparently contradictory Soviet moves on the global chessboard.

As viewed by Stalin, many such proximate "goals," that is, openings and middle-games, lay along the long path to eventual Soviet world domination. In the welter of unpredictable and conflicting events, trends, and the vicissitudes of foreign leaders and their personalities, particularly in the democracies, retreat sometimes seemed to Stalin to be the best policy. At other times, offense was required. Sometimes offense meant waging offensive war, as against Finland in December 1939 or against South Korea in June 1950 in the North Korean war plan backed, if not developed by Moscow.

In operating in the seas of contingency in this way "dialectically" while seizing the initiative when the situation warranted, Stalin, like Lenin, would often rely on Napoleon's old standby, which Lenin was fond of quoting: "*S'engage et depuis on vôi.*" ("Try it and see what happens.")

In other words, the "world-historical" game of grand strategy and diplomacy was viewed by Stalin as a protracted, stage-by-stage process. He conducted it flexibly, advancing Soviet interests bit-by-bit. He also set about realizing the sacred "pledge" that he had made symbolically to the Party in his funeral oration at Lenin's bier in January 1924, and that he often repeated throughout the 1920s: namely, to extend the borders of the U.S.S.R. and forward world revolution As former head of Soviet foreign intelligence in the 1940s, General Pavel Sudoplatov, has written,

> Stalin's . . . first priority was the fulfillment of their geopolitical aspirations to transform the Soviet Union into the largest superpower in the world.[6]

Collaboration with the Western capitalist Allies in World War II together with the indispensable Lend-Lease aid given the U.S.S.R. did not, in the last analysis, deter Stalin from the Marxist-Leninist grand strategy of world domination in the name of Soviet-style socialism. The "world-historical" chess match, as viewed from the Kremlin, was always still on—during and after the war. As before, the Soviet play continued moving forward by phases. And, it was Lend-Lease that had helped it move forward.

Joseph Vissarionovich (Djugashvili) Stalin ruled the Soviet empire for a quarter of a century, or about as long as Queen Victoria reigned in Great Britain. Like the queen and all rulers who have held power for almost a generation—even those who held it for a shorter, eventful period, as did an extremely powerful Napoleon Bonaparte—Stalin cast a long shadow over the land, and, in fact, the world. He left his mark on every facet of his country's society that he sought to shape, even on the contours of buildings known as "Stalin wedding cake." If ever there was a tyrant of whom it could be said that he regarded himself as an "engineer of human souls"—including, as it turned out, the souls of foreign diplomats—that leader was Stalin.

In the initial, 1941 Lend-Lease negotiations as well as in the wartime and postwar conferences with the other members of the Big Three, Roosevelt and Churchill and their emissaries, Stalin was always in command of the proceedings, in the sense that the other two summiteers routinely deferred to him. This was an advantage that he knew how to skillfully exploit. Always chesting his cards, his true designs, Stalin's effect on these leaders, while not "hypnotic," was at least extremely potent in its persuasiveness and firmness.

Above all, it was part of Stalin's methods to rapidly shift tactically *in medias res* as though he were buffeted by objective, Newtonian forces while at the same time helping to direct the vectors of those forces to his own advantage. How else to explain his expansion into eastern Europe during and after World War II—that is, his retention of the lands he had won during the short period of his collaboration with the Nazis (1939–1941) and Western toleration of violation of agreements made at Yalta? A chess master always keeps his eye on potential plays lying several moves ahead. As he does, he attempts to deceive the opponent by keeping him in the dark as to the master's basic strategy.

Memoirs written by lower-echelon Western participants in Big Three meetings always later expressed their awe mixed with dismay at the way Stalin would maneuver and tack, the way he would wind up generally getting his way over his other Allied conferees. The "Boss" (*Khozain*) and "*Vozhd*" (Leader) were names applied to him by his cohorts and propagandists. These cognomens indeed caught the essence of Stalin's nature and style. A true tyrant, like Ivan the Terrible in Russian fact and legend, Stalin was not satisfied unless he had penetrated and controlled tyrannically every facet of Soviet society, including especially the minds of his immediate aides. In this respect Stalin left his colleague-dictator, Adolf Hitler, way behind. Stalin's aides' loyalty to him, as with Tsar Ivan III and his obedient entourage, was a matter of life and death to them.

Stalin's curiosity about key foreign countries, their systems, leaders, and exploitable vulnerabilities knew no bounds. This was especially true in connection with his interest in America—as principal helper in Soviet industrialization, possibly as a future Soviet ally and donor of vital military aid in the "inevitable" war to come. That Stalin perceived this possibility, if not likelihood, by 1940–1941 now seems undeniable.

The Soviet dictator inserted himself into every possible field, a fact American Lend-Lease negotiators in Moscow were to discover to their surprise from the very opening of the talks in July 1941. This included Stalin's command of every item to be shipped on his long, initial Lend-Lease wish list.

Once briefed on whatever matter, he considered himself to be an authority. This included everything from belles lettres to linguistics, from military science, biology, and agronomy to constitutional law and the types of military equipment to be sent via Lend-Lease. His memory has been described as prodigious. True, he would arrive at his conclusions as a rule only after consulting specialists. But once he had immersed himself in the nitty-gritties of whatever endeavor or subject, Stalin would make the final decision absolutely on his own. He chose whichever plan, conclusion, tactics and strategy, work of art—or assassination and execution—that he thought best filled the bill of "socialism" or "socialist realism" as he interpreted it. This, of course, buttressed his own personal power. At the same time whatever policy he and his aides crafted toward other countries had to advance the Soviet global cause of world revolution and Soviet domination.

It is said that his method of conducting Politburo sessions was to hear input from the other dozen-plus members of that highest body. Stalin would then follow Russian alphabetical order duly placing himself near the end of the list of speakers. He would then sort out the views he had previously heard as he arrived at his own conclusion.

It is testified by Soviet Army memoirsts that this likewise was his procedure, as commander in chief, when conducting sessions within the councils of military high command, or Stavka, during the war. Unlike Hitler during the Russian campaign, Stalin—at least, by 1942 during the Great Patriotic War—would carefully weigh what his commanders had to say before making the final decision. Poets and novelists, architects, economists, cinematographers, composers, scientists, marshals, admirals and generals, and diplomatic service officials—anyone performing a public function in the society or for the State—knew that whatever party line or decision would be reached, it would be Stalin alone who would ultimately color it and approve it. And woe to those who did not take this into account. Perhaps this is what Hitler meant when he described his Soviet counterpart as an outstanding organizer and administrator.

Stalin would likewise keenly observe how policy was being carried into effect. This, too, directly affected Lend-Lease, sometimes in adverse ways, since lower officials feared to act unless they thought the Boss would approve. Decision making at lower levels was thus often hamstrung. Typical, totalitarian bureaucracy, developed to the nth-degree in Soviet Russia, also complicated execution of Lend-Lease assistance at the middle and grassroot levels.

Everyone was expected to think and work as Stalin thought they should. The penalty for failing to understand Stalin's methods and the system could mean, and often did, prison, the Gulag, or the firing squad. Unlike some of other dictators in history, the Soviet *Vozhd'*, Stalin, himself set very high standards of *"rabotosposobnost'"* (capacity for work, diligence). Vacations for the Boss were working vacations. He was an indomitable toiler at his job of Soviet leader (unlike Lenin who was essentially lazy, spending little time at his desk). Any number of foreign diplomats, such as those discussing Lend-Lease and other sensitive matters with the Soviet leader in 1941 and throughout the war, noticed how shrewdly and intelligently Stalin conducted himself and the affairs of state.

Stalin, the Georgian, totally lacked the emotional instability—that is, on the job—that interfered so disastrously with Hitler's distorted sense of reality. Stalin's alleged "paranoia" is often cited by biographers and historians, whether Russian or Western. Yet the less clinical expression might better be "suspiciousness" with which to describe the dictator's eagle eye. In any case, this trait seldom interfered with the Soviet leader's conduct of foreign affairs. If and when it did, it arose only near the end of his life in 1952–1953. This was when Stalin definitely showed signs of pathological paranoia. It could be seen in his irrationally blaming Jews for plotting various, nonexistent conspiracies and crimes, and planning, as some maintain, a World War III against the capitalist world.

Yet even in 1952–1953, when he was in his early seventies, Stalin's suspiciousness, when directed, at least, at his "comrades" in the Politburo and Secretariat, was hardly misplaced. It may even have been warranted. For, as it turned out, evidence of active plotting against Stalin among his cohorts, especially by 1952, has slowly surfaced through recent historical research. Some evidence points to Stalin's murder in early 1953 by means of a plot centered around Lavrenty Beria and Georgy Malenkov, along with others at the top.

The Soviet dictator's work day started mid to late morning. He would then work far into the night and early morning hours. His day could last anywhere from ten to twelve, even fifteen hours. At "dinners" towards midnight at his nearby dacha fifteen minutes from the Kremlin or at his "distant" dacha twice the time away, Stalin would often hold informal, semiofficial meetings with a half-dozen key members of the Politburo. At these informal conclaves, most of the other comrades would down large amounts of vodka. Stalin, however, generally kept to Georgian wine, a regimen that some believe permitted Stalin to keep his cool while observing his colleagues as they got progressively drunk. They would perhaps thereby reveal some unpleasant things that Stalin should know about. (It is said that Stalin's physicians recommended wine as a remedy for the dictator's notorious insomnia.) Only on rare occasions Stalin would allow himself to cross the line.

Unlike many of his cohorts, Stalin was frugal in his private life. At Kremlin banquets in honor of foreign dignitaries during World War II, Stalin would pretend to be drinking toasts in 100-proof vodka like the rest of the Politburo and the guests. Actually, however, his glass contained wine of low alcoholic content. In talks with American negotiators as Lend-Lease and collaboration in the war got underway, Stalin would let the guests drink while keeping himself sober. Stalin was always in control of himself and, as he hoped, others, not infrequently in order to take them in or as happened several times during the war as when he insisted angrily on the Western Allies' opening of a second front in Europe.

STALIN'S WEAPON OF DIPLOMACY

As one studies the conduct of Stalin's favorite business in the Kremlin, namely, *diplomacy*, it is important to keep his various personal characteristics in mind.

Diplomacy to Stalin was to be used with utmost seriousness like a well-tooled weapon. To Stalin's mind actual war fought with lethal weapons was not always necessary or preferable. Diplomacy, with which by contrast Hitler had little patience, could prove its effectiveness, in Stalin's mind, short of a clash of arms. In fact, in brandishing diplomacy *like* a weapon, often in tandem with scarcely cloaked extortion, Stalin calculated that the Soviets could reap the same rewards via diplomacy—the extension of Soviet power and territory and the enhancement of the international prestige and influence of the Union of Soviet Socialist Republics—that might not otherwise have been achieved through risky, outright war.

In going along so readily with U.S.-donated Lend-Lease, Stalin had obviously calculated that as a powerful dictator, he could control the risky "fall-out" of friendliness toward the capitalist donor country. As he knew, such gratitude would inevitably be felt among his own subjects toward this well-known aid from the rather romantic place to many ordinary Soviet citizens, "*Amerika*." Russian historians today admit that Lend-Lease had a tremendously positive effect on the morale of Soviet civilians and soldiers. Stalin himself, aware of this, not unpainfully, was not above expressing gratitude for the American aid—for public consumption, at home and in America.

Observers have said that Stalin considered diplomacy to be "the continuation of war by other means." At same time, when diplomacy did not or could not get the results under urgent conditions and sought by the *Vozhd'* in the short term, he would resort to arms. A case in point was his three-month war against Finland beginning in December 1939. This was as it had been earlier with the enforced Sovietization of the former Russian imperial borderlands through the 1920s—in which Stalin, the Georgian, personally played an important part as Commissar of Nationalities—Stalin would not hesitate. Yet he resorted to arms only when he thought application of the Red Army was absolutely necessary. In the Winter War against Finland 1939–1940, actual war fighting was one such last resort. To Stalin, outright war inevitably entailed dangers that he was not as a rule willing to face. In contrast to Hitler, Stalin seldom acted impetuously like a risk-taking gambler.

The Finnish "Winter War" had come about this way. In his application of forceful diplomacy to acquire the Finnish territory he wanted from the Helsinki government in autumn 1939, the usually cautious Stalin, in launching a war against "little Finland," had counted on the Red Army's risk-free, large superiority in numbers of men and arms with which easily to overwhelm the enemy. But his aggression failed. Casualties mounted astronomically on the Soviet side. So, Stalin again resorted to diplomacy. With the result that the treaty with that scrappy country to the north, signed in March 1940, gave the dictator only half a loaf—less than the large swatches of Finnish territory, if not the whole of Finland as an additional Soviet Republic, that he had originally sought. The compromise assured that this bloody war—for the Soviets—would not continue. And with it a mounting antipathy abroad towards the U.S.S.R.

At same time, Marshal Kirill A. Meretskov, the strategist who had drawn up the Soviet Finnish invasion plan, wrote in his postwar memoirs that he had been ordered by Stalin after the March peace treaty to develop a further plan for capturing and annexing all of Finland.

The Winter War and the treaty marked the final abandonment, in fact, of overt Soviet attempts ever again to try to convert Finland into a vassal state or Soviet Republic. In its way, the settlement of March 1940 and its aftermath became a symbol of the way in which Stalin operated.

STALIN AND FDR

"It is beyond all question that later on [Roosevelt] will be accessible to our influence."

—Maxim Litvinov in a letter to Stalin[7]

As mentioned earlier, Stalin had always shown a mixed attitude toward America. He would sometimes display flashes of apparently genuine admiration for that rich country. It seemed that he regarded the United States as a special case. Only rarely did he express the view that America was ripe for Soviet-style revolution; he acted as if this were only a remote possibility. Yet his direct involvement in the subversive, espionage affairs of the GRU and NKVD-NKGB activities as well as the aboveground propaganda line of the CPUSA in America were anything but perfunctory.[8]

During preparations for Lend-Lease in 1941 and in wartime conferences, Stalin also seems to have understood that President Roosevelt's Cabinet along with lower officials in the executive branch—Department of State, War Department, etc.—was relatively united around the head of state and government.

This unity in Washington at times contrasted with that of the British government. The government in London, operating under conditions of less stable, virtual coalition parliamentary democracy, was shot through with officials who either wanted nothing to do with Stalin's Russia or who welcomed the mutual annihilation of Germany and Russia in war. Of course, there were partisans of this point of view within the American government as well. But there they were outnumbered by others of the opposite persuasion. In any case, the strength and unity of the American presidential system of government as contrasted to the British parliamentary system, not to mention Roosevelt's own personal charisma, were positive factors adding to the contrast in policy making and the difference between American and British attitudes toward the U.S.S.R. Churchill's own charismatic influence in England was to arise only later. (Roosevelt, after all, had been in office since 1933, Churchill since 1940.)

Some in high places in London also regarded Soviet Russia as a useful pawn in deflecting Hitler eastward. There were partisans of this view in Washington as well. Yet Churchill was not far behind Roosevelt and his team in regarding Stalin and the U.S.S.R. as a strong, potentially dependable co-combatant against Hitler. In some respects, Churchill's government led the way in paving a road to Moscow for extending American Lend-Lease aid to the Soviets. Suspicions on one or the other side of the "strange alliance" during the war—namely, that either the eastern or western half might defect and at some juncture strike a deal with Hitler— was never too seriously entertained, it seems, either in Moscow or the Western capitals at least not in the earliest period of spring and summer 1941. In any case, such suspicions, when they cropped up, came and went.

Stalin knew that Roosevelt's authority over his own governmental team was extremely strong. He knew the American president had his will in most areas of domestic and foreign policy making (e.g., he was even trying to pack the U.S. Supreme Court in violation of the U.S. Constitution). FDR's reelection to a third term in 1940 only buttressed the Soviet view of the President's nearly autocratic as well as popular rule. Therefore, from Stalin's point of view, working with any of FDR's several closest associates was the best way to influence American policy in preferred, Soviet directions. This became obvious at those very first Lend-Lease talks in Moscow in July 1941 in which Stalin personally took part.

While debunking the American boast of its being eminently if not uniquely the most democratic of all countries in the world, there were often hints from Stalin that he thought America and Americans to be industrious and relatively peaceloving, imbued with a commendable "bourgeois-democratic" spirit and entrepreneurial initiative. He was also informed of Roosevelt's and the American public's long-standing, anti-Nazi posture. These characteristics, to Stalin's mind, evidently, were quite unlike those of any other capitalist state.

According to Russian historian, Yu. B. Basistov, as early at 1939 Stalin considered the USA to be a "pro-Soviet" country among only three so classified. Besides America, only Greece and Yugoslavia were so designated.[9] American power, of course, helped make it preeminent over the others.

SPIES AND AGENTS OF INFLUENCE

The task is to penetrate into those places where policy is born and developed, where discussions and debates take place, where policy is completed. Penetrating the surroundings of Roosevelt himself is the goal that we seek in our everyday work.[10]

The Soviet leader also appears to have thought that a certain naïve streak ran through the American people and its leaders. This was true of the Americans in ways that were quite unlike the traits found in the jaded, old European states and their encrusted systems. If Churchill compared Stalin to a burglar, Stalin once compared Churchill to a common pickpocket. Nothing like these negative views were ever expressed by Stalin toward Roosevelt.

On the other hand, Soviet security chief Lavrenty Beria's son, Sergo, writes in his memoirs that Stalin and leadership regarded democratic countries as essentially hobbled by their "slow-moving" democratic political system.[11] Unlike dictatorships, democracies must contend with public opinion, and leaders of totalitarian countries would have to take this into account as well, Sergo Beria pointed out, citing attitudes held by his father and Stalin. This put the democracies at a disadvantage with countries ruled by one-party dictatorships. The latter could expedite matters pretty much as they wished and whenever they chose. The so-called parliaments of dictatorships merely rubber-stamped the dictator's prior decisions.

The point is that democratic countries' openness and democratism allowed—indeed, invited—Stalin and the Moscow leadership to influence public opinion. This was especially the case with the United States. Here such influence was brought to bear by squads of Soviet "illegals" and "legals" and fellow travelers. These measures were carried out far more successfully in the United States than in any other leading capitalist country during the prewar and war periods.[12] As a result, it seems undeniable that Lend-Lease, as tenuously supported on the American side in Congress and among the people—it had to be supported in order for it to be put into effect—*probably would have been inconceivable without such influence and Soviet penetration in America.*

It is therefore ironic in retrospect that Soviet spies and agents of influence operating in Washington, D.C., New York City, and elsewhere in a sense actually paved the way to such closer approaches to the U.S.S.R. This was represented and symbolized by, and culminated, above all, in Lend-Lease, which in turn helped save Russia from Nazi conquest and as a consequence prevented German control over Eurasia.[13]

Such domination had been Hitler's ultimate goal. Under the influence of his reigning authority on geopolitics, Professor and General Karl Haushofer, the Führer was convinced that dominating Eurasia would lead ultimately to victory across the oceans over the United States. Precisely for that reason, Hitler was building long-range bombers and rockets while working earnestly in Norway on atomic fission in order ultimately to develop nuclear weapons. Having left the war against England unfinished, Hitler had sought to conquer Russia as a guarantee against America that in entering the war, would tip the scales against the Axis. Hitler calculated he could preempt this likelihood by conquering the Russian giant to the east and thereby also inherit its rich resources. As Austrian historian Heinz Magenheimer points out,

> Hitler reckoned with the probability of the United States entering the war if it were prolonged, and this was to play an important role in his considerations of how best to deal with the Soviet Union. That he clearly recognized the growing weight of the United States was revealed, in early July [1940], by the Z-plan—the temporary resumption of the Kriegsmarine's ship-building programme—and the discussions of the basic principles with leaders of the OKW and the branches of the Wehrmacht in summer and early autumn. [The plan to attack the U.S.S.R.] was likewise designed to anticipate intervention

by the United States on Britain's side. On the one hand, the issue was to establish an impregnable empire in continental Europe, on the other, to ensure that Japan kept its back free for a confrontation with Britain and the United States in eastern Asia and the Pacific.[14]

As we saw, the Soviet dictator held an unusually favorable opinion of the American president. How much of his reputed personal admiration for Roosevelt stemmed from purely exploitative motives is hard to say. He fullsomely described FDR as a skillful leader of his people. At same time, Stalin regarded the American leader as a foxy character and *"politikan"* (politician) whom only he, Stalin, could outwit. After FDR's death in April 1945, Stalin lamented the fact that the "vulgar" anti-Soviet Truman, whom he disliked, had taken over in the White House.

Too, there is evidence that Stalin had his suspicions regarding America's alliance with Britain. At times in the pre-June 1941 period he seems to have entertained the notion that America, like the British, was egging Soviet Russia into war with Germany. Both Western countries thus relished a coming fratricidal struggle between the two totalitarian states. The Americans, through their ambassador in Moscow, Lawrence Steinhardt, repeatedly, routinely, vehemently denied such motives. Russian and Western historians of one school of thought maintain, on not entirely convincing evidence, that Stalin, right up to the cataclysm of June 22, 1941, sincerely sought continued long-term, peaceful relations with Nazi Germany.

As to Stalin's two other colleagues of the Big Three, it was clear to everyone that Stalin liked Roosevelt but disliked Churchill. How much of this reflected Stalin's pre-June 1941 attitudes is not known. Yet it could not have been lost on Stalin that Churchill had always been a dyed-in-the-wool anti-Communist whereas Roosevelt seldom cast the U.S.S.R. in an unfavorable light. Memoirists close to Stalin write that he actually heard Stalin make bitter criticism of Churchill. Before becoming prime minister, Churchill, indeed, had once exclaimed that Bolshevism should have been "strangled in its cradle."

Moreover, the British government as a whole was always an object of suspicion on Stalin's part. Within the Moscow's Commissariat of Foreign Affairs, it was hard to find any Soviet official who thought, or who dared to think, highly of the British. Meanwhile, officials like ex-Foreign Minister Maxim Litvinoff (who was returned by Stalin as a deputy minister in the Foreign Commissariat in late 1941 as well as being posted as ambassador to Washington), as with the bearded, deputy commissar of Foreign Affairs, S. A. Lozovsky, an apparent Litvinoffite, had obvious sympathies for America.

The latter, like Litvinoff a Jew, was executed in 1952 on false charges stemming from Stalin's then anti-Jewish campaign. Litvinoff himself barely escaped such punishment in the latter years. The Jewish aspect is interesting in that Stalin was convinced, not unlike Hitler, that Washington was run by "Jewish money."[15] When Harry S. Truman replaced Roosevelt at FDR's death in April 1945, Stalin reasoned that, unfortunately to his mind, a new, "non-Jewish" group was now in charge in America.

Another sore point with Stalin vis-à-vis the British was the content of the information relayed secretly to the Kremlin by such agents as the "Cambridge Five" in London as well as from his alert ambassador there, Ivan Maisky. Namely, that when the U.S.S.R. invaded Finland in December 1939, Britain was seriously considering the military contingency of RAF bombing of the Caucasus oil fields, the main source of Soviet petroleum and gasoline. This unprovoked, naked Soviet aggression had caused an uproar of pro-Finnish sentiments in England. It did also in America but nowhere near as potently as it did in Europe. Finland, after all, was just around the bend to the north from the British Isles. Moreover, many of the military and civilian officials who were to oversee such dire measures against Soviet targets in the Caucasus remained in the British government after Churchill took over in May 1940, of which continuity Stalin was kept fully informed.

Some historians, both Russian and Western, believe that Stalin never forgave the British for these and other "sins." He thus remained permanently suspicious of the British Prime Minister's motives despite other indications that Churchill's motives in 1940–1941 could have been interpreted differently. Namely, that the British leader merely hoped in all honesty that if Germany invaded the U.S.S.R., as he surely thought it would, his country would welcome Stalin into the Allied, or later United Nations, fold as an ally and encourage U.S. Lend-Lease aid to the U.S.S.R.'s war effort. It is another piece of irony that the only country capable of giving such aid on a large scale was the United States, not the disliked (by Stalin) Great Britain (although the British, of course, contributed to Lend-Lease shipments to the U.S.S.R.).

Russian historian Ivanov writes of U.S.-Soviet relations in the immediate pre-June 1941 period as one, he says, in which the "two great powers, the U.S.S.R. and the USA, though not yet participating in the Second World War, realized that their positions were not all that different." He continues,

> The USA and the U.S.S.R. were potential allies in the sense of their both opposing complete German domination on the European Continent. Both the Soviet Union and the U.S., moreover, were mutually alarmed by Japan's aggressive policy in the Far East that threatened the national intersts of both

countries. To Stalin's mind, the ultimate authority in all matters, including foreign affairs, was Lenin. Soon after World War I, it was Lenin who had predicted that that conflict between Japan and the U.S. was inevitable. This at once meant that by further analysis relations between America and the Soviet Union were bound to become closer . . . Once they both did enter the conflict, a vast reorientation of forces did, in fact, take place on a world scale. It would be one in which the USA would play the leading role. By taking all this into account, warnings sent by Washington to Moscow could not help but have alarmed Moscow . . . Ideological and political factors between countries belonging to antagonistic social and economic systems do play a decisive role in their relations. Nevertheless this role need not be all-determining.

Geopolitical factors operating in the relations between states do assert themselves. They can, in fact, assume the dominant position over ideological, political, and class factors . . . Similarly, in World War I, geopolitical determinants of policy led to a reorientation of forces so that the main countries of the Entente—Russia, England, France, and the USA—all found themselves on the same side of the barricades.[16]

The Russian historian implies that despite Stalin's miscalculations concerning the timing of German aggression against the U.S.S.R. and his "stubborn refusal" to face that fact, he nonetheless surely did understand these geopolitical truisms.

Stalin's singling out of America took various forms. Not infrequently at the wartime summits Stalin tried to pit FDR against Churchill. He knew FDR disagreed with the latter on various postwar issues, particularly those that might negatively affect the integrity of the British Empire. He also greatly admired FDR's number two man, Harry Hopkins, with whom he had gotten along so well in the pre–Lend-Lease talks in Moscow in mid-1941. Hopkins was the official who had smoothed the way to carrying out this vital assistance. Ex–foreign spy chief, General Pavel Sudoplatov, has described Harry Hopkins as a "Soviet agent." Hopkins is so described in the *Venona Papers*.

Soviet spy penetration within the upper echelons of the American government was incredibly extensive. It was a strong factor in the Soviet realignment toward America. Agents and spies included among others the Assistant Secretary of the Treasury, Harry Dexter White; the American diplomat and policy-making aide, Alger Hiss; Laughlin Currie, Roosevelt's economics assistant within the White House itself and a spy courier. Secret Soviet agents operating for the U.S.S.R. as spies were at work in the War Department, OSS, Air Corps, War Production Board, Office of War Information, Departments of Agriculture and Commerce, administration of Lend-Lease; Mrs. Eleanor Roosevelt was said to have had a woman Soviet agent as a personal friend; and so on. In all, this activity made the administration look like Swiss cheese. To appreciate the scale of this Soviet penetration, imagine that such a situation existed and was exposed today within the administrations of, say, Reagan, the Bushes, or Clinton. The shock and public outcry would be—justifiably—deadening. That such penetration could be occurring would seem unbelievable.

It is hard to deny that this widespread penetration by Soviet agents of influence, not to mention the many unnamed Soviet sympathizers in the American bureaucracy and at the highest levels in Washington, D.C., all became potent factors that led Stalin, before World War II and Lend-Lease, in the direction of accommodation with the U.S. government, which he calculated he could influence so well. As, in fact, he did.

Hopkins was the top American official chosen by Roosevelt who had first approached Stalin in July 1941 with offers to ship large amounts of aid to the beleaguered U.S.S.R. That country was then fighting for its very life against Nazi Germany after only a month of war. The Soviet leader's expressed admiration for Hopkins might well have stemmed from the American official's known sympathies for Soviet Russia as well as his putative admiration for Stalin personally—and, of course, because of Hopkins's proximity to FDR.

Roosevelt once remarked to former U.S. Ambassador to the U.S.S.R., William C. Bullitt, after the latter had expressed strong doubts about the trustworthiness, not to mention brutality, of Stalin,

> Bill, I don't dispute your facts, they are accurate. I don't dispute the logic of your reasoning. I just have a hunch that Stalin is not that kind of man. Harry [Hopkins] says he's not . . . and I think that if I give him everything I possibly can [by way of Lend-Lease aid] and ask nothing from him in return, noblesse oblige, he won't try to annex anything and will work with me for a world of democracy and peace.[17]

Early in 1942, Roosevelt wrote to Churchill as follows:

> I know you will not mind my being brutally frank when I tell you that I think I can personally handle Stalin better than either your Foreign Office or my State Department. . . . He thinks he likes me better, and I hope he will continue to do so.

Again, as in chess, Stalin tried to figure out Roosevelt's "game" as it was being played out before his eyes—as, for instance, in the pre–Lend-Lease negotiations of the summer and fall of 1941 and at the Big Three wartime summits in Tehran and Yalta. He always applied to foreign leaders and their aides the considerable talents that he had put to such good use for twenty years as the Soviet Communist Party's General Secretary in charge of vetting top Party and Government officials in the Soviet Union. He played this key role after his appointment to this post in 1922 by Lenin, amid the latter's extravagant praise of his talented Georgian, Stalin. Stalin's card file memory concerning the party and government officials' personalities, the vulnerabilities and strengths of hundreds of his chosen, key Nomenklaturists selected for top positions, was extraordinary.

In other words, sizing up people, including foreign diplomats and leaders, became Stalin's stock in trade, at which he excelled. Stalin always insisted on having and reading ahead of time from his intelligence sources the bulging files on any and all officials and leaders with whom he was to come into contact.

As Robert Sherwood writes in *Roosevelt and Hopkins*, Harry Hopkins described Stalin favorably this way after his first meeting with him in late July 1941:

> There was no waste of word, gesture, nor mannerism. It was like talking to a perfectly coordinated machine, an intelligent machine. Joseph Stalin knew what he wanted, knew what Russia wanted and assumed that you knew . . . He wore no armament, military or civilian . . . His hands are huge, as hard as his mind.

When Stalin looked at America in the 1920s, he saw a country that was, relatively speaking, an industrial giant, and that was in general peace-minded. For instance, in diplomacy, such as at the London Disarmament Conference (1935–1936), it was the "out-of-area" Americans alone who favored virtually unlimited disarmament. By contrast, the British refused to negotiate serious reductions in naval armaments while the Germans and Japanese altogether boycotted the conference. Fascist Italy participated only as a nonvoting member.

Too, Stalin understood well the phenomenon of virulent American isolationism. At the same time he perceived that business interests in America, especially after the financial crash in Wall Street of 1929, were eager to make deals with the U.S.S.R., regardless of ideological differences and Soviet revolutionist propaganda. Stalin, like Lenin, was well aware of the apolitical, nonideological nature of profit-seeking American businessmen. (The analogy today might be Fidel Castro's wooing of pacifists or certain ideologically numb, profit-minded American business interests, especially the wheat farmers and their lobbies in Washington, in his pursuit of lifting the U.S. embargo on American trade with Communist Cuba.)

Stalin, moreover, was reassured when FDR, in his first year in the White House, decided as one of his first acts in foreign affairs to recognize the U.S.S.R. (in 1933). America was the last Western country to do so some ten years after most European countries had extended recognition. Roosevelt perceived, even that early in the pre–World War II years, that the U.S.S.R.

might one day join Great Britain, France, and the United States in opposition to any aggressor nations. Secretary of State Cordell Hull was convinced, notes an American scholar, that "only such a union could recall the jingoist nations to their senses. The serious deterioration in the prospects for world peace were uppermost in the President's mind as he prepared his approach to Russia [in 1933]."[18]

What immediately followed during the 1930s were large and significant American business deals with the U.S.S.R. The result was that no less than two-thirds of all Soviet industrial enterprises were built with sizable American aid in the form of machines and technical assistance by qualified personnel.

In his time, Lenin had set a precedent for capitalist aid to the Soviet Republic. He had allowed large Western capitalist concessions to exploit Russian oil, gold, and other natural resources. These at first were granted by Moscow to the British—exploiting to Soviet benefit resources in the Caucasus and in Siberia. Yet Lenin had spoken especially positively of potential American assistance. He was aware, of course, of the aid dispensed through the Hoover ARA food program that had saved the lives of some 4 million Soviet citizens in the early 1920s.[19]

These earlier precedents of Western, and especially American assistance in the form of the ARA and the help given Soviet industrialization in the 1930s by Ford, General Electric, et al., served as significant, tangible forerunners of Lend-Lease aid. They were also the prelude to post–World War II American relief aid to the Soviet Ukraine dispensed through UNRRA in 1945–1946. This U.S. aid tradition might even have been continued under the Marshall Plan after 1947 had Stalin not vetoed U.S.S.R. and Soviet East European satellite participation in the large and effective American aid program for Europe.

Not to be forgotten either was the fact that Stalin the Georgian was an avid student of Russian history. By all intents and purposes he was a Russophile in the romantic, nationalist sense. Yet, he disdained, as Lenin did, certain negative characteristics that he found in individual Russians. He often touted "Great Russian" superiority and Russian expansionism of the tsarist past—that is, Russia as a "civilizing force" over the "backward" borderlands to the south and east. He was flattered when his writers described him as a latter-day Ivan the Terrible or Peter the Great. Whether he bestowed such fullsome praise on *Rus'* and Russians for purely opportunistic reasons is hard to say. Yet it appears his feelings along this line were genuine. Also genuine was his interest in Russian culture, toward which he was by no means indifferent. His attendance at performances of the Bolshoi opera and ballet seemed not to be merely perfunctory. Stalin ably played on these sentiments when in conference with Westerners. The latter were thus favorably impressed with Stalin's

"Russian patriotism."

As a result of his consciousness of Russian history and his personal role as an updated tsar-turned-commissar, he therefore was aware of the long, positive tradition in cooperative American-Russian relations. This "nationalistic" awareness on Stalin's part seems to have in a sense abetted the Soviet leader in pursuing an alliance with America and the West, if an often stressed one, before and during World War II. Of course, the factor of sheer desperation was primary in Stalin's mind after June 22, 1941.

By playing on Russo-American traditions of cooperation, Stalin was, above all, able to win American favor. This paid off in the dispensing of Lend-Lease aid and monetary credits to the U.S.S.R. during and after the war. It could also be used as a diversionary tactic by the Soviet dictator to get his way when it came to the territorial giveaways—for example, at the Yalta Conference of 1945. Playing upon FDR's sympathies was one example of this.

ARMAND HAMMER'S ROLE

The millionnaire industrialist, Armand Hammer, also played a key role in laying the foundations of Lend-Lease. As a dyed-in-the-wool collaborator of Lenin's and Stalin's in procuring Western, especially American, assistance in the industrializaion of the U.S.S.R. going back to the 1920s, Hammer was an old hand at such machinations in the Soviet interest.

In his well-sourced biography of Hammer, espionage expert Edward Jay Epstein describes the active role played by this interlocutor in nailing down Lend-Lease. Epstein notes that in November 1940—ironically around the time of the famous Stalin report to the Politburo—Armand Hammer met with FDR in the White House. He and the President discussed the idea of developing American military assistance to Britain, the Neutrality Act and Roosevelt's campaign promises not to embroil the United States in the European war to the contrary. Roosevelt thereupon suggested to Hammer that he discuss this plan with Harry Hopkins. Hopkins twice traveled to New York City, Hammer's base of operations, to discuss this idea with officials and businessmen there.

Did they also perhaps discuss extending such aid to Hammer's favorite country, the U.S.S.R.? One author, Peter Niblo, author and former U.S. intelligence officer, surmises that this indeed was the case. He writes,

> Could this Lend-Lease idea also have been received—possibly conceived—in Moscow just as a massive German buildup of of forces along the borders of Eastern Europe [facing the U.S.S.R.] was being reported to the Kremlin? Could a desperate need for military supplies by Moscow have been envisioned by Stalin by late 1940? One might answer that Stalin was still Hitler's ally. Why,

then, would Lend-Lease be of any interest to him? . . . The Kremlin's main objective as war approached became immediate U.S. military aid without a need for compensation.[20]

NOTES

1. William Taubman, *Stalin's American Policy From Entente to Détente to Cold War*, New York, W. W. Norton & Company, 1982, 18.
2. Robert Ivanov, *Stalin i Soyuzniki 1941–1945* (Stalin and the Allies, 1941–1945), Smolensk, Rusich, 2000, 122. Ivanov notes that the "USA and the Soviet Union were potential allies since both countries sought to prevent Germany from dominating Europe" (92). Post-Soviet Russian authors also note that both Lenin and Stalin said that they regarded the United States as relatively peaceminded compared to other capitalist countries. Radical U.S. disarmament proposals at European conferences after World War I are examples of such peacemindedness. So was its own domestic disarmament.
3. Cf. Albert L. Weeks, *Stalin's Other War: Soviet Grand Strategy 1939–1941*, Lanham, Rowman & Littlefield, 2002, for Stalin's expansionist plans according to evidence found in the latest archival documentation and research by post-Soviet Russian historians.
4. Weeks, *Stalin's Other War* chapter 1, "Soviet Expansionist Ideology: Propaganda or Blueprint?"
5. Paul Johnson, *Modern Times*, New York, Harper Collins, 1983, 202.
6. Pavel Sudoplatov and Anatoli Sudoplatov, *Special Tasks*, New York, Little, Brown and Company, 1994, 96.
7. Amos Perlmutter, *FDR & Stalin: A Not So Grand Alliance, 1943–1945*, Columbia, University of Missouri Press, 1993. 90.
8. Herbert Romerstein, and Eric Breindel, *The Venona Secrets: Exposing Soviet Espionage and America's Traitors*, New York, Regnery Publishing, Inc., 2000, 100–101.
9. Yu. B. Basistov, *Stalin—Gitler Ot pakta do voiny* (Stalin-Hitler From the Pact to War), St. Petersburg, Blitz, R.F., 2001, 34.
10. Peter B. Niblo, *Influence*, Oakland, OR, Elderberry Press, 2002, 49. Cf. Romerstein, *Venona*, on this point.
11. Sergo Beriya, *Moi otets Lavrentii Beriya* (My Father, Lavrenty Beria), Moscow, Sovremennik, 1994, 119.
12. The authors make this point in Romerstein, *Venona*.
13. A. N. Yakovlev, ed., *1941 God*, vol. 1, 779.
14. Heinz Magenheimer, *Hitler's War: German's Key Strategic Decisions 1940–1945*, London, Cassell, 2002, 40.
14. Romerstein, *Venona*, 391 passim.
15. Robert Ivanov, *Stalin i soyuzniki 1941–1945* (Stalin and the Allies, 1941–1945), Smolensk, Rusich, 2000, 92–93.
16. George N. Crocker, *Roosevelt's Road to Russia*, New York, Da Capo Press, 1975, 161–62; George C. Herring, Jr., *Aid to Russia 1941–1946: Strategy, Diplomacy, the Origins of the Cold War*, New York, Columbia University Press, 1973, 29.
17. William E. Kinsella, Jr., *Leadership in Isolation: FDR and the Origins of the Sec-*

ond World War, Boston, G. K. Hall & Co., 1978, 63.

18. The ARA was continually attacked in Soviet reference books, such as the *Large* and *Small Soviet Encyclopedias*. In them the ARA was described as a spy organization.

19. Niblo, *Influence*, 86; 88.

4

✢

Historical Roots of Lend-Lease—I

America is a very rich country to which all countries are subordinated.

—V. I. Lenin, July 1920

* * *

From every source at my disposal . . . it looks as if a vast German onslaught on Russia was imminent . . . Should this new war break out, we shall, of course, give all encouragement and any help we can spare to the Russians, following the principle that Hitler is the foe we have to beat. I do not expect any class political reactions here, and trust a German-Russian conflict will not cause you [President Roosevelt] any embarrassment.

—Prime Minister Winston Churchill's cable to Roosevelt, June 15, 1941

* * *

I would not minimize the personal capabilities of [Franklin D.] Roosevelt—his initiative, courage, and decisiveness. Without doubt, of all the captains [*kapitany*] of the contemporary capitalist world, Roosevelt is by far the strongest figure.

—J. V. Stalin, July 23, 1934

* * *

The Russians had recognized much earlier than our leaders the importance of having a secret service that functioned efficiently, and the effectiveness of their methods and organization won the highest praise from our specialists.

—Walter Schellenberg, Chief of Counterintelligence, *Memoirs*

When you get right down to it, it should have been no surprise when the United States and Russia (that is, the Soviet Union) hitched up as allies in World War II.

The history of any countries' relations with each other are likely to be determined to a large extent by precedents. If the precedents over a long period of time are generally positive, traditional friendship will probably follow generation after generation. Yet such relations are not "predestined" to be friendly. They are as much a function of the wills of the leaders of such countries as they are the common interests that tend to unite them.

That said, when Russia became the U.S.S.R. in late 1917, the historical tradition of Russo-American friendship was severely challenged and nearly severed altogether. Lenin and his Bolsheviks had sworn eternal enmity against what they called the "bourgeois-democratic" and "imperialist" countries of the West. In 1919 they set up a "general staff of revolution," known as the Third Communist International (Comintern). Its task was to spread Bolshevik-style subversion worldwide. Moscow's hate America propaganda became a key element in this undeclared war against the "old bourgeois order" in the West. After the Bolshevik coup d'etat of November 7, 1917 (falsely described as a "revolution" by Soviet propagandized historiography and swallowed whole by the naïve), Lenin had proclaimed that he had established a new order in Russia. It was one, he said, that would be emulated inevitably throughout the whole world. Ironically, Lenin's expression, "new order," along with much else Soviet as well as totalitarian was borrowed by the Nazis in Germany after 1933.

Despite this break with the Russian past as concerned America, Lenin was not above turning to the United States when aid was urgently needed. As a remote republic left out of World War I's destruction, unlike most of Europe including Russia, America in its homeland enriched itself from the war. During the postwar period until the crash on Wall Street in 1929, America's was a thriving economy that had been free of the turmoil of the Great War (1914–1918).

Every nation-state in the world in the interwar period was, of course, aware of the exceptional country, America. Its prosperous industry, its natural resources, its abundant agricultural production were widely known. The broad oceans on both of its sides, east and west, the long-standing isolationist spirit of its people were also known. These factors insulated that country from the machinations and wars of European countries at the turn of the twentieth century. The European countries, Soviet Russia included, were cognizant of what this could mean in terms of their own national interests, their foreign policy, and grand strategy. If America remained in the background, that was one thing; if it emerged to tip the scales of diplomacy and war in Europe, that was another. All these factors meant that

America was a "special case." It was viewed abroad as a reluctant, latecomer ally of one or another side involved in a European war (as in World War I).

From the several major European wars of the nineteenth century fought abroad, America remained entirely aloof. As an ally of a European combatant or alliance, however, it would be of inestimable value. This was amply proved in the Great War in terms of the assistance America lent to the Entente Powers led by England and France and in the East lent to Tsarist Russia. Shipped American aid, a small-scale World War I "lend-lease," and the American Expeditionary Force sent to fight against the Central Powers in France were invaluable assets in the Allied victory over the enemy. This also meant that America's riches in future might again be made available to those powers with whom it was allied or with whom it enjoyed traditional friendship in the diplomatic-military sense.

Soviet Russia became increasingly menacing as did its ideology. It began an almost yearly process of enlarging itself throughout the 1920s. Forcible annexations of the former tsarist borderlands were made by the Red Army in the Caucasus and Central Asia. Lenin and the Comintern talked about "world revolution" and setting up, in their very words, a "Soviet of the Whole World."

As this militancy was expressed in tangible ways, the U.S.S.R. drew even further away from traditional, prerevolutionary friendship toward America. Since 1918, that now had to lie dormant in the face of Soviet Comintern "internationalism," outright subversion, extensive espionage, and war. On the diplomatic level, Soviet-American contacts—even after the belated U.S. official recognition of Soviet Russia in 1933—were often accompanied by bitterness and/or varnished over with false "amity."

Nevertheless, communism and Marxist-Leninist ideology to the contrary, the nearly 200-year tradition of Russo-American friendship going back to colonial America was never totally disrupted. The Cold War era's "proxy wars" (notably in Korea in the 1950s and Vietnam in the 1960s), in which the U.S. and U.S.S.R. were indirect enemies, were phenomena of the post–World War II period, not of the pre–World War II years. But even in these wars—plus the other local conflicts and tensions as well as with the dangerous, U.S.-Soviet "brushes" in the air and on the high seas, the tensions over the status of Berlin, and many other crises—the two superpowers still had never fought each other directly in large-scale military combat.

TRADITIONAL RUSSIAN-AMERICAN TIES[1]

In promoting cordiality in Russian and American relations, geography played a positive role. The very remoteness of the two countries from each other had precluded any direct confrontation or clash. Their border-to-border contact is up in the Bering Strait between Siberia and Alaska. They have never met as enemies on the field of battle. The Scriptural injunction against being "dipped in the blood of thine enemies" does not apply. In fact, until the North Atlantic Treaty Organization (1949) and the Warsaw Pact (1955), the two countries had never even been lasting members of opposing alliances.

If it had not been for America's physical remoteness from Europe (a gap that began to be closed only with the invention of the steamboat and the airplane), America and Russia might have contended with each other during the nineteenth century. For in Europe, Russia under the tsars and later under the commissars played—and still plays—an important role in the traditionally competitive, balance-of-power "Quadrille of Europe" consisting of itself, Britain, France, and Germany (before Germany, Austria-Hungary). Strong and persistent Russian assertion of its expansionist aims in Balkan Europe and in the Black and Mediterranean seas was always met with stern resistance on the part of the other members of Quadrille. One major result of this unstable rectangle of forces was the Crimean War (1853–1856), during which America played a totally hands-off, neutral role.

Fortunately for long-standing Russian-American friendship, the United States remained largely aloof from the European machinations and conflicts of the nineteenth century. Geography and the essentially neutralist, isolationist American foreign policy since the days of George Washington in their way likewise helped protect Russian and American cordiality.

EARLIEST PHASE OF FRIENDSHIP

The United States and Russia were and in many ways still are at opposite poles with respect to cultural background, traditions, and political philosophy. Despite these differences, during a major part of the nineteenth century a peculiar relation of cordiality existed between these powers. Upon close examination, one can see that this tradition has little other basis than the existence at given times of a common enemy. But the tradition was also abetted by the absence of competing national interests.

Although the first of the European powers to recognize American independence, the Russia of Empress Catherine the Great did not sincerely sympathize with the democratic ideals of the Declaration of Independence or the views of Thomas Paine. Quite a different motivation impelled the Empress in St. Petersburg to recognize that distant, new republic: St. Petersburg saw that the American colonial rebellion provided an opportunity for her to weaken the power of Russia's maritime competitor, Great

Britain. "The enemy of my enemy is my friend." Britain was a naval power, the principal country standing astride Russia's valuable egress from its ice-free ports on the Baltic Sea and Arctic Ocean. Not surprisingly, Catherine had always refused to lend any of her Cossack soldiers to George III and his colonial enterprises.

With the dispatch in 1780 of the first American envoy, Francis Dana (representing the Continental Congress), to the Russian court, it was expected that the American would be favorably received. Britain by this time appeared to be hopelessly bogged down in its futile war against the American colonists, and there seemed to be a basis for establishing a Russian and American diplomatic and commercial relationship. But this did not affect the Dana mission. Accompanied by the 14-year-old John Quincy Adams, who in several years was himself to become American minister (quasi-ambassador) to Russia, Dana was not once granted an audience by the largely uninterested Russian ruler during the two years of Dana's sojourn in the Russian capital.

At one point the American minister to Russia optimistically requested that Congress appropriate a sum of money equivalent to 6,000 rubles, the Russian fee which had to be paid to each of the four Russian ministers empowered to sign a treaty. But the money was never sent. The Empress's delay, the end of the war in America, and the ensuing American policy of disengagement from Europe led the United States to table its efforts toward détente with Russia.

With the accession to the throne of the (initially) liberal Tsar Alexander I in 1801, a new upward trend in U.S.-Russian relations seemed in the offing. Adams, now the new American envoy to the court of St. Petersburg, was now graciously received by the Tsar, an event that had been prepared by the friendly and rather sentimental correspondence that had previously taken place between Alexander and Thomas Jefferson.

Sentiment aside, Russia had a no-nonsense reason for courting America's friendship. As indicated above, there was a "common enemy," in this case Britain. There was also the factor of potential bilateral commercial intercourse. American merchant ships were appearing in increasing numbers in Russia's Baltic seaports. The broad-beamed schooners carried such commodities as pepper, coffee, tea, cotton, tobacco, and especially sugar. These were traded for such Russian goods as hemp, flax, sailcloth, cordage, linen sheeting, iron, furs, and the inevitable caviar. Because the trade was valued in the millions of dollars, Russia was quite as interested in preserving it as the United States. Also, the threat of British interference with American and Russian ships hung over both countries.

As for France on the European continent, Alexander's stated willingness to comply to the terms of Napoleon's "blockade" (refusing entry into Russian ports to all neutral as well as English ships engaged in trade from the British West Indies) was more honored in the breach than in the observance. These imports were too essential to Russia for Alexander permanently to respect a formal agreement. Instead, he invoked the qualifying principle of *rebus sic stantibus* ("as long as things remain thus"). Russia therefore pursued its own interests, which ran counter to those of some of its European counterparts in the Quadrille. Yet they harmonized with those of the U.S. Russian and American amity and bilateral commercial intercourse thus continued unabated.

Napoleon, seeking hegemony over Europe for himself and France, declared war on Russia in 1812. Thus opened the Fatherland War from which came the title, "Great Fatherland [or Patriotic] War" of World War II. Alexander joined forces with England. This was in a *marriage de convenience* directed against the dictator of France. When this happened, America found itself in a war—the War of 1812—with England, Russia's newfound ally. St. Petersburg knew that there was no danger that America would become involved in Napoleon's adventure. This was not only because of the U.S. policy of neutrality, but because France, like Britain, had interfered with American shipping on the high seas. Nevertheless, Russia wished to make sure that America would not be drawn into Napoleon's orbit. Thus, Russia used the tactic of offering its good offices as mediator in the British-American War of 1812. This anticipated a similar American offer to be of service to Russia almost a century later. This was when the United States acted as mediator in the Russo-Japanese War of 1904–1905.

President James Madison, eager to get off the hook of an untenable war with Britain, sent Secretary of State James Monroe and Secretary of the Treasury Albert Gallatin to St. Petersburg in 1813 to join the U.S. minister to Russia Adams. They were and to act as a team of American troubleshooters seeking the help of Russia as mediator in the War of 1812. At the same time they were commissioned to sign a trade treaty with her.

However, international communications being as primitive as they were in 1813 (it took weeks for messages to be carried across the Atlantic by ship), the American envoys were surprised to learn upon their arrival in St. Petersburg that Britain had meanwhile let it be known that it had no intention of agreeing to Russian mediation. The war was going badly for its adversary, America, and the British were suspicious of the Tsar's motives. British-Russian rivalry on the seas, despite their alliance, had continued to be the *bête noire* in the relations between the two European powers.

Meanwhile, President Madison was being subjected to vehement antiwar criticism in the U.S. press. ("Madison's War" was an even more frequently used epithet than "McNamara's War" over 150 years later.) A contemporary journal, *Niles' Register,* attacked Madison from another angle: namely, for having tried to do business, either diplomatic or commercial, with "Alexander the Deliverer." His regime, said the influential journal, was a "government of horror" that ruled over an empire composed of *"conquered* countries, *usurped* provinces, and *ravaged* territories."

The eventual failure to win Russian mediation in the War of 1812 was not the result, however, of these and similar anti-Russian attacks. Delays in communications, British obduracy, and the Tsar's absence from the Russian capital (he took personal command at the front where the Russians were driving the French westward) all militated against mediation. Finally, the two belligerents, Britain and the United States, agreed on their own to a ceasefire. The war ended. However, just before this occurred, Tsar Alexander, seeing that his efforts to mediate were failing, offered to defray the expenses incurred by the American envoys during their stay in Russia.

As a result of the tsar's show of good will during this American time of troubles, there ensued a friendly relationship, which was to remain intact for most of the rest of the century.

RUSSIA IN THE AMERICAN NORTHWEST

The Monroe Doctrine of 1823, which was later to be applied in South America, was actually first inspired by a U.S.-Russian encounter in North America. (Likewise, in the Cuban missile showdown of October 1962, application of the doctrine was again applied to Russia in a dangerous confrontation of the two countries when the U.S.S.R. attempted a *coup de main* in this hemisphere by deploying medium-range, nuclear-tipped missiles on the island ninety miles from U.S. shores.)

The Monroe Doctrine contained two basic ideas: (1) noncolonization of the Western hemisphere by European powers, and (2) nonintervention by European powers in the affairs of nations of the New World, with the consequent threat to their newly won national independence. It was the first idea that was evoked by Russian actions along the northwest littoral of North America. But application of the doctrine was otherwise exceptional since it was directed more at Britain, France, and Spain.

During the first two decades of the nineteenth century, both America and Russia had chartered companies and established settlements in the North Pacific area stretching from the rocky Aleutian Islands off Alaska (both the Russians and the Americans were also active in the Hawaiian Islands) to the then Spanish-ruled province of California. The Russians had established themselves in these areas as a consequence of the voyages of Vitus Jonassen Bering (1681–1741), Danish expatriate and an officer in the tsarist navy. On his frigate *St. Petersburg* in the 1740s, Bering and his men sailed into the treacherous strait, now named for him, separating North America (at Alaska) from Asia.

Pursuant to these voyages, the Russian-American Company was chartered under the authority of Tsar Paul I in 1799 as Siberian traders and fur hunters began to settle southward to what is now the area around San Francisco. Under a monopoly granted to it in a ukase issued by Tsar Alexander I in 1821, the company was given complete control over all Russian settlements from the ring straits to 51° north latitude. America was thus confronted with the possibility of a large Russian colony on the western littoral of North America an outpost of the tsarist empire in the Western hemisphere, with Sitka (then called Novy Archangel) in Alaska as its capital.

Although the Russians in "Russian America" endured every imaginable hardship under a governor-general and units of Cossacks as they sought to retain their tenuous hold upon the long strip of territory in the New World, it eventually became impossible to maintain a liaison with the home country, even to receive adequate assistance to defend the possessions. When American minister to Russia Adams protested that the Tsar's ukase of 1821 had unwarrantedly designated the 51st rather than the 55th parallel north (as had been previously designated by Tsar Paul I in 1799) as the southern boundary of Russian America, Alexander yielded. The result was the signing on April 17, 1824, of the Convention as to the Pacific Ocean and Northwest Coast of North America. This was the first formal accord to be reached between the two countries, which the American press even then called the "two colossi."

An American and Russian conflict over the continued expansion of the United States into the far west was thereby avoided. The southern boundary of Russian America was moved northward to 54' 40' (today the southern border of Alaska). After "Seward's Folly" in 1867, the Russian presence in the Western Hemisphere was ended altogether. The Monroe Doctrine was vindicated in its first practical application. Furthermore, with the sale of Alaska to America (see below) no fallout of hard feeling remained from the territorial settlements. In the presidency of Boris Yeltsin in the 1990s the subject of Russia's sale of Alaska was to become a joking matter even if a rival politician in Russia trumpeted to largely deaf ears that Alaska should be "returned" to Russia.

RUSSIA AND THE AMERICAN CIVIL WAR

Some time before the Russian support for the Union in the American Civil War materialized, several events took place which were to further solidify Russian and American friendship in the post-1824 period. This was to pave the way for the anti-Confederacy, pro-Union policy upheld by St. Petersburg.

John Randolph, who succeeded Adams as the American minister to the court of Tsar Nicholas I, was to stay in the Russian capital for the shortest period of time for any American envoy to date. Although compelled to distract himself from his ill health with alcohol and drugs, the erratic envoy from Roanoke, Virginia, nevertheless proved to be an able diplomat at the tsar's court. He succeeded in paving the way toward a new understanding on Russian and American commerce and neutral rights, both countries pursuing similar policies with regard to the protection of neutral commerce and free trade. For various reasons, however, the fruits of Randolph's efforts had to await the passage of various events which then occupied the attention of the tsar (among them the revolts in Poland).

During the stay of America's next envoy, James Buchanan, another very well-known American politician, the second important milestone marking the emergent tradition of Russian and American friendship was passed: the Russo-American Treaty of Commerce and Navigation of December 18, 1832, signed in St. Petersburg and ratified in Washington the next year.

At about this time a major international crisis, eventually escalating into the Crimean War, was facing Russia; it was a crisis, however, like many others of the nineteenth century that significantly left unaffected the tradition of Russian-American cordiality. By mid-century, the Ottoman empire and Turkey, "the sick man of Europe," became the objects of competing national interests between the members of the European Quadrille as well as various European "bystanders." It was largely the expansionist ambitions of Nicholas I in the Near East, however, which helped ignite the various rivalries into a major war.

Leaving aside the details of the war, it is important here to note that the United States maintained the strictest neutrality in the conflict. An important document—the Convention as to the Rights of Neutrals on the Sea—was signed on July 22, 1854, as testimony of these U.S. intentions. It became the third major agreement between the two countries. By the time of the outbreak of the American Civil War, then, Russian and American relations were at a high point of friendliness.

On April 19, 1861, President Lincoln proclaimed the blockade of the southern U.S. seaports. This was a measure that immediately affected U.S. relations with foreign states. Great Britain and France thereupon offered their support to the Confederacy, an event which caused some observers, both in Europe and America, to predict the outbreak of war between America and the two European powers.

As for Russia, it had supported the Union from the very beginning. What were its motives?

The key Western protectorate of the Russian empire, Poland, was the scene of serious uprisings [taking place in Russian Poland] in 1830, 1846,

1848, and 1861–1864 under the banner of separatism. These events further aggravated relations between Russia on the one hand and Britain and France on the other, the two latter countries supporting the Polish rebellion. This weakness at home was a potent factor impelling the Russians to extend the hand of friendship toward America.

Moreover, early in the American Civil War, the Tsar Alexander II's able foreign minister, Alexander Gorchakov, assured the U.S. minister in St. Petersburg, Cassius Marcellus Clay, that American naval vessels would be permitted to bring "prizes" (i.e., captured British ships) into Russian ports. Russia, meanwhile, would display "unequivocal" support to the North in the war. The tsar made good on his pledges, amid a public fanfare of sentimental twaddle in both countries. Russia's firm moral and diplomatic support undoubtedly deterred Great Britain from large-scale intervention in the American War Between the States.

In 1863, at the climax of pro-Russian euphoria in the United States and the year of Union victories in the battles of Gettysburg, Chancellorsville, and Vicksburg in the East, two squadrons of the Russians' Pacific and Baltic fleets made surprise visits to San Francisco and New York. These moves could not have been better timed. The Polish revolts were beginning to increase tensions between Russia and Britain and France. In case of a new war with the two West European powers, Russia would have found herself more "land-locked" than ever, as the British fleet would surely have been able to block her exits from the Baltic and the Black seas. Thus, the tsar, on the advice of one of his admirals, decided to take the precaution of moving out the two squadrons to keep them from being bottled up by the British as well as to keep them ready to attack British shipping in the event of war. New York and San Francisco became the logical loci for setting out on any such anti-British action; and in any case, there were no other suitable friendly ports for the Russians to use.

An emotional hoopla accompanied the presence of the Russian ships in the two American harbors. As Foster Rhea Dulles described it,

> In New York delegates from every neighboring state came to the city to visit the Russian vessels lying at anchor in the bay; their officers were invited to cities throughout the East for memorial banquets. Secretary Seward [later to figure in the sale of Russian Alaska to the U.S.] received the Russian admiral at Washington and the Navy Department offered him the full facilities of the Brooklyn Navy Yard. On the West Coast too there were gala receptions for the officers. Everywhere the American people were drinking enthusiastic toasts to Lincoln the Emancipator and Alexander the Liberator . . . The nation echoed Secretary of Navy Welles' heartfelt "God bless the Russians."

One of the more ostentatious expressions of pro-Russian enthusiasm occurred when the Russian flagship *Alexander Nevsky* was treated to a twenty-one-gun salute banged noisily in New York Harbor by no fewer than five U.S. frigates all firing simultaneously! The next day the *New York Herald Tribune* rhapsodized,

> Hardly one but understands that while the great Protestant power of England, and the great Catholic power of France, had entrenched themselves behind the bristling abatis of diplomacy, ready to quarrel, to grumble, and to contend for the ninth part of a hair, Russia, far distant from us, but, in her turn, intent in an opposite quarter of the globe, upon the extension of popular civilization, has preserved those relations of friendship, which, when they become ancient, may also become indissoluble.

In New York City, an elaborate "grand ball" was staged in the Academy of Music on (at that time) fashionable 14th Street. The gala event was attended by hundreds of couples. Ladies in their satin hoopskirts were escorted by gentlemen sporting beards and long hair and sideburns. The Russian naval officers, with their elaborate beards, St. George's crosses, gold buttons and epaulettes, and exotic, animated dancing were, of course, the center of attention.

Under these euphoric conditions, needless to say, little or no thought was given in the press to the contrasting social, economic, and political systems of the two friendly countries. In Russia, pro-American feeling was running as high as pro-Russian feeling in New York and San Francisco. In both countries rather far-fetched comparisons were made. The most common one was that the liberation of Russia's some twenty million serfs by Tsar Alexander's ukase of 1861 was the exact analogue, if not homologue, of Lincoln's Emancipation Proclamation of the year following which freed some four million black slaves. But, one writer observed,

> The social and juridical resemblance between Russian white serfdom and American Negro slavery, both of which were hindrances to a free capitalist society, did not lead the countries along similar lines. . . For almost half a century more the Russian landlord or baron continued to exploit his former serfs, and they were obliged to pay him endless indemnification . . . The Russian peasant had no chance to become anything like an American farmer . . . In the United States the immense grants of land under the Homestead Act and other less spectacular confiscatory measures made slowly possible the creation of a farmer class whose dreams could be realized without revolution or rebellion . . . The opposite is true for post-Emancipation Russia.

This episode of nearly delirious pro-Russian sentiment in America during the Civil War is as instructive as it is prophetic. It illustrates the degree and the rapidity with which political and diplomatic decisions taken in the two distant capitals, St. Petersburg and Washington, could unleash a spontaneous wave of popular feeling.

This type of virulent euphoria was to crop up again in both countries less than a hundred years later during World War II. Lend-Lease was the trigger for this new flush of friendship in the war period, 1941–1945.

"SEWARD'S FOLLY"

In 1787, Thomas Jefferson had met in Paris, where he was the American minister, with one John Ledyard, woodsman and explorer of the Lewis and Clark type, who was eager to return to America by way of Siberia, the Pacific Ocean, and the unexplored wilderness of the North American continent. The Virginian proposed to him that he "go by land to Kamchatka [on the Russian Pacific Coast], cross in some of the Russian vessels to Nootka Sound, fall down into the latitude of the Missouri [River], and penetrate to and through that to the United States."

That same year, Ledyard started out on his mission, having received permission of Empress Catherine the Great to traverse Siberia to reach the Russian Pacific northeast. However, after Ledyard had reached and wintered in Kamchatka and was preparing to resume his journey into the North Pacific waters in the spring of 1788, the Empress asserted her woman's prerogative and for some unknown reason changed her mind and retracted her permission for advancement of the American project. And there the matter rested until the United States was able to explore the North Pacific area by beginning from the American side.

With Russia's withdrawal from the California and Canadian Pacific coast, there followed a protracted period of Alaska's decline together with a corresponding lack of interest in the area on the part of the Russians, the British, and the Americans. Following Russia's defeat in the Crimean War, and with the sizable decrease in the population of fur-bearing sea otters in Alaskan waters, the Russians were finally persuaded to give up their last outpost in Russian America. No force, verbal or otherwise, had been applied by Washington.

Before the end of the Crimean War, the U.S. initiated efforts to acquire Alaska. Secretary of State William L. Marcy (1853–1857) and Senator William M. Gwin of California had tried to interest the Russian envoy in Washington, Baron Edward von Stoeckl, in making a deal on Alaska. In 1859 President James Buchanan (the former minister to Russia) sanctioned Senator Gwin to approach von Stoeckl with the concrete offer of $5 million. But the Foreign Ministry in St. Petersburg delayed, despite von Stoeckl's enthusiastic support of the offer. After a delay on the American side because of the Civil War, the question of selling Alaska was reopened with the Russians, who meantime had decided that the bankrupt Russian American Company, which was barely hanging on in Alaska, was not worth continuing.

With the support of President Andrew Johnson, Secretary of State Seward in 1867 once again proposed the price of $5 million. But this time the Russians doubled their selling price to $10 million. Finally, a compromise of $7.2 million was agreed upon. On March 30, 1867, the treaty was signed in a friendly atmosphere, and was followed by Senate ratification just a week later. The deal had been "signed, sealed, and delivered" so fast for the purchase of a territory that was practically unknown to most Americans that a public uproar broke out. Most famous among the epithets used to describe the new territory was "Seward's ice-box."

NOTES

1. The historical background of this chapter and part of the next is derived from Albert L. Weeks, *The Other Side of Coexistence: An Analysis of Russian Foreign Policy*, New York, Pitman Publishing Corporation, 1970, chapter 4, "Grounds for Convergence."

5

Historical Roots of Lend-Lease—II[1]

> Considering as necessary the future development of economic relations with capitalist countries... and the application of the technology of the foremost capitalist states for accelerating the industrialization of the U.S.S.R., the party congress stresses the great significance of Bolshevik tempos in Socialist industrialization of the country in order to provide economic self-sufficiency for the U.S.S.R.
>
> —Joseph Stalin, June 26, 1930

RUSSIAN-AMERICAN ECONOMIC TIES

Reliance on capitalist know-how in order to attain economic self-sufficiency—this was Stalin's program in the area of foreign economic involvement. It was successful largely because the West—and especially the United States—was glad to do business with the Russians. An important economic link between East and West was thereby formed.

Under the tsars, imports amounted to only a small part of total world trade, some 3 percent. The Bolsheviks had inherited a degree of Russian autarky from the previous regime even before they themselves deliberately set economic self-sufficiency as their goal. But the degree of industrialization in Russia lagged far behind that of the other great European powers. To achieve self-sufficiency in the modern world, it was first necessary to accelerate Russia's own industrialization. For this to be accomplished, however, partial dependency on foreign nations and foreign technologies became necessary for attaining independence from those same foreign states.

One of the first feelers put out by the U.S.S.R. for financial help was in the direction of the United States. In the 1920s, the Chase Bank of New York extended a $20 million credit to the new Soviet Republic, an unusual action for a Western country in the early period of Soviet rule. For dozens of years, no other Western bank was to make loans to the Soviets, although the Chase credit was dutifully repaid within a few months.

In speaking of the early period in the 1920s up to Stalin's first Five-Year Plan, the most outstanding case of U.S. economic assistance to Russia was the case of the emergency assistance under the American Relief Administration (ARA). The ARA was of immense importance in saving untold millions of Russians from outright starvation during the years 1921–1923. The U.S. House of Representatives authorized an appropriation (which was approved by the Senate) of $20 million in food, medical, and other supplies, which, when added to other contributions from the United States, amounted to a staggering (for that time) $66.3 million. Although the Soviet government eventually provided transportation and housing for ARA officials under Herbert Hoover, then Secretary of Commerce, negotiations for undertaking the mission were delayed because of Russian suspicions of the Hoover mission's motives. As part of the agreement, the United States promised no discrimination and no anti-Soviet activities. An auxiliary arrangement flowing from ARA was the Soviet payment of $10 million in Russian gold bullion for the purchase of seeds and additional foodstuffs.

The aid was received at the time with strongly but unofficially expressed gratitude on the part of the Russians, who pronounced the initials "ARA" as an acronym, "Ara." Officially, however, the aid has not been so received. The *Small Soviet Encyclopedia*, one of the most widely read Soviet reference books in the U.S.S.R., asserts,

> "ARA," headed by H. Hoover, claimed officially that its task was to give foodstuffs and all other types of aid to any European country suffering as a result of the First World War. In fact the principal aims of the "ARA" was to conduct a struggle against revolutionary movements and strengthen the economic and political positions of American imperialism in the European countries. . . . In a number of instances, "ARA" undertook espionage and underground activities and support of counterrevolutionary elements.

What is suspect here is not so much ARA's alleged motivations in 1921–1922, but the motivations of the party-directed editors of the Soviet encyclopedia in 1958 for painting a negative picture of the work of ARA. (The encyclopedia, moreover, omits any mention of the millions of Russians who received the aid.)

When the subject of U.S. economic aid to Russia is brought up, one immediately thinks not only ARA, but especially of Lend-Lease aid during World War II. It is a relatively recent expression of American aid to Russia, and it was a very large contribution.

Total U.S. Lend-Lease aid is put at about $12 billion (this figure does not include the contributions made to Russia by the other Allies). If the aid supplied by the three "Anglo-Saxon" Allies (the U.S., U.K., and Canada) is taken together, it amounts to this (rounded-off estimates):

- 10,000 tanks
- 10,000 artillery pieces
- 14,500 airplanes
- 100,000 tons of rubber
- 500,000 tons of nonferrous metals
- Nearly 500,000 trucks
- 2.3 million tons of food provisions
- Hundreds of ships
- $3 billion-worth of machinery, including whole factories
- Military cloth sufficient to clothe 3 million Red Army soldiers

The American scholar and Russian specialist, Ellsworth Raymond, who was on the scene in Russia working as an economic analyst in the U.S. Embassy in Moscow during part of the war, has offered this guarded opinion:

> Most Lend-Lease reached Russia in the later years of war, when the Red Army was winning on its own . . . thus the Russian claim is probably true that the U.S.S.R. fought the war mostly with weapons made in Soviet factories from Soviet raw materials. On the other hand, Allied machinery and transportation supplies were very great. The most objective estimate is that Lend-Lease was marginal assistance, coming rather late in the war. Only the Kremlin knows whether or not this marginal aid was crucial for Soviet victory. But the grand 1,400 mile Russian offensive from Stalingrad [1943] to Berlin [1945] would certainly have been much slower had there been no Lend-Lease.

However, later research in Russia into Lend-Lease throws into question Raymond's partial minimization of the importance of this aid.

Beyond Lend-Lease there was still a longer, broader form of American assistance to Russia that is is often ignored. It is directly relevant to Soviet Russia's staying power in World War II. It is doubtful, in fact, whether Russia could have been able to tool up for war in the late 1930s and in the 1940s as rapidly as it did had it not been for the foundations laid by long-standing American technical assistance. Doing business with Russia not only predates U.S. recognition of the U.S.S.R. in 1933, it goes back to before 1917—in fact, to the beginning of the last century. In the section that follows is an account of this foundation-laying technological assistance.

EARLIEST PERIOD OF U.S. TECHNOLOGICAL ASSISTANCE

As far back as 1783 the U.S. Minister to Russia Francis Dana predicted that "in the nature of things" future relations between the United States and Russia would be commercial rather than political.

Dating from the time when U.S. Army Major George Washington Whistler was called to St. Petersburg by Nicholas I in 1842 to serve as consulting engineer for the building of Russia's largest and best-equipped railroad to that date, every facet of the Russian economy has felt the influence of American technology, inventions, know-how, and assistance. The American role by no means diminished in the twentieth century when the establishment of the Soviets was undertaken in the late 1920s and early 1930s, despite non-recognition of the Soviet regime by Washington.

Dependence of Russia upon the West generally for the development of its economy dates back to the reign of Peter the Great. Carpenters and blacksmiths from Holland visited the palace of the enterprising tsar, the builder of the new city of "Sankt-Petersburg," named for his patron saint. Scientists, scholars, and specialists of various kinds also were solicited by Tsar Peter I. The resultant great reforms in education and in the military and state structure of Russia reflected these direct Western influences. But until the West itself had begun to employ the manufacture of goods at the end of the eighteenth century, Western Europe's influence upon Tsarist Russia earlier in the century had been intellectual and cultural, affecting mainly the small aristocratic elite or the court. The vast majority of the Russian population was left unaffected by the various Western influences; Peter's reforms only kept the Russian peasant more hopelessly subordinated to the landowning nobility.

However, during the reign of Nicholas I (1825–1855), Russia at last showed signs of becoming conscious of its incredible backwardness, compared to the Western standard of living. The tsar's personal awareness of this fact was reflected, for example, in the law of 1840 which gave factory owners the option of liberating serfs bound specifically to their factories thereby opening the way for creation of a class of "free hired labor." This law meant little when the small size of both the middle-class entrepreneurs and their serfs are taken into account. Still, it signified the beginning of the Russian government's interest in laying the basis for industrialization of Russia, a country rich in natural resources and full of great potentiality.

"Some time in 1840," a U.S. engineer and traveler to Russia at that time, John S. Maxwell, tells us, the Emperor Nicholas assembled his counselors and requested their opinions as to the possibility of a railroad from St. Petersburg to Moscow. Everyone opposed it except Count Kleinmichel, the minister of Ways and Communications. After due consideration it was concluded that railroads "as they are constructed in the United States" were the most suitable for the empire. Major George Washington Whistler, "an American gentleman of distinguished ability in his profession," was invited to visit Russia and superintend the making of the proposed road, subsequently called the Nicolayevsky Railroad. Neither money nor influence at court was of any importance, and all those who had built their hopes upon these two considerations were thrown aside for other foreigners who were known in Russia to possess the needed intelligence, energy, and perseverance. As soon as it was reported that the Americans had won the contract, reports Maxwell, "a prolonged growl was heard in the English quarter."

This early Russian dependence upon U.S. know-how in railroad building and maintenance was to lead to the journey of two Russian Army engineers, emissaries of Tsar Nicolas I, to the United States to acquaint themselves with American railroad techniques on-the-spot and to prepare themselves for application of this experience, with U.S. help, to Russia. The Russian engineers were especially impressed by Major Whistler's use of steep grades, sharp curves, machinery, and steam excavating devices—all these being applied by the Baltimore & Ohio Railroad, with whom Major Whistler had served as chief engineer.

The Russians also admired the American system of bridge building. As a result, Major Whistler was invited to work for the Russian government for seven years on its ambitious railroad building enterprise. It was on Whistler's advice, by the way, that the Russians adopted their well-known broad, five-foot wide gauge tracks which, as one version goes, resulted only accidentally from Russian misreading of Whistler's blueprints, by measuring track width from the outside edges of the rails instead of from the inside! (The wide gauge is still in use in the Russia.)

The actual railroad-building project was initiated with the construction in Russia of foundries and iron factories, together with the importation of those U.S.-made locomotives and machinery (steam pile drivers, earth excavators, machine tools, etc.) which had already been used so profitably in railroad construction in the United States.

"Human capital" was also lent to Russia by the United States at this time. American firms sent over to Russia numerous technicians, engineers, millwrights, bridge builders, and other specialists in fields relating to railroading. Maxwell reports that almost every steamer brought to Russia some "enterprising son of New England." Among them were Harmon and Eastwick of Philadelphia and, of course, Major Whistler himself, who received the Order of St. Anne from the tsar before the American railroader's death in St. Petersburg in 1849.

One of the most outstanding achievements in this early Russian railroad building was the construction of one of the largest railroad foundries in the world at that time—the Alexander Foundry, sprawling over some 160 acres. It had been built by U.S. engineers and was staffed in the beginning with American technicians. It employed over 3,000 skilled workers. Hundreds of locomotives and thousands of railroad cars were built in this foundry. The Russian government was so pleased with it that it bestowed awards upon the U.S. technicians for the help they had given in its construction. Maxwell, who had become secretary of the U.S. legation in Russia at that time, predicted that a great economic future awaited Russia if it continued its railroad expansion. He added that U.S. engineers with experience in their own country could effect a regeneration of the economy of the Russian empire if they were invited to help and if their activities were not hampered by the barriers of passports and police. Such a regenerated economy, he said, would usher in extensive Russo-American trade. Perhaps if it had been a comprehensive program, it could have prevented revolution.

In addition to railroad construction, the United States played still another important role in the Russian economy in the early nineteenth century, in its most important sector—agriculture. Eleven times in the nineteenth century famine swept Russia, largely because of its inadequately plowed fields and the low level of agricultural science and technique. Even as late as 1905 the peasants, 80 percent of whom each held fewer than eighteen acres of land as his share, "tickled" the soil with ancient, shallow wooden or iron plows and had in use a mere 138 tractors. What little agricultural innovation was made in the early as well as late nineteenth and early twentieth centuries most often bore a "made in the U.S." stamp. Illustrative of this is the following story told by Maxwell:

> One of the most amusing incidents attending our visit to this institution [an imperial farming institute near St. Petersburg] was to find there an American who had but lately arrived in the country. He spoke nothing but English and could hold no conversation whatever with those around him except through the medium of signs and gestures. He was a tall, thin man with a thoughtful countenance. He had brought with him a number of improved instruments of agriculture such as were never seen before in Russia . . . He found the pupils of the farming institute reaping wheat with the old-fashioned sickle, mowing with a short scythe attached to a 10-foot pole, and plowing in every way but the right one. He perfectly astonished [the Russians] . . . with his long, straight furrows, his clean cut sward, and his gigantic strides with the mysterious cradle. One blustering day he saw the scholar cleaning grain by

throwing it up in the wind which carried off dust and chaff while the grain fell to the ground. One countryman did not like this antiquated process and constructed [on the spot] a winnowing mill out of such materials and such tools as happened to be on hand . . . [He was] elected an honorary member of the Imperial Society for the Improvement of Agriculture.

Data are lacking on the quantity of U.S.-made farming equipment that found its way into Russia in the early period. By comparison with the amount imported at the end of the nineteenth century from the U.S.—when Russian foreign trade in general was coming enough into its own to start the country down the road to its first industrial revolution—it is of little significance.

ASSISTANCE IN THE NINETEENTH AND TWENTIETH CENTURIES

Although Russia and the United States differed considerably in their political customs and general outlook, various factors encouraged Americans after the American Civil War to visit Russia. The abolition of slavery in the United States and of serfdom in Russia was looked upon—somewhat mistakenly—as a strong bond between both these countries. The visits of the Russian squadrons to the United States in 1864 and of the U.S. fleet to Russia in 1867, the assistance of the Russians to the North in the Civil War, and the purchase of Alaska—all contributed toward the travelers' sympathy and feeling of unity between the two developing countries. The economic growth of Russia, however, was sorely frustrated by various paradoxes in its national economy.

The tsar levied high tariffs on imports (for example, 58 percent on pig iron) to protect the small amount of domestic industry, setting at the same time relatively low prices on grain, Russia's largest export. The result was that industrial goods were immeasurably higher priced than their foreign counterparts. Moreover, the purchasing power to buy them in Russia was severely restricted by the low income from grain sales and the general bankruptcy of both small peasant holders and the landowners themselves. Foreign imports of manufactured goods, once the tariff had been levied upon them, were also restrictive in price. In spite of the protests of the small, relatively powerless but rising industrial class, tsarist legislation did little to release peasants from the village (the low agricultural technology required an abnormal amount of peasant labor in the fields) to become free labor in the urban areas. As a result, the country groaned on frustratedly until the significant financial reforms of N. K. Bunge, the brilliant minister of finance under Alexander III, and of the talented Count Sergius Witte, minister of finance and influential in Russian finance after 1901. These able statesman started Russia up the road toward an industrial revolution.

RAILROAD BUILDING

An official Soviet textbook on Russian economy, *History of the National Economy of Russia*, published 1947–1948, by Peter I. Lyashchenko, admits candidly (for a Soviet-period book) that the period of the 1890s in Russia under Tsar Nicholas II witnessed "an industrial upsurge . . . one of the important stages in the history of the capitalist industry and national economy of Russia as a whole. . . . With respect to its tempo of development during these years, Russia outstripped nearly all countries." The rate of expansion of industry—excluding its own perennial stimulus, railroad building—was indeed phenomenal.

For example (according to Lyashchenko's figures), in the 1890s smelting of pig iron increased 190 percent (England, 18 percent); iron 116 percent (U.S., 63 percent) coal industry, 131 percent (Germany, 52 percent). The key industry of the railroads also showed huge advances and its influence over the rest of the economy was tremendous and crucial. A Russian government newspaper in 1897 assessed this influence as follows:

> The building of railroad lines opened a new branch of industry for production of materials needed for them, the repercussions of which have not only been the building of large new factories and shops, but has caused large mining companies to busy themselves with ore extraction . . . materials necessary for building and use of railroads. Such influences of railroads upon the development of iron and steel and mechanical industries are immediate. Less direct influence, however extends to all the other branches of industry, and also to trade.

Perry Collins, a U.S. businessman and explorer, predicted in the 1850s that if railroads could be strung across Siberia and industry developed there—a great possibility, he thought, after his explorations along the Amur River—Russia would enjoy the same upsurge of economic activity as did the United States when America began stretching itself westward, developing and lacing together new industries with railroad networks.

Figures given by the Tsarist government newspaper *Pravitel'stvennii Vestnik* for the pace of railroad building in the 1880s and early 1900s are quite striking. For example:

1882–1896   14,106 *versts* of track laid
1881–1893   44 percent increase in number of passengers carried;
            43 percent increase in *versts* traveled
            108 percent increase in freight per *verst* (one *verst* = 1.067 km; .6629 mi)

The newspaper also listed industries that were stimulated because of their close connection with the maintenance of railroad transport and the production of fuel (domestic kerosene, coal, and gasoline industries).

The *financial* role of the United States was relatively small during this period (France's was much larger) as it had always been and continued to be. *But so far as its influence upon actual production know-how, equipping the railroads, and the setting up of construction facilities were concerned, the U.S. role was great and crucial.* The various forms that this American assistance took in railroad building—in the construction of the Chinese Eastern Railway and the Trans-Siberian Railway—were valued respectively at $286,260,000 and $172,525,000 (initial outlay), and can be categorized as follows:

- U.S. inventions
- U.S. advanced techniques made available to the Russian government
- U.S.-made machinery and equipment

Moreover, certain basic inventions in the railroad field had their home in the United States. Among the important ones that found their way into Russia were the electric locomotive (invented by Page in 1851); diamond rock drill (Herman, 1854); sleeping car (Woodruff, 1856); air brake (Westinghouse, 1869); automatic coupler (Janney, 1873); and the development of any number of automatic railroad and signal devices, and so on, coming out of the rich railroading experience of manufacturing New England and Western U.S., with the largest rail networks in the world. Even more significant was the advanced American technique for producing and applying these and other non-American inventions in railroading.

Such American businessmen and travelers as Collins and Maxwell, Daniel Butterfield, Alexander Ford, and George F. Kennan were proved correct in their predictions. They had prophesied that opening the Siberian lands for routes to the Pacific and the Far East for Russian trade, industrial expansion, and national defense would in turn open up trade with the United States, which itself had expanded to its own Pacific Coast. Not even the lack of a single U.S. banking house in Russia for conducting credit and foreign currency transactions prevented the U.S. from playing a large and varied role in Russia's eastward expansion, reflected in the construction and growing importance of the two Pacific ports of Vladivostok and Port Arthur.

Alexander Hume Ford, an American traveling engineer who was on hand at the time of the building of the Trans-Siberian railroad wrote at that time,

> American activity was abroad in the land, and while Russian engineers at first laughed at the idea of American manufactures competing with Europe, they were induced to give a few orders [for goods]. To their astonishment the

goods arrived in less than three months and proved the most durable and efficient tools up to that time . . . The Russian officials suddenly realized that just across the Pacific pond, not 5,000 miles away, they [the Americans] could supply all the needs of the new railways and all hurry orders were promptly cabled [on the United States–British-made transatlantic cable] to America, whose markets were some 15,000 miles nearer eastern Siberia than those of Europe.

Realization of these facts of proximity through acquiring high-quality American goods and technology resulted in the following events:

1. Visit of two Russian engineers in the 1890s as a committee empowered to make purchases of U.S. railroad equipment in the United States; they reported that three-quarters of the necessary equipment could be purchased in the United States.
2. The importation or construction in Siberia of U.S.-made steel bridges; track-laying tools; steel rails (production of steel rails instead of iron rails started on a small scale in Russia after 1874); air-brake system; automatic couplers; turning lathes; quartz mill; railroad machine shops; steamrollers and steam pile-driving machines; electric light plants; mogul machines for tearing up stumps, etc.; rolling stock of various types; telephone and telegraph wire; rock drills necessary for ripping through the Yablonoy, Baikal, and other highlands; railroad-car wheel lathes; construction of the Saimova Railroad Works, and others.

AGRICULTURAL MACHINERY

In this field the U.S. role was also significant. What little agricultural machinery there was in Russia before Soviet importation of it and the Five-Year Plan production of agricultural implements and machinery (see below) almost always bore an American trademark. During Russia's boom periods of the 1890s and the early 1900s, when imports of machinery escalated along with domestic industry, huge amounts of U.S.-made farm equipment and almost every type of machinery were sent to Russia. While the United States "supplied the world" with agricultural machinery in the 1890s, its biggest customer was Russia. More than one-third of American agricultural machinery used outside the United States was found in Russia. Russian imports of American agricultural machinery quadrupled in five years during the 1890s. In 1901 alone, about 410 million was spent by Russia for U.S. agriculture machinery. It is hard to fix the figures for this accurately because of the fact that German shippers would sometimes fasten German labels over the U.S. labels during the machinery's transshipment.

In the 1890s the Russo-American Black Sea Steamship Line was established, thereby avoiding the expense of German or English transshipment. After these cargoes were unloaded, the machinery would then have to be transported by rail or river, which in turn stimulated construction of better land and river routes. Alexander Ford, an eyewitness at the wharves of Black Sea ports, particularly in Odessa at the time when these ships were arriving into port, related that he saw miles of American equipment lining the docks and trains. He also saw huge river barges on the Dnieper River, departing daily with loads of McCormick reapers, binders, movers, threshers, cleaners, and rakes—all of which were made in the United States. And where the railroads or rivers ended in trans-Urals Russia, camels took up the journey for the rest of the way into Siberia! In the spring of 1901 record shipments of agricultural machinery left New York bound for Russia: for example, 20,000 tons in twenty days.

Ford gives an account of the fading of the Russian peasant's initial suspiciousness of the machinery as "the inventions of the Devil":

> After the man in the white blouse of the Russian soldier had been seen on the vast private estates of the Tsar, learning the use of the threshers and mowers, prejudice began to vanish, and village communes discussed the necessity of procuring harvesting that would enable the village mir [commune] to compete with the great overlords and pay taxes.

American business agents, completing orders for machinery personally with representatives of the village peasant communes, helped this peasant institution thrive and compete with both its tsarist and landowner competitors. *Pravitelstvennii Vestnik* reported in 1896 (No. 224) on the creation of a fund for purchasing agricultural implements to the peasants. It was named Funds for Purchase of Implements and Agricultural Machinery to the Peasants, under the administration of the Kiev Syndicate for Agriculture in the Counties (uyezdy). These banks were located in the cities and rich-soil provinces of Svenigorodsk, Kanevsk, Kiev, Bratislavl, and Mogilev-Podolsk. "The business is going well," the newspaper reported. Now the peasants, instead of relying on insufficient local industry, could "get the best foreign-made scythes, plows, harrows, machinery for cleaning grain, winnowing machines, sorting machines (sortirovshchiki), and others."

The arrival of U.S.-made agricultural machinery by river (to those thatched-roof Russian villages fortunate enough to receive it) was heralded with the ringing of the village church bells. Led by the *Starosta* (head or elder) of the commune, the peasants would gather around the old Scottish-made river barges to watch the unloading of the valuable cargo. These barges were also employed for the "floating gardens" used to demonstrate and propagate the latest agronomical techniques, an idea employed by Russian government agronomists and well-suited to the river-oriented villages of the Ukraine.

In addition to the agricultural and other machinery purchased from U.S. concerns and sent to Russia, there were displays of American agricultural implements and machinery (and railroad equipment, locomotives, etc) at Russia's famed Nizhni-Novgorod (now Gorky) fair of 1896. For the preceding nine years the fair had displayed an average of $89 million worth of goods and included some 4,000 booths for both the "outer" and "inner" fair grounds and the splendid palace built in 1890. A list of the American agricultural goods on display, many of which had already been ordered or purchased, included the following:

- grain sorters (*sortirovshchiki*)
- cotton-gins and presses (most often sent to Central Asian provinces and Vladivostok and elsewhere in Siberia)
- rice-milling machines, threshers, cleaners, rakes, scythes, sulky plows, grain elevators, binders, mowers
- dredging machinery (to deepen Russian rivers which in turn expedited transport of machinery to the villages)
- lathes for turning axe handles and other wooden parts

Reports appeared daily in *Pravitel'stevenii Vestnik* (*Government Messenger*) in the late 1890s on the fair in the column headed "Around the Provinces." One such article (in No. 136, 1896) cited the fact that in the "First Division" of the fair grounds were displayed reapers (*zhneiki*) and reaper-binders (*zhneiki-sopovyazalki*) from "four famous American firms." The exhibit housing most of these American samples was the "Second Exhibit of Agricultural Machines and Equipment," set up by the Moscow Agricultural School.

It was perhaps no exaggeration when Ford stated that the regeneration of Russian prairies was "left entirely" to American influence and to the fact that during the late 1890s "our shipments of mowers, reapers, and binders doubled in one year." The importation of motor-driven equipment, such as the tractor and bulldozer, came in the later Soviet period (see below).

U.S. RAILROAD COMMISSION IN RUSSIA, 1917

The United States government sent the Root commission to Russia in the spring of 1917 "for the purpose of welcoming Russia to the sisterhood of republics," but, more realistically, to ensure Russia's continued support of the allies in World War I. Out of this commission, which toured throughout most major parts of the country, came an economic recommendation: that a commission of American railroad specialists be appointed to improve conditions on the Russian railroads to relieve both the military and civil bottlenecks of supply during World War I.

The Allied Missions of England, France, and Italy by prior agreement had assigned responsibility for all the transportation systems of the Russian provisional government to the American ambassador—West European recognition of America's stake in the railroad. At the suggestion of U.S. Ambassador David R. Francis, a five-man advisory commission of railway experts to Russia was appointed. The noted railroad engineer, John F. Stevens, was made chairman.

This commission arrived in Vladivostok in June 1917 and set about immediately to devise plans to alleviate congestion at Vladivostok and "to improve generally the transportation facilities of the Siberian railway." When the American Railroad commission went to Petrograd late in the summer, the experts reported to Ambassador Francis that they had inspected the Trans-Sib and had begun the erection of an assembly plant near Vladivostok. Soon, in October, at Ambassador Francis's suggestion and with the support of the Russian Ministry of Ways and Communications, the commission inspected the Donets system of railroads in the Ukraine. This inspection had just been completed when the Bolsheviks staged their coup in Moscow. Further work by the commission, and by Stevens in particular, was halted by disruption caused by the Bolshevik revolt. Ambassador Francis wrote of the frustration of any further helpful activity of this commission in western Russia as follows: "The Bolshevik revolution prevented the consummation of the well-laid plans of these railroad experts." As a result, all the members of the commission returned to the United States, except Stevens. He remained in Russia, where he was established in the government's Ministry of Ways and Communications in the capacity of special adviser so that he could assist in the indeterminate future in carrying into effect the measures that the commission and Russian officials had agreed were vital for supplying the people of Russia with food and clothing.

Meanwhile, in Washington in September 1917, there had assembled, at the request of the Russian provisional government upon the recommendation of the railway advisory commission, a party of 288 Americans consisting of railroad-operating men, engineers, and interpreters, all under the command of Colonel George Emerson. This group, called the Russian Railway Service Corp, was organized by the U.S. War Department under the authority of President Wilson for the purpose of maintaining transportation between the Russian eastern front and the base of supplies at

Valdivostok and of thus averting the threatened collapse of the Allies' eastern front. The Russian Railway Service Corp left the United States November 1, 1917, and arrived at the end of the month in Vladivostok. Because of the Bolshevik coup and widespread disorders in Russia, the "Corp," only after March 1918, managed to accomplish improvement of the Trans-Sib Railroad when it was able actually to direct the operation of the road, to maintain the road and equipment, and to supervise the movement of troops, supplies, and ordnance of the Allied armies in the Allied intervention.

It was this U.S.-administered Russian Railway Service Corp which saved large numbers of the Czechoslovakian army in transit east through Siberia on their way to the United States and eventually to the West European front. But perhaps the Corp's chief accomplishment in its five years of existence was the feeding and supplying of the population of Siberia at the time of great civil upheaval. The population of west Siberia and the forces of Admiral Kolchak were entirely dependent on the Corp for assuring that supplies on the Trans-Siberian and other railways reached their destinations. The Kolchak anti-Bolshevik government arranged for the purchase of medical and other supplies under the Red Cross and was supplied transportation and protection for these shipments by Stevens's Corp and U.S. Army units under General William S. Graves stationed in Siberia.

MISCELLANEOUS TECHNOLOGICAL ASSISTANCE

A list of other manufactured goods which came from the United States to Russia throughout the period 1894–1917 includes

- tin plate
- cast iron
- oil well machinery
- pipe-line tubing (supplied for the Odessa sewage system)
- boilers (from the Ames Iron Works)
- iron and steel railroad rails (Maryland Steel Company)
- piers; carriages; bicycles; railway cars—freight and passenger
- rock drills (Westinghouse; Ingersoll and Sergeant Company)
- gun lathes (Niles Company)
- machinery for turning out crankshafts for the Russian navy and shipbuilding tools including punching and sheering machines; pumps; plate-straightening and bending rolls (from Hilles and Jones Company, Wilmington, DE)—some of this machinery was located in the Nevsky Mechanics Works, St. Petersburg

- machinery and ammunition (Bethlehem Steel Corporation and Remington Arms Company)
- Singer sewing machines
- screw, universal-milling, surface-grinding, and universal-grinding machines (Brown and Sharpe Manufacturing Company Providence, RI)
- shingle-cutting machine (for the peasants' small-scale artel economy)
- electric-propelled, so-called American dredger (Linden W. Bates Engineer Works, Chicago)
- locomotive boilers and locomotives (Baldwin Locomotive Company, Altoona, PA) (Russian "Decapod" Locomotives first made here)
- office machines (International Business Machine Corporation, New York, NY).

Technical and material aid rendered Russia by U.S. firms in the field of dredging and ice-breaking was notable also. At the request of Tsar Nicholas II, Linden W. Bates, a famous dredging expert, visited some of Russia's frozen ports and drew up plans for both icebreakers and dredgers. Bates used his Chicago company's experience in these activities on the Great Lakes. The result of Bates's Russian travels was the building of the world's largest dredger up to that time, the electric-propelled "American Dredger." A contract for $7,000 was hence made with an American company to dredge the Pacific Ocean harbors of Russia. Among the completed projects was the important Alexander III Canal in St. Petersburg.

Moreover, at least one committee of Russian engineers appointed by Tsar Nicholas II visited the United States in the 1890s to study the building of the Chicago Barge Canal. It had been constructed on land somewhat resembling Russia's flatland steppes. With the data on this American experience in their hands, the Russian engineers returned to their native country and set to work with U.S.-made dredgers, removing the shifting river and harbor shoals in various points of Russia.

Among the U.S firms doing business inside Russia at this time were the Walk-Over Shoe Company, the Singer Sewing Machine Company (the building still stands in today's St. Petersburg), and the International Harvester Company, all with branch offices in Russia. Also, two U.S. bankers published reports on Russian economic problems. The banker, Wharton Barker, told how he had been invited to Russia in 1879 by the Grand Duke Constantine and Prince Sergius Dolgoruky to confer with them and other ministers on railroads and the coal, iron, and steel enterprises that were to be constructed or expanded in the south of Russia. In 1878 he had been appointed financial agent in the United States for the Russian government and had directed the building of four naval cruisers. Samuel McRoberts, vice president of the National City Bank in New York, upon U.S. Ambassador David R. Francis's advice and with the support of the tsar, investigated sources of Russia's wealth and its proposed plan for industrial development in 1916 preparatory to negotiating a loan to obtain the working capital necessary to finance several projects to aid Russia's war effort. A loan of $50 million was eventually negotiated through the Russian Foreign Minister Sazonov.

U.S. TECHNOLOGICAL AID DURING THE SOVIET PERIOD

The following quotations from Soviet sources suffice to illustrate the Russian attitude toward American technical know-how:

> Let the American capitalists leave us alone. We will not touch them. We are even ready to pay them with gold for machinery, tools, and so forth, useful for transport and production, and not only with gold but even with raw materials.
>
> —Quoted in *The Current Digest of the Soviet Press* (C.D.S.P.), Vol. 111, No. 1, p. 6, from Lenin's *Works*, Vol. XXXI (1920)

* * *

> The Soviet people rate highly that American businesslike approach to things [*Amerikanskaya delovitost'*] which, by Comrade Stalin's definition, is "that indomitable strength which neither knows or accepts any impediments . . . not letting a single thing come in the way of carrying an assigned task to the completion."
>
> —From a *Pravda* editorial, June 11, 1943

* * *

> Is Russia prepared to enter into business relations with America? [Lenin]: "Of course she is ready."
>
> —From *The Current Digest of the Soviet Press* translation of an article from *Pravda* (April 22, 1950) and *Bolshevik* (No. 7, 1950) on publication of Vol. XXXI of Lenin's *Works* containing previously unpublished documents of Lenin. C.D.S.P. Vol. II, No. 17, 1950

* * *

> Another of the most powerful countries is the United States of America. Our relations with them, both as regards our agriculture by American agriculture which has been brought to a high technical level, develop apace. Not only has engineer Cooper [Colonel Hugh Cooper], to the great benefit of the concern, become the consulting engineer for the construction of the Dnieper Hydroelectric Station, but a large number of other important and skilled American engineers enable our skilled workers and engineers to become familiar with the industry and are be-

ing conducted with very big American firms with a view to concluding new agreements for technical assistance.

—Report on foreign affairs by A. I. Rykov, president of the Council of Commissars, to the Fifth Congress of Soviets, May 1929

* * *

Stalin to General Dwight D. Eisenhower, August, 1945:

There are many ways in which we need American help. It is our great task to raise the standard of living of all Russian people, which has been seriously damaged by the war. We must learn all about your scientific achievements in agriculture. Likewise, we must get your technicians to help us in our engineering and construction problems, and we want to know more about mass production methods in factories. We know that we are behind in these things and we know that you can help us.

—From Eisenhower's *Crusade in Europe*, 1948

* * *

Thanks to mass production, Americans have succeeded in raising their material standard of living. I think we can learn from the Americans on how quickly and well to produce shoes and pots and pans. . . . In a relatively short time America built up an amazing technology. I saw how fast she can build skyscrapers, how accurately and well she can produce automobiles in Detroit, and how many inventions she has which lighten the life of man.

—Ilya Ehrenburg in *Izvestiya*, July 17, 1946, an article "In America" written on his return from a trip to the United States in 1946

* * *

We observe the United States with interest, since this country ranks high as regards science and technology. We should be glad to have American scientists and technicians as our teachers and in the technical field to be their pupils.

—Stalin (in 1932), as quoted in Amtorg's *Economic Review of the Soviet Union*, No. 2, February 1934, p. 45, in an article entitled "Soviet Industry and U.S.," by Z. Sukhov

* * *

The Soviet Union is indebted to Mr. [Henry] Ford. He helped build our tractor and automobile industries.

—Stalin, quoted in Eric Johnston's *We're All in It*, 1948

Congratulations and greetings to the victorious workers and to the leading staff of the first gigantic tractor plant in the U.S.S.R., the "Krasno-Znameni" [Stalingrad] plant. Our thanks to our technical teachers, the American specialists and technicians, who have helped us in the construction of the plant.

—Stalin's telegram to the Albert Kahn engineers working on the Stalingrad Plant; reproduced in *Economic Review of the Soviet Union*, August 1, 1930, 314

One could hardly find any other country which has such great possibilities of developing its exports to the U.S.S.R. as the United States.

—Statement by Commissar of Foreign Trade P. Rosengoltz in a speech on April 23, 1933, quoted in *Handbook of the Soviet Union*, published by the American-Russian Chamber of Commerce, 1936

* * *

Like the United States, the U.S.S.R. is a country of great distances, of rich and multiform natural resources. . . . We have found, generally speaking, of all foreign technical men, Americans are best equipped to give advice on our development projects and American-type machinery is in most cases best adapted to our needs.

—Statement to the press by U.S.S.R. ambassador to the U.S., A. A. Troyanovsky, January 1934; quoted in *Handbook of the Soviet Union*, 380

The Soviet period witnessed not only continuation of the tsarist policy of 1890–1917 of borrowing technically and materially from the United States in particular. It also saw a great increase in the volume of this assistance and a greater than before role played by the United States in helping the Russian people overcome backwardness.

In fact, the United States has sold and shipped more commodities of all types to the U.S.S.R. since the October Revolution of 1917 than any other country. According to Soviet figures the U.S. supplied the U.S.S.R. with more exclusively industrial necessities in the period since the revolution than the U.S.S.R. was able to buy from *all* other countries in the ten-year period of the first two Five-Year Plans (1928–1937). Technical personnel from the U.S. numbered between 600 and 700 persons in 1930 alone, according to Peter Bogdanov, chairman of Amtorg, in a speech delivered in that year.

The United States did not formally recognize the Soviet government until November 16, 1933. Despite this fact, American businessmen, in many cases sympathetic to Soviet economic goals, although often deploring the methods of industrializing and advancing the country known as "backward Russia," sold or leased valuable machinery, equipment, or technical personnel to the Bolshevik government. All this was done despite unabating Soviet propaganda against "bourgeois imperialism." It was also done without full legal protection to U.S. businessmen, which could be provided only by stable diplomatic relations between the two countries.

Enterprising U.S. businessmen seemed to echo the words of the American ambassador to St. Petersburg at the end of the eighteenth century, Francis Dana. Even then he had proposed establishing "a good understanding between both countries and intercourse to the mutual advantage of both nations." He predicted that "in the nature of things" future relations between Russia and the U.S. would be *commercial rather than political*.

That attribute of the U.S. businessman cited by the Soviet humorists Ilf and Petrov in "They and We" (from *Little Golden America*) and by Stalin (see quote above) of keeping his word was utilized by the Soviet government in its dealings with Americans. Dependence of the developing Soviet economy upon the advanced capitalist economy of the United States appeared in all the most basic sectors of the economy of the U.S.S.R.

A thoroughgoing assessment of the U.S. contribution to the industrialization of the Soviet Union can be found in Elisha Friedman's *Russia in Transition: A Business Man's Appraisal*. The author was a traveling businessman to the U.S.S.R. in 1931 and formerly lecturer on finance at New York University and the New School for Social Research. Friedman's assessment reads as follows:

> The Soviets lean strongly toward America for technical advice, because Russian and American conditions are so similar. Both countries are rich in natural resources, both constitute large free-trade areas with populations well over 100 million, and neither has political designs against the other. America has advanced far along the road that Russia wishes to travel, namely of mechanization of industry, the emancipation of the worker from the heavy physical toil, the high productivity per man, and the resulting increase in the consuming capacity of the worker. For this reason the Soviets are looking toward American corporations to realize the Five-Year Plan. They are offering American engineers salaries far in excess of the maximum wages paid to Soviet engineers, and in addition give them numerous privileges and advantages.

Russian engineering schools had not yet succeeded in turning out a sufficient number of trained men. Even though the courses in some of the schools were cut down to as little as six months, and the students worked day and night in order to finish their training, the number of graduates was found inadequate for the jobs. As a result the Soviet government planned to import approximately 13,000 additional foreigners, in order to keep up with the Five-Year Plan. These were to include about 3,000 engineers, 3,000 foremen, and 7,000 skilled laborers. About 5,000 were to be Americans. This is a large number in view of the fact that more than 4,000 foreign experts were already under contract with the Soviet government and 2,000 additional were employed by the 124 foreign corporations which had contracts for technical aid to the Soviets. The Depression forced the Soviets to curtail this program.

According to official Soviet figures *the United States was the chief supplier of commodities of all types of the U.S.S.R. for the period 1921–1947*. However, up to 1939, or the beginning of World War II, the United States ranked second among the top three suppliers of goods to the U.S.S.R. since 1921. The figures for the *pre*-World War II period are as follows.

Exports of All Types (1921–1938) (in dollars)

Germany	2,016,000,000
United States	1,445,000,000
Great Britain	907,000,000

During the war, shipments from Germany, of course, ceased while imports from Great Britain (excluding Lend-Lease) were insignificant. But with the establishment of Lend-Lease, Soviet importation of U.S. goods received a boost. The figure for U.S. imports to the U.S.S.R. during the whole period 1921–1947 soared high above that for any other country exporting to the U.S.S.R.

U.S. Shipments to the U.S.S.R. (1939–1947) (in dollars)

1939–1940	137,000,000
1941	120,000,000
1941–1945	9,500,000,000
1946–1947	501,000,000

Breaking down the figures for U.S. exports in terms only of *metals* and *machinery*—the two major items in an industrialization program—the period 1921–1947 yields the following:

U.S. Shipments of Machinery and Metals to the U.S.S.R. (in millions of dollars)

	Machinery	Metals
1921–1936	257	108
1937–1941	204	78
1941–1945	1,325	922
1946–1947	278	39
	2,064	1,147

Meanwhile, during the period of the first two Five-Year Plans (1928–1937) the U.S.S.R. imported from all other countries a total of only $1.8 billion of machinery (*oborudovaniye*) and $981 million worth of metals: a total of only about $2.8 billion. In other words *the total value of shipments of machinery and metals from the United States to the U.S.S.R. since the revolution (to 1947) is almost one billion dollars more than the total machinery metals shipments made to the U.S.S.R. by all other countries during the period of the first two Five-Year Plans.*[2]

Stalin himself acknowledged the overwhelming U.S. impact upon Soviet industrialization. During a conversation with Eric Johnston in June 1944, Marshal Stalin asserted that no less than *two-thirds of all the large industrial enterprises in the Soviet Union* had been built with United States material aid or technical assistance.

NOTES

1. The data in this chapter are reproduced from Albert L. Weeks, *The Other Side of Coexistence An Analysis of Russian Foreign Policy*, New York, Pitman Publishing Corporation, 1970, chapter 2.

2. Yet Stalin, after praising Americans' democratism and describing the United States as the "stronghold of world capitalism," could also declare: "[We Soviets] do not worship everything American" (to Emil Ludwig in 1931), "Historicus," "Stalin on Revolution," *Foreign Affairs*, January 1949, 210. After the war (1947), Stalin admitted to Harold Stassen that the "Soviet Union would have cooperated with Germany as much as with any other Capitalist country if Germany had desired." "Historicus," a pseudonym of George Morgan, a U.S. State Department Russian specialist, adds that Stalin had long believed "that proletarian forces were backward" in America. Labor leaders there are "reactionary" and "reformist." "It cannot be denied," he said, "that American life offers an environment that favors the Communist Party's falling into error while exaggerating the strength and stability of American capitalism." The U.S. then, according to Stalin, would be among the last countries to go communist, 210–11.

6

Western-Soviet Relations before "Barbarossa"

We knew perfectly well Hitler was trying to trick us with the [Nazi-Soviet non-aggression] treaty. I heard with my own ears how Stalin said, "Of course, it's all a game to see who can fool whom. I know what Hitler's up to. He thinks he's outsmarted me, but it was I [Stalin] who has tricked him!"

—N. S. Khrushchev[1]

* * *

Hitler is not so foolish as to think as to think that the Soviet Union is simply another Poland or France or Britain, or all them taken together!

—J. V. Stalin to Marshal Zhukov, spring, 1941[2]

* * *

It is generally accepted to criticize Stalin for not giving timely orders for moving up more of our forces from the rear of the country to meet and repulse an enemy attack. I am not about to theorize what might or might not have happened for good or ill if this had been done. It is quite likely that since our forces lacked anti-tank and anti-aircraft defenses and had limited mobility as compared to the [Wehrmacht] enemy, we could not have withstood the enemy's cutting, penetrating onslaught by its panzers and therefore might have gotten into the same difficult straits that our forward-deployed forces did in certain front military districts during the first days of the war. Nor is it known what consequences would have ensued from this in terms of the defense of Moscow, Leningrad, and in the south.

—G. K. Zhukov[3]

* * *

During the opening days of the war Stalin did not neglect his duties as the country's leader [as claimed by Khrushchev and echoed in Western books] . . . Hitler's war against the U.S.S.R. was lost long before the last German offensive against Moscow [December 1941]. The parade of units of the Red Army in Red Square on Nov. 7, 1941 marked the beginning of a new war that was called by the British military historian, John Erickson, "Stalin's war against Germany."

—Zhores and Roy Medvedev[4]

* * *

The first priority of Stalin and his aides was the fulfillment of their geopolitical aspirations to transform the Soviet Union into the largest superpower of the world.

—Pavel Sudoplatov, former lieutenant-general, first deputy in charge of foreign intelligence, NKVD[5]

Communist Party General Secretary Joseph Stalin, by appointing himself on May 6, 1941, in no uncertain terms signaled the world, and Germany in particular, that the U.S.S.R. was readying itself for war. As Stalin told Red Army graduates in a forty-minute secret speech in the Grand Kremlin Palace the next day, that future war would be with Germany, not, as previously indicated in official Soviet statements, with Turkey, Japan, or Poland (before 1939).[6]

Within days after the German invasion in the early morning hours of Sunday, June 22, 1941, Stalin, following a pause of seventy-two hours to think things through, abruptly turned a friendly face to the democratic Western countries of the United States and Britain, but particularly to the United States.

The readiness and relative ease with which the Soviet leader made this demarche might be and has been attributed by some solely to the blunt fact of the Soviets' desperate situation as the Germans smashed into Soviet Russia.

Is this assumption, however, entirely convincing—especially in the light of recent information that has come out of post-Soviet Russia? It seems possible that Stalin made this decision so rapidly because he had years earlier contemplated the possibility of East-West collaboration against the common Nazi enemy.

AMBIVALENCE TOWARD GERMANY

Unlike the timely decision to turn to the West, it had taken Stalin several years to make a deal with Hitler's Germany that culminated in the mutually profitable Nazi-Soviet agreements of 1939–1940. Of this "unnatural" demarche Stalin from the beginning had stated to intimates that he regarded it as a strictly short-term proposition. Following Lenin's tactics toward Germany, one of the Versailles "loser countries," Stalin had secretly sought state-to-state relations with Nazi Germany. Yet this was true of Soviet relations with some other countries, too, including fascist Italy. Such overtures were made despite mutually hostile Soviet and German propaganda combined with Stalin's sometimes off-hand, though non-publicized friendly remarks about Hitler or Nazi Germany.

On his part, Hitler, too, had made feints in Stalin's direction soon after becoming the German chancellor in 1933. But this had been repulsed by Moscow. One version goes that it was Hitler and the Germans who first approached Stalin's Russia to make a trade deal.[7] Whichever, it was Stalin who had unleashed the Communists' global antifascist campaign that lasted some six years—1933–1939. This campaign was later the subject of jokes between Stalin and German emissaries after the signing of the first Nazi-Soviet Pact of late August 1939.

Despite propaganda noise, throughout the 1930s right up until 1939, there were repeated soundings by Russian emissaries in Berlin. On Stalin's orders they were testing the waters there in terms of opening up, at the very least, mutually beneficial state-to-state relations. A major aim was to encourage robust Soviet-German trade.

Above all, a major precedent for Soviet-German cooperation had already been established—secretly—in the 1920s. On Russian soil the German military tested weapons, some of them Soviet made, and tried out combat tactics in violation of the Versailles Treaty. Junkers produced military aircraft presaging the infamous Ju-87 Stuka dive-bomber as well as testing chemical warfare, a Soviet specialty. This cooperation also included Soviet and German exercises in "blitzkrieg" war-fighting tactics on the Russian steppes.

This mutually profitable German-Soviet cooperation enlightened the military strategies and equipment of both non-Versailles countries. Ironically, a number of the participants on the German side later turned out to be leading Wehrmacht generals and field officers waging war against the U.S.S.R. after June 22, 1941. Secret Soviet-German military collaboration, however, was abruptly terminated when Hitler came to power in 1933.

It should be noted, too, that a residual feeling of respect toward Germany and German culture (Soviet ideology's holiest of holies, Karl Marx and Friedrich Engels, after all, were both Germans) was imbedded in the minds of Lenin and some of his aides, such as Karl Radek, the influential Politburo member and Germanophile. Lenin had always admired the German wartime administration of Chancellor Ludendorff. However, the

Russian attitude toward that central European country was crossed with a deep feeling of suspicion, even fear of the "Prussian spirit" of Germany, which, indeed, again manifested itself so patently with the rise of Adolf Hitler as German chancellor.

Not to be forgotten, moreover, was the fact that Germany had been Russia's bitter foe in World War I. Too, in 1918 with the sacrificial Brest-Litovsk territorial deal concluded under Lenin, the Germans succeeded in coercing the Soviets into granting them control of the resource-rich Ukraine, much to the despair of many of Lenin's closest comrades. Brest-Litovsk was the price Lenin was prepared to pay, his comrades' objections to the contrary, to shut down the eastern front. It allowed Germany to shift its troops conveniently westward facing the capitalist nations, former World War I allies of tsarist Russia.

AMERICA AT A DISTANCE

In contrast to this, toward the non-European, New World country of America, as discussed above, there had always been a deep Russian respect. This long tradition even shows through subtly in some of Lenin's writings, despite his harangues against "capitalist imperialism." America was far enough away geographically for it not to be directly involved in opposing Lenin's and Stalin's plans for spreading communism into the central and west European capitalist countries—their immediate goal after World War I. Or for America to become another *direct* poker player in the post-Versailles balance-of-power game being played in earnest on the European continent after 1918.

Moreover, during the short-lived Allied intervention of 1918 up to the Armistice of November, the United States represented far less of a threat to Lenin's new Soviet Republic than did Britain or Japan. America's main interest in the intervention of 1918, Soviet propaganda aside, was, as George Kennan has pointed out, to protect Allied military assets stored at Russian ports to the north and far east in the Allied war against the Kaiser.

In Bolshevik eyes, in fact, America could be and was viewed as an offstage newcomer rival to British and French "imperialism," and of the Japanese in the Far East. Nor was it a direct participant, as the larger European states were, in the colonization of Africa and Asia and in protecting European metropolitan countries' colonies throughout the Third World. In addition, virulent American isolationism throughout the 1930s kept the United States out of such machinations in Europe. These were facts of life that were not lost on the Soviet rulers in Moscow as they glanced toward the overseas colossus, America.

As to the European powers in contrast to the United States, what most engrossed Stalin was what he perceived, or what he said he perceived, as Franco-British plotting by means of their Munich-appeasement policy of the mid- to late 1930s, that is, to turn Germany eastward, egging that country into war with the U.S.S.R. Meanwhile, Stalin was aware of the fact that in 1939 President Franklin D. Roosevelt had been urging British Prime Minister Chamberlain to encourage collective security collaboration between the West and Stalin's Russia to stem the tide of Nazi expansionism.[8]

Stalin once remarked in 1940:[9]

> The French government of Daladier and the British government of Chamberlain have no intention of involving themselves in war with Hitler. What they hope is to encourage Hitler to wage war against the Soviet Union. Refusing to join us in an anti-Hitler bloc, at the same time they did not wish to keep Hitler from committing aggression against the Soviet Union. They were to pay for this shortsightedness.

PERISHABLE NAZI-SOVIET ALLIANCE

Austrian historian Heinz Magenheimer has noted the significance of the Roosevelt administration's overt anti-Nazi posture before World War II. He also observes that FDR was bent upon influencing Stalin to reconsider his alliance with Hitler:[10]

> The "anti-Axis" policy of the United States, in fact, dated back to the pre-war period. It was evidenced, for example, immediately before and after the German-Soviet treaty of 23 August 1939, when Roosevelt initially urged Stalin to take sides with Britain and France; even after the treaty was signed [Roosevelt] did nothing to isolate the Soviet Union. The President's mild and lenient policies towards the Soviet Union, stemming from his conviction, even prior to the outbreak of war, that Russia could be a potential ally against Germany and Japan.

During the less than two-year period of the Nazi-Soviet honeymoon, late 1939 to mid-1941, Moscow ostensibly, but by no means permanently, tabled whatever notions it may have entertained of improving relations with its future west European allies. Instead, the Soviet government lent whatever support it could to the Nazi cause.

Trade was a big factor in the bilateral relationship built between Berlin and Moscow. During the period 1921–1938, Germany exported to Russia over $2 billion in commodites; the U.S., $1.4 billion. After Hitler came to power, the Soviet security police, or NKVD, collaborated with the German Gestapo. One noxious by-product if this collaboration was the Soviet invention of a mobile gas wagon for liquidating enemies of communism. Dr. Berg's lethal wagon was emulated in the form of the gas chambers of

Nazi Germany. The Soviet gulag table of organization likewise was shared with Heinrich Himmler's emerging camp administration

Following Germany's occupation of the western half of Poland and the Soviets of the eastern half in autumn 1939, the Axis powers opened hostilities in early 1940 against democratic France and Britain, the Lowlands, and Norway. Here the Soviets' own "Lend-Lease"—actually, it was mainly a cold, barter arrangement—took the form of billions of German marks' worth of supplies of all types that were transported by rail punctually by Soviet Russia to Germany.

On February 11, 1940, the wartime German-Soviet Commercial Agreement was signed in Moscow. By this deal, the Soviets were to ship billions of Reichsmarks' worth of war-related materials and goods to the Germans. These were freighted by rail to Brest-Litovsk, then offloaded from the wide-gauge Soviet railroad cars to freight cars on the narrower-gauge tracks leading west to Germany. In the first eighteen months following the signing of this important agreement, the following were shipped to the Germans:

- 1,000,000 tons of grain for cattle plus legumes valued at 120 million Reichsmarks;
- 900,000 tons of mineral oil coasting about 115 million Reichsmarks;
- 200,000 tons of cotton costing approximately 90 million Reichsmarks;
- 500,000 tons of phosphates;
- 100,000 tons of chrome ore;
- 500,000 tons of iron ores;
- 300,000 tons of scrap metal and pig iron;
- 2,000 kilograms of platinum;
- Manganese ore, metals, lumber, rubber, and numerous other raw materials including especially grain were shipped to Germany.
- In addition the Russians granted Germany the right of transit for German traffic to and from Rumania, Iran, Afghanistan, and other countries of the Near and Far East. Russian freight rates for any foodstuffs purchased by the Germans from Manchukuo (under Japanese occupation) were reduced by 50 percent.

This aid helped Hitler in his war against Britain, France, Norway, and the Lowlands. At same time, Soviet Russia got German technology in return. The aid from Soviet Russia continued to roll westward from Brest-Litovsk where the railroad cars were altered to fit the narrower western gauge. The shipments were generally sent on time right up until the German invasion of the U.S.S.R. in late June 1941, although Stalin was capable of delaying such shipments to make a point with Hitler. This Stalin did in early 1941 to remind Hitler of his vulnerability.

In the in August 1940, the Soviet ice-breakers "Lenin," "Stalin," and

"Kaganovich" cleared a path for the German Navy raider "Comet" through the Arctic Ocean route to the Pacific. "Comet" then proceeded to disrupt shipping in that region sinking or capturing ten Allied vessels.[11] Soviet ambassador to London Ivan Maisky sarcastically informed newsmen and foreign diplomats that the Soviets listed German and British war losses "not in two columns but in one."[12]

When France fell in June 1940, Moscow sent congratulations to Berlin on what it called the Germans' "splendid victory." Significantly, Stalin himself sent no such message; this was left up to the Soviet commissariat of foreign affairs.

As each smaller European country fell under the Nazi heel, Moscow dutifully broke off relations with that occupied democratic country, be it Norway, Denmark, Holland, or Belgium. This policy resembled Moscow's abandonment of Czechoslovakia, with whom it had a friendship treaty, just before and after the Wehrmacht occupied that hapless country in 1938.

Besides this egregious Stalinite policy of helping Nazi Germany, the Communist International (Comintern), following the Molotov-Ribbentrop Non-Aggression and Friendship Pacts of August-September 1939, was instructed by the Kremlin to launch a peace campaign. This was aimed at weakening the security of the Allies, America included. Workers' strikes were called by communist-controlled unions in European defense plants. There was even some communist sabotage at these plants. The U.S. Allis-Chalmers plant in South Carolina was one such target. European and Communist Parties, like the CPUSA, obediently condemned efforts by the governments of England and France, and the Roosevelt administration as well, to bolster their nations' defenses as war broke out on the continent and on the high seas.

By far the most drastic measures of this type, however, were applied against France and Britain, not America. Such Soviet-inspired actions tended in any case to let up by late 1940. This was, significantly, when relations between the U.S.S.R. and Germany were headed toward a downturn from which they never recovered.

WARMING TOWARD THE U.S.?

In all, it was abundantly clear that at this point in time Stalin acted as if he thought he was in a phase of a "middle-game" on the world chessboard. Yet he seemed unable or unwilling to anticipate the possibility that Hitler would deceive him in the nearest term. Or, on the contrary, did he, in fact, anticipate such a double-cross in near future? If he did, this might account for a certain warming, albeit scarcely perceptible, in U.S.-Soviet relations before June 22, 1941.

Along this line, a new Russian study by Academy of Sciences historian Dr. Robert Ivanov shows that by late 1940 Stalin was having serious doubts about the durability of his alliance of convenience with Hitler.[13] There is evidence, too, that Stalin was even ready to recognize the tangible danger of a German military threat to the U.S.S.R. In 1940, Soviet agents in Germany and elsewhere were already reporting new, sizable German army troop deployments in the east.

It has long been obvious to historians that Molotov's crucial talks with Hitler in Berlin in the autumn of 1940 had ended in a serious rift. Some contemporary German historians maintain that Hitler's decision finally to attack the U.S.S.R. came as a result of these bumpy talks. Some Russian historians concur. The historians defend this perhaps untenable theory despite the fact that Hitler had first initiated such an attack as early as June 1940. Yet in November Stalin's emissary, Molotov, had made new, impossible demands on Berlin, especially in the Balkans. This seriously compromised Germany's perceived interests in that key region. Aggressive Nazi behavior in the Balkans, a mirror image of equally aggressive Soviet diplomacy in and designs on that same region, inflamed bilateral Soviet-German relations. So did perceived German activity in Finland.

NEW TENSIONS WITH GERMANY

An agreement for a Quadpartite Pact, which would include the Axis powers and Soviet Russia, never materialized. It seems not to have been realized largely because of new demands put on the Germans by Moscow, the latter prioritizing these demands in the short term above the Soviet-Axis global carve-up in the long term.[14] The new, barbed Soviet demands were mixed with complaints about German moves in closing ranks with Finland, which had been the victim of Soviet aggression from December 1939 to March 1940 and which sought German aid.

Molotov made additional demands, especially concerning the Balkans. Among other things he stipulated that Bulgaria should be part of the Soviet security sphere. A Soviet military base should be built at the Dardanelles. Both Italy and Germany should assist the Soviet Union in realizing its goals in the Balkans and at the Straits, especially if Turkey should resist Soviet pressures toward the latter. "Hitler had every reason to fear," writes Topitsch, "that as soon as their present wishes were granted, the Soviets would be making new and even more dangerous demands . . . Molotov's further, extravagant claims amounted to nothing less than an encircling movement from Poland to the Balkans—one which would have made a successful defense against [Soviet] attack from the east impossible, and which would reduce Germany's role from representative to satellite."[15]

Georgy Dimitrov recorded in his diary on November 25 that Molotov had remarked to him, on the latter's return from Berlin, that "our relations with the Germans look lively but there exist serious differences between us . . . We are pursuing a course of demoralizing the German troops that are occupying the various countries. But we're going about this without shouting about it." To which Dimitrov responded, "But won't this intefere with Soviet policy [toward Germany]?" Molotov replied, "Of course. But it must be done anyway. We wouldn't be Communists if we didn't follow such a course. It's only that it must be done quietly."

SHIFT TOWARD THE WEST

These strains between Moscow and Berlin that arose so obviously by 1940 can be viewed as a prelude for a realignment of Soviet Russia toward the Western Powers.[16] As Ivanov shows in his book, *Stalin i Soyuzniki 1941–1945* (*Stalin and the Allies 1941–1945*, published in 2000), back home Stalin was drawing some pregnant conclusions about the degenerating state of his relationship with Hitler especially as concerned the Balkans and implicitly the geostrategic Turkish Straits, Russia's egress out of the Black Sea.[17]

A case in point in this emerging realignment is the Politburo meeting in the Kremlin of November 14, 1940. In it, according to a well-informed eye-witness, Ya. Ye. Chadayev, Administrator of Affairs of the Council of People's Commissars (the top executive organ of the government, known later as the Council of Ministers), after Molotov had reported on his talks in Berlin, Stalin made his extended comments. He also inserted this interesting observation when the subject came up of expanding into Iran, which was one of Hitler's "generous suggestions" proffered by the Führer to Molotov and that the latter had reported at the Politburo meeting,

> Of course, the Soviet Union does not intend to be taken in [by Hitler]. Look, this is our neighbor. We must have very warm and good relations with it.

Then Stalin ticked off the following pregnant observations that not only indicated his awareness of the German danger but implicitly, at least, pointed toward a possible alliance with the West, Hitler's warring enemies since 1939:

1. Germany is concentrating troops along the Soviet border. "It is preparing to attack our country. The Führer used the talks in Berlin [with Molotov] in an attempt to cover up his true intentions."
2. The Soviets made their agreements with Nazi Germany, Stalin disclosed, "merely to forestall an attack by fascist Germany... This provided us with a temporary breathing spell. While the immediate threat of armed aggression against us was somewhat weakened, it was not entirely eliminated." (Stalin was to make this same point in his first postinvasion speech to the Soviet people, July 2, 1941.)
3. Meanwhile, he continued, *"The Reich's ruling circles have increased their hostile actions toward us as though to accentuate the fact that the attack on the Soviet Union was a foregone conclusion."*
4. *"So, what are the Führer's intentions with respect to further cooperation with the Soviet state?"* Stalin asked rhetorically. *"Can we assume that at some time Hitler would abandon the plans inscribed in 'Mein Kampf'? Of course, we cannot make this assumption!"*
5. "Hitler has subdued six European countries in his victorious war against them," Stalin said. "This was, of course, a great strategic achievement for fascist Germany. Now Hitler has set the task of settling matters with England in forcing her to capitulate. Yet this is not Hitler's main goal. The main thing for him is to attack the Soviet Union... **We must always keep this in mind as we prepare to repulse the fascist aggression**" (emphases mine—ALW).
6. Stalin told the Politburo of what must be done to strengthen defenses against such an "inevitable" attack. The new western border must be fortified by deploying troops from the rear to that broad, more than 1500-mile front.
7. Thereupon, Stalin made this significant statement: *"Strong **diplomatic** measures must be undertaken in order to enhance these defense preparations"* (my emphases—ALW). In this context he then mentioned the Soviet effort to conclude a neutrality pact with Japan as one such necessary measure to be taken on the diplomatic front. "She must be neutralized," said Stalin as he indicated the need to protect the eastern, Asian rear of the U.S.S.R. lest the Soviets get embroiled in a two-front war. Moreover, nationalist China, Japan's enemy but no friend, either, of the U.S.S.R., must be approached, he said, by means of Soviet economic and military aid (presumably of a type that was already forthcoming to China from the U.S. as part of the Lend-Lease program). Stalin then asserted bluntly, *"Everything must be done to weaken the Hitlerite coalition, to attract to our side those satellite-countries brought under Hitler's sway."* Here Stalin was referring to Czechoslovakia, Romania, and other Central and East European countries occupied by the Germans or sufficiently tamed by them.

PREINVASION DÉTENTE TREND

Despite the frigid relations with the countries in the British bloc, by the end of 1940 a tendency toward cautious rapprochement set in . . . Tensions arising and growing in relations between the Soviet Union and Germany by the autumn of 1940 acted as a premise for improving Moscow's relations with Great Britain and its allies. Although in June 1940 Molotov had turned down a meeting on trade proposed by British Ambassador S. Cripps, by October the Soviet Government expressed no hesitation in concluding a limited barter-trade agreement with Britain.[18]

Actually, Stalin began lending aid to those governments in exile of the occupied countries of eastern Europe. According to newly discovered Soviet documents, Stalin, by now a rather poor ally of Nazi Germany, began a process of secretly arming underground forces in some of these countries; earlier Stalin had ignored these governments.

This represented a significant shift on Stalin's part. For here was Stalin, right under Hitler's nose, in the throes of initiating a process of drawing away from the much-touted Soviet-German friendship. At same time he was giving encouragement to liberation movements in Nazi-subjugated countries.

Hitler and Goebbels were well aware, as they not infrequently said, of a potential alignment between the America and its anti-Axis European allies and the U.S.S.R. This prospective Soviet-U.S. alignment was cast in terms of what the Nazi leaders called the "pro-Soviet clique" around Roosevelt. To their minds, such a shift by the U.S.S.R. toward America was always a nightmarish possibility. Goebbels's diaries of 1939–1941 are replete with such worries. Also worrisome was Stalin's earlier putative pursuit of "collective security" with the capitalist states against Nazi Germany in the mid to late 1930s. Hitler surely knew what the combined power of the Western powers, including the U.S. plus the U.S.S.R., would mean for the destiny of Germany.[19]

On his part, Stalin occasionally let the cat out of the bag about his true attitude toward America as a potential ally. After some heavy drinking (a rarity for Stalin who tended to control his drinking) at a late-night party in the apartment of Georgian friend G. A. Egnatashvili, someone expressed the fear that one day Soviet Russia would find itself in a war with America. Hearing this, Stalin blurted out, "My dear Liliya Germanova. We won't be fighting America. We will be fighting Germany! England and America will be our allies. So, don't be worried . . . Here's to your health!" Stalin exclaimed lifting another glass in a toast.[20]

At his famous reception for Red Army cadet graduates, May 5, 1941, Stalin designated Germany as the main Soviet enemy. He then observed significantly, "In Europe [Hitler] doesn't have the resources. Only the USA and the U.S.S.R. has them. It is these two world powers who will determine the outcome of the struggle."[21]

Ironically, perhaps deliberately so, this budding new policy of Stalin's coincided with the time when both London and Washington first began informing Stalin of Hitler's true plans—namely, to attack the U.S.S.R. Churchill's first message to Stalin—with a general warning of hostile German intentions toward the U.S.S.R.—had been sent in summer 1940. The two Western capitals had derived this information, though shared with only handful of officials in both countries, from Enigma Machine decryptions made at Bletchley Park near London. This activity, code-named "Ultra," apparently was not penetrated by Soviet agents until later in the war, or roughly by 1943. Probably, it was never completely penetrated to the point where Soviet agents thoroughly knew the Ultra decryption process for translating Enigma-coded traffic.

It is significant that the British leader was apparently ahead of the American president in initiating détente with the Soviets before "Barbarossa." As Soviet Ambassador Ivan M. Maisky noted in his diary on May 12, 1941, or five weeks before the German invasion,

> [Churchill] is counting on the USA and only on the USA [although] Wall Street is far more hostile toward the U.S.S.R. than the London City. Consequently, it turns out that when the British government tries to take a given step toward improving Anglo-Soviet relations, Washington shoves a stick into the wheel.[22]

Maisky had established friendly personal relations with Winston Churchill in London as far back as autumn 1939, in contrast to his relations with Prime Minister Chamberlain. Maisky's talks with Churchill and his immediate circle were generally positive. At that time Churchill told Maisky that Soviet and German interests would eventually clash in Eastern Europe despite the Nonaggression Pact of August. Maisky agreed and noted in his diary that Churchill's "perspicacity in this regard" meant that he thought Britain should oppose Hitler's attempt to apply his expansionist "*Lebensraum*" policy to the Balkans. This, in turn, meant, noted Maisky, October 6, 1939, that British and Soviet interests were in harmony. This attitude strongly contrasts with the atmosphere of German-Soviet cooperation emanating from the just concluded Molotov-Ribbentrop agreements of August and September.

In June 1940 Hitler had signed on to the invasion plan that later came to be called "Operation Barbarossa." (It was finalized and given that designation by the German General Staff in December 1940.) The plan was at first to be put into effect in spring 1941. However, the Nazis' "last-minute"

Balkan campaigns against Greece and Yugoslavia forced postponement of the operation until late June. This was, as it turned out, a perhaps fatal delay. Hitler calculated that even with the postponement to summer 1941, he would be able sufficiently to subdue the "weak" Soviet Russia, a "house of cards," so as to avoid being bogged down in the notorious Russian winter.

Interestingly in the successful, if short-term, coup against the pro-Nazi government in Belgrade in early 1941, the U.S., British, and Russians all cooperated, if indirectly, yet knowingly, in separate ways. The future allies were aware of their joint stake and their efforts to prevent Yugoslavia from becoming another German satellite, which it did in any case since these efforts failed after the one week of an anti-Nazi regime adorned with a Yugoslav-Soviet mutual assistance pact signed with the U.S.S.R.[23] The German penetration of the Balkans in general alarmed all three capitals—Washington, London, and Moscow. All three were aware of the common interests in preventing that penetration that included Hungary, Romania, and Bulgaria, and might ultimately include Turkey and the geostrategic Straits at Constantinople.

"IGNORING" WARNINGS OF ATTACK

Stalin *publicly* regarded the several warnings of aggressive German intentions that he received from London and Washington in 1940–1941 as "provocations."

To his mind—as far as can now be determined from documents from the still only partially opened archives made available to date to researchers by Russian authorities—Stalin thought that the British, and to a lesser degree the Americans, were giving him "disinformation." Their hidden intention, he said, reflected what he said he thought all along since mid-1939, was to propel Germany and Soviet Russia into war. This, Stalin believed, was the Western imperialists' self-interested hope that was aimed at deflecting the Germans eastward against the Communist power in order to destroy it. There seems little doubt that Stalin entertained these suspicions, at least, in 1939 to mid-1940, and not, seemingly, without some grounds. At least, as this policy expressed the views of certain influential British officials in London as well as Americans in Washington.

However, by early late 1940 and 1941, the Soviet leader seems to have had a change of heart. By then he had decided—on the basis of intelligence information he had received (that may have included, it is believed, significant parts of the actual planning for Operation Barbarossa)—that Germany, indeed, was actively planning such an attack. Yet, perhaps for show, in order, as he thought, to mislead the Germans, Stalin together with his security chief, Lavrenty Beria, and other top intelligence officials in Moscow summarily, publicly dismissed such warnings and intelligence information that came pouring in to the Kremlin by 1941 from their well-placed own agents in Berlin, Tokyo, and elsewhere.

As an illustration of how far Stalin could carry this ruse, if that is what it was, just days before the invasion on June 22, the Soviets, apparently on Stalin's direct orders, decreed that a young German officer, who had defected to the Soviet side on the western front producing documents showing that Operation Barbarossa was for real, was to be shot. Other such "German provocateurs" were similarly dealt with. So were Soviet army trigger-happy "alarmists."

Stalin's much-touted "paranoia" aside, these publicized actions appeared to be exploited as a form of propagandistic "advertising." They were at very least an overt signal in the form of disinformation to the Germans indicating how little credence the Kremlin and personally Stalin supposedly placed in such "provocations" perpetrated by individual German line officers at the eastern front, or by Stalin's own informers.

On his part, Stalin also issued orders to his forces on the line to do nothing to "provoke" the Germans into waging war. These, too, were advertised. Broadcasts over Moscow Radio and items published in the party newspaper *Pravda*, such as the famous one of June 14, 1941, were nuanced so as to suggest that Moscow would not be "enticed" into hostilities with Germany by such "tricks" and "provocations." To further emphasize the Kremlin's determined "peace-mindedness," shipments of Soviet supplies to Germany continued to roll westward on schedule.

Yet as post-Soviet archives indicate, Stalin was kept well informed of German troop movements in the spring of 1941. To suggest that he simply ignored or repudiated all this espionage warning of German war plans against the U.S.S.R. is simply not credible. That Stalin, in fact, sought to exploit the information *is* credible.

THE WELLES-UMANSKY TALKS

Stalin had been warned in another way that involved Sumner Welles, the U.S. undersecretary of state and one of FDR's closest aides, and a reputed "dove" on Russia.

In a series of interesting talks undertaken by Welles and Stalin's prickly ambassador to Washington, Konstantin Umansky, in July 1940 (note the early date), a number of points of "mutual interest" were struck off.[24] Roosevelt had initiated these discussions, Gaddis notes, in order to make a "concerted effort to try to improve United States relations with the Soviet Union." These talks, which began in that eventful summer, are noteworthy given the fact that U.S.-Soviet relations were apparently at a low ebb at this time. As Foreign Minister Molotov put it in his address to the U.S.S.R. Supreme Soviet on August 1, "I will not dwell on our relations with the United States of America, if only for the reason that that there is nothing good to that can be said about them." Yet "both Moscow and Washington had by this time developed enough common concerns to keep the negotiations going."[25]

The Umansky-Welles discussions revolved round the following:

1. Obviously reflecting Stalin's thinking (no Soviet ambassador ever dared to "wing" it on his own), the Russian ambassador, Konstantin Umansky complained that given "common concerns" concerning the European situation, Soviet Russia should not be subjected to such discrimination as the U.S. embargo on aircraft equipment.
2. The Russians, the ambassador complained, had increasing difficulties obtaining export licenses on for strategic materials that they wished to purchase. The Americans, he insisted abrasively, should "sell the Russians whatever was necessary for their defenses." As the author notes, few concrete results came out of the protracted Umansky-Welles talks. But the "psychological atmosphere," notes Gaddis, "had definitely improved." Even Molotov admitted that the United States had demonstrated, if "in very small way," a desire "to improve relations with the Soviet Union."

Gaddis further points out that since the Russians feared a German attack, as reported to Washington by U.S. ambassador to Moscow, Laurence A. Steinhardt, "they would never risk such an attack merely to improve relations with the United States or Great Britain." Yet Welles went ahead, with FDR's approval. On March 1, 1941, the Secretary gave Umansky some earth-shaking information—about the coming German attack on the U.S.S.R.—after which "Umansky turned very white" while also expressing thanks.

Meanwhile, at this moment the Roosevelt administration began developing plans to assist the U.S.S.R., when and if it chose to accept such assistance, when a German invasion materialized. (Lend-Lease for England and several other friendly, anti-Axis nation-states was to be approved by the U.S. Congress in March 1941.)

The prospect of adding Soviet Russia to the list of Lend-Lease recipients certainly seemed remote in early 1941. Yet, as the author writes, Roosevelt was now in possession of secret information "suggesting that the prospect [of a Nazi war against the U.S.S.R.] was not remote at all [and] refused to accept amendments [to the Lend-Lease bill] that would have excluded the U.S.S.R."

On March 11, Lend-Lease became law in the flexible form that the President had demanded, and especially with the wording in the law that gave the White House the leading hand in seeing through and staffing this aid. Significantly, this was just over a week after Welles had shared with Umansky the Enigma information—without, of course, revealing that top-secret source to the Soviet ambassador.

At same time, Stalin was pleased to have achieved Japan's neutrality by means of the treaty signed between the U.S.S.R. and Japan in April 1941. Yet it is noteworthy that the pact was one of mere neutrality, not nonaggression or active friendship. It thus fell short of expectations—probably on both sides. The ebullient Soviet dictator purportedly told the Japanese negotiator, Foreign Minister Yasuke Matsuoka, as he saw him off at the Moscow railroad station after some heavy toasting in the Kremlin, "Japan will straighten out the East, and the Soviet Union and Germany will take care of Europe, and later on between them they will take care of the Americans."

Despite such public pronouncements, which in some respects read more like propaganda than real policy, the Americans and the British all but bombarded Stalin and his aides with secret information concerning Germany's invasion plans. Throughout May and June, on the very eve of Hitler's perfidy of June 22, 1941, Washington and London were sure they could convince Stalin of the coming attack. Yet apparently they could not. However, until Stalin's private papers (assuming they still exist) are examined, we will never know how seriously Stalin took these warnings. There are hints that he took them very seriously.

The assumption to date is that the Soviet dictator, who was said to be proud of his own private sources of intelligence information (neither Stalin nor the NKVD-NKGB had any objective intelligence-assessment office) received them with "paranoic disbelief." That may or may not be true. It may be truer to say that Stalin reacted that way for *public, that is, German consumption.*

Moreover, it seems the Soviet leader simply could not believe that Hitler would be so foolish as to entail a two-front war *at that time*—with Britain in Germany's rear to the west, huge Russia to the east and with summer approaching and the usual "early frost" in Russia not far behind. At any rate, no public display of such suspicions of an imminent German attack, Stalin seems to have reasoned, could be allowed. To his mind it would mean giving the Germans a pretext for initiating hostilities.

However, that the Soviet leader could not but have secretly welcomed Roosevelt's and Churchill's repeated offers of future help to the U.S.S.R. should that country be attacked cannot be denied. Later during the war Stalin admitted as much when he expressed his gratitude for Allied, and American Lend-Lease assistance. *Both Western leaders, as Stalin well knew* before June 22, were publicly and undeniably committed to the idea that of the two dictatorships, German and Russian, the latter was far less threatening to American and British interests. "At the present time," said President Roosevelt in late 1941 and he had made similar statements earlier, "Russia is in no sense an aggressor nation—Germany is."[26]

This contrasted with an anti-Soviet statement Roosevelt himself had made in autumn 1939, on the eve of the Soviet against Finland:

> The Soviet Union, as everybody who has the courage to face the facts, knows is run by a dictatorship as absolute as any dictatorship in the world. It has allied itself with another dictatorship, and it has invaded a neighbor [Finland] so infinitessimally small that it could do no conceivable harm to the Soviet Union.

A similar view documenting the flexibility of Stalin's policy making, his diplomatic chess play during the several months preceding Barbarossa is offered in a classic study of American and Soviet foreign policy by two Harvard and Amherst scholars, William L. Langer and Everett Gleason, in their comprehensive work published in 1953 at the height of the Cold War. While showing no sympathy at all for Stalin or his tactics in the foreign arena in the years 1940–1941, the authors nevertheless found evidence of a shift in Stalin's attitude toward the West, and toward America in particular. As they wrote,[27]

> Yet for all the bitterness and controversy engendered in [U.S.-Soviet trade talks] and a number of other issues, there were more than mere hints that politically the two governments [American and Soviet] were finding common ground. Oumansky himself suggested that if Soviet trade with Germany were to be an insurmountable obstacle to the development of Soviet-American trade, it might be well to be "good sports" about it. "It is our belief," he added, "that many common denominators may be found in the long-range policy of both the American and Soviet governments and certainly in the immediate future there should be common denominators in the economic policies of the two governments" . . . In the same spirit the ambassador somewhat later was frank to say that the German invasion of Greece and Yugoslavia must be "profoundly disquieting" to his government, and to remark how useful it would be for both the United States and the Soviet Union, as well as for the whole world, if the foreign policies of the American and Soviet governments were "identical" . . . He stressed the common interest of the United States and the Soviet government in supporting nationalist China [in its war against Japan]

Then the Soviet ambassador dropped this bombshell, doubtlessly knowing the boss in Moscow would approve:

Without doubt the Soviet Union and the United States will eventually be on the same side anyway.

Bearing the above in mind and looking back at the Welles-Umansky talks, the authors suggest that Welles's efforts to normalize relations with Moscow, while also warning the Soviets of German intentions, may have "provided at least a foundation for closer relations." The talks, they continued, "may even have influenced important decisions of the Kremlin with respect to broad policy."

They further pointed to the limited nature of the neutrality agreement with Japan. Its modest terms may have been motivated by an emerging, new Kremlin attitude toward the West. That is, by neither pushing for a nonaggression pact with Japan nor membership in the Axis alliance, Stalin was possibly hedging his bets against the future—that is, "so as not to estrange the democracies by seeming to associate the Kremlin with the Tripartite Pact."

On the twenty-fourth anniversary of the Bolshevik revolution, November 7, 1941, Roosevelt ordered the shipping of Lend-Lease aid to the U.S.S.R.

This began across the waters of the Pacific Ocean and southward via the Atlantic and Indian Oceans to Iran.

* * *

In the last analysis from reviewing the evidence (to the degree that it is available), one gets the impression that while Stalin ostentatiously and highandedly dismissed the reports of a German doublecross by Hitler (as in the famous June 14 *Pravda* article denying Soviet belief in German perfidy), his motive in doing so stemmed from genuine, total disbelief in the likelihood of a German attack at sometime in the future. Rather, it appears that he could not believe that the attack would come so soon. Germany, after all, was still fighting England. Molotov and Ribbentrop were forced, after all, to meet in November 1940 in a Berlin air-raid shelter! For Germany, Stalin appears to have reasoned, in this case fatally, to risk a two-front war under the conditions of spring or summer 1941 could not truly have been Hitler's intention. The German dictator could not be that foolish.

DEMARCHE

At same time, Stalin was fully aware of the positive effect of U.S. Lend-Lease aid to the British war effort. Too, he was aware of the consequences that would follow from a Nazi defeat of England. As espionage specialist authors Jerrold and Leona Schecter observe in *Sacred Secrets: How Soviet Intelligence Operations Changed American History* (Brassey's, Inc., 2002,

127): "Despite the 1939 Nazi-Soviet Pact of Nonaggression Stalin did not want Great Britain to fall because it would free Hitler to attack the U.S.S.R." That may be only part of the story. The other part may have been Stalin's awareness of the positive use that would follow from allying the U.S.S.R. with an undefeatable West. Indeed, one of the main tasks of the Soviets' well-developed espionage in London was to track U.S.-British relations, Lend-Lease, and the drift of America into war against the Axis, Russia's prospective enemy. How, after all, could Stalin have ignored the importance of an America involved in the war? How could he ignore the efficacy of the multifarious Lend-Lease aid coursing to Britain over the North Atlantic? Moreover, had he not been informed well before June 22 that such aid would be extended to Soviet Russia if it ever itself got into a war with Nazi Germany?

Moscow Ambassador Steinhardt's virtual plea to Stalin in April 1941 via Deputy Foreign Minister Lozovsky could not help in this respect but to have made an impression on the ever-vigilant Soviet dictator.[28] Stalin assiduously followed the input and diplomatic innuendoes he received from the highest levels of the Commissariat of Foreign Affairs, headed by Molotov, as well as his other secret sources of information. Stalin always played his cards very close to his chest. He kept deep secrets even from his closest aides, including Molotov, Beria, Golikov (head of military intelligence), and the rest.

It seems he must have at least put on his own mental scales what many historians call his "paranoic suspicions" weighed against his rational concerns about Germany's aggressive intentions. On one side of such scales were his suspicions directed against Hitler, buttressed by the many reports that came into the Kremlin, and which he himself had voiced at the Politburo meeting back in November 1940. On the other end of the scales were his unwarranted suspicions of the intentions—unwarranted at least, by late 1940 and into 1941—of the Western Allies and their "provocations" to get Soviet Russia into the war. However, until Stalin's own, most top-secret papers are made available—on the assumption that they were not entirely destroyed in March 1953 upon Stalin's fatal stroke and death—it will be hard to determine just how these scales were tipped. At that time they were purloined by Beria's men.

At some future time perhaps the president's office in today's Kremlin might choose to release the documents. Until more is known, we will not know exactly what Stalin was thinking or planning by way of 1) waging war himself against Germany and ultimately the West—for which there are rather solid grounds for suspicion; 2) continuing to postpone Soviet involvement in the "inevitable" war; or 3) planning a demarche toward the United States and Britain. On Prime Minister Churchill's part as on Roosevelt's, the choice was clear. As the PM declared in a radio speech on the night of June 22, 1941, just after the German attack,[29]

The danger now threatening Russia is the same danger threatening us and the United States . . . We shall double our efforts and will fight together as long as we have the strength and life to do so.

Churchill's show of a flexible attitude toward the U.S.S.R. as a potential ally of the West against Hitler can be traced at least as far back as 1939, a year before he became prime minister. In this respect the British PM may have possessed more foresight than President Roosevelt. Yet Roosevelt himself may have entertained such ideas years before "Barbarossa" despite contrary opinions about Soviet Russia within his own circle.[30] Whatever the case, Stalin executed his next major turnabout in Soviet foreign policy by closing ranks with America and Britain. Lend-Lease became the centerpiece of this enormous sea change.

NOTES

1. N. S. Khrushchev, *Khrushchev Remembers The Glasnost Tapes*, Boston, Little, Brown and Company, 1990, 128
2. G. K. Zhukov, *Vospominaniya i razmyshleniya* (Reminiscences and Reflections), Moscow, Progress Publications, 1995, vol. 1, 384.
3. Zhukov vol. 2, 26–27.
4. *Voprosy Istorii*, No. 6, 2002, 33.
5. Sudoplatov, 96.
6. Medvedev, 26.
7. Cf. Weeks, *Stalin's Other War*, Chapter 3, "The Soviets' Pro-German Posture."
8. Sudoplatov, 97. Cf. William E. Kinsella, Jr., *Leadership in Isolation: FDR and the Origins of the Second World War*, Boston, G. K. Hall & Co., 1978, chapter 3.
9. Sokolov, 43
10. Magenheimer, 39.
11. Suprun, Mikhail. *Lend-Liz I severniye konvoi 1941–1945* (Lend-Lease and the Northern Convoys, 1941–1945), Moscow, Andreyevskii Flag, 1997, 7.
12. Suprun, 7.
13. Ivanov, 98.
14. In his book, *Roosevelt and Stalin*, Prof. Nisbet appears to overrstate the Soviet interest in joining the Axis. Robert Nisbet, *Roosevelt and Stalin: The Failed Courtship*, New York, Regnery Gateway, 1988.
15. Ernst Topitsch, *Stalin's War: A Radical New Theory on the Origins of the Second World War*, New York, St. Martin's Press, 1987, 29.
16. As Goebbels noted in his diary.
17. Ivanov, 97–98.
18. Suprun, 7.
19. Basistov, 36.
20. Sokolov, 83.
21. Russian State Archives of Literature and the Arts (RGALI), Folio 1038, quoted in Afanas'iev, 132. There are three extant versions of this secret speech by

Stalin. The above quotation is from a version found in the diary of the Soviet writer, Vasili Vishnevsky, who heard the speech.

22. V. V. Sokolov, "*I. M. Maiskyi mezhdu I. V. Stalinym I U. Churchillem v perviye mesyatsi voiny*" ("I. M. Maisky Between I. V. Stalin and W. Churchill During the First Months of the War"), *Novaya i noveishaya istoriya*, No. 6, 2001, 19.

23. Sudoplatov, 119 and 234. Cf., Kostin, A. A. "*Pozitsiya SShA v otnoshenii Yugoslavii v yanvarye-marte 1941 goda*" ("The Position of the U.S.A. in Its Relations with Yugoslavia January–March 1941"), *Voprosy istorii*, No. 1, 2002, 107–15.

24. John Lewis Gaddis, *We Now Know: Rethinking Cold War History*, Oxford, Clarendon Press, 1997, 140–41; Jones, 29; Suprun, 8. Note that Umansky was an ex-NKVD officer, not an unusual double career for key Soviet ambassadors.

25. Gaddis, 140.

26. Gaddis, 146.

27. William L. Langer and S. Everett Gleason, *The Undeclared War 1940–1941*, New York, Harper & Brothers Publisher, 1953, 344.

28. A. N. Yakolev, *et al.*, *1941 god*, vol. 2, 80–81.

29. V. A. Nevezhin, *Sindrom nastupatel'noi voiny* (The Syndrome of Offensive War), Moscow, Seriya Pervaya Monografiya, Airo-XX, 1997, 24. Cf. Weeks, *Stalin's Secret War*.

30. Sudoplatov, 97 and Nisbet

7

✛

The "Strange Alliance" Is Born

May I express in conclusion the great admiration of all of us in the United States for the superb bravery displayed by the Russian people in defense of their liberty.

—Harry Hopkins, letter to Stalin, July 25, 1941[1]

* * *

That these countries of diametrically opposed social and political were able to put their differences aside in the name of forming the anti-Hitler coalition was an outstanding milestone in world history.[2]

* * *

The Russian dictator went into detail as to [Lend-Lease] supplies required, listing them in order of priority as tanks, anti-tank guns, bombers, anti-aircraft guns, armor plate, fighter and reconnaissance planes, and barbed wire. . . . Stalin again stressed his need for transport, for American jeeps and trucks. "Winning this war depends on the gasoline engine. The country that can produce the greatest number of gasoline engines will be the victor."[3]

* * *

Your [President Roosevelt's] decision to grant the Soviets an interest-free loan in the value of $1 billion . . . is accepted by the Soviet government with deep gratitude as crucial aid to the Soviet Union in its tremendous, arduous fight against our common enemy.

—J. V. Stalin, message to Roosevelt, November 4, 1941

* * *

Second in size to the British aid program, this Soviet [Lend-Lease] package presented a gigantic challenge to the infant United States war industry in addition to the tremendous problem of delivery and annoying factor of surliness on the part of the Soviet Union itself.[4]

* * *

During the war the strategic materials and foodstuffs shipped to the U.S.S.R. under Lend-Lease played an important role and to a significant degree contributed to to the successful outcome of the war against the common enemy, Hitlerite Germany.

—J. V. Stalin, message to President Truman, June 11, 1945[5]

* * *

The abnormal situation [in the Southwestern Sector] is such that the tank corps are so under-strength that the only strength they have is in their name, "tanks."

—Chief of the Main Administration of the Red Army's Motorized Forces, General Lieutenant Ya. N. Fedorenko, in a message to Chief of the General Staff General G. K. Zhukov, July 1941[6]

The war on the eastern front, 1941–1945, known as the Great Patriotic War, lasted 1,418 days. Russian (meaning "Soviets" of all nationalities) deaths totaled upwards to 27 million. Material destruction to the U.S.S.R.'s villages, towns, and cities and their industrial-agricultural bases was horrendous.

THE GREAT PATRIOTIC WAR BEGINS[7]

At 3:15, June 22, 1941, under the first light at dawn (Russia's far north location meant an early twilight), Germany launched its massive attack against the Soviet Union.

No less than 153 German divisions consisting of 118 infantry divisions, 19 tank divisions, 15 panzer divisions plus thousands of warplanes and cavalry units—a total of over 5.5 million men including Germany's allies—smashed over the Soviets' new, post-1939 western border along a 1,200-mile front. Joining the Wehrmacht in the assault were almost 40 divisions of its allies—Finland, Romania, and Hungary. The Wehrmacht troops amounted to 75 percent of the entire German armed forces. German planes freely carried out devastating bombing of frontline forces, airfields, railway stations and junctions, and of cities, towns, and villages.

Opposing the invaders, according to German sources, were 118 Red Army infantry divisions, twenty cavalry divisions, forty motorized and tank brigades, and 6,000 aircraft. Soviet forces along the front numbered upwards to 3 million. In some sectors the defenders were outnumbered on the order of two to one, in some places by three to one. The damage wrought on the defenders was tremendous.

The Soviets were outnumbered in many places along the front by nearly two to one—a disproportion they soon made up for against the invaders in the months and years ahead. Along the border the defending Soviets had amassed 190 divisions. These consisted of 5.5 million men, 3,712 tanks, 4,950 planes, 47,260 guns and mortars, and in the Baltic over 190 naval ships.

In the opening two months of the invasion, the Germans had captured over 1 million Red Army POWs; the Soviets had suffered over 700,000 dead or wounded. By August, the Germans had advanced 500 miles into the western part of the U.S.S.R. They were a mere 200 miles from Moscow with a ribbon of concrete pointing to the capital, and only 100 miles from Leningrad.

Of all the destruction wrought in the opening days and weeks of Operation Barbarossa, perhaps none was more most critical than the severe loss in aircraft. No fewer than 1,200 were caught like sitting ducks on the ground or in their forward-positioned hangars. Soon the Germans had occupied a good deal of the Soviet Baltic states of Estonia, Latvia, and Lithuania, as well as the western territories of Belorussia and Ukraine. They were poised to cross the Dvina and Dneiper Rivers.

In the mayhem, thousands of Soviet soldiers performed unparalleled acts of bravery as they were to do on many fronts and in many battles during the war. By mid-July 1941, the enemy was halted near Kiev for seventy-three days. The Wehrmacht killed or captured more than 660,000 Russians—about one-third of the Red Army—in the battles around the capital of Ukraine. These encounters, along with some others were the greatest defeats in Russian history. As a result of the defeat, the north, center, and the south were left vulnerable to rapid German advances.

By November of 1941, the Germans had taken and occupied the Baltic states, Byelorussia, Moldavia, most of Ukraine, and the Crimea, and a large part of Karelia. They had also seized a considerable territory around Leningrad and Moscow. Before the war, those parts of the country that were occupied by November 1941 had contained 40 percent of the total population of the Soviet Union and produced 63 percent of the nation's coal, 58 percent of its steel, and 38 percent of its grain. Human losses were enormous.

ONWARDS TO AID

As noted earlier, after the German invasion of the Soviet Union, the governments of Britain and the United States immediately declared their support for the U.S.S.R. in its struggle against the aggression by Germany and its allies. On June 23, 1941, President Roosevelt informed the media that "Hitler's armies are today the chief dangers to the Americas." This first, official statement contained no clear promise of Russian aid. On the next day, however, Roosevelt announced at a press conference that the United States would give all possible help to the Soviet people in their struggle against Germany and its allies; preliminary discussions with Soviet officials began on June 26, 1941.

A number of conservative senators and congressmen argued that America's aid ought to be restricted to proven friends, such as Great Britain and China. In late July and August, Congress debated this subject. Isolationists insisted that aid to Russia meant aid to communism. On the other hand, some thought the Russian front might be America's salvation.

A public opinion poll taken in July 1941 indicated that 54 percent of Americans opposed Russian aid. Yet by September, those opposed to giving aid declined to 44 percent. Those favoring helping Russia rose to 49 percent.

Basing himself on slowly changing American public opinion on this issue, Roosevelt proceeded cautiously yet stubbornly in the matter of aiding the Soviets. He distrusted Soviet Russia. Yet he did not think that the Soviets, in contrast to the Germans, intended to conquer Europe. He seems also to have regarded the Soviet state as at least quasi-democratic. Against a large body of opinions among officials within various Cabinet departments, civilian and military, Roosevelt calculated that the Russians would resist the German assault longer than anyone anticipated. This would help the British. Perhaps it would even keep the United States out of the fray in Europe.

Roosevelt used a "fireside chat," December 17, 1940, and his State of the Union address, January 6, 1941, to introduce to the American public and the world for the first time the two historical terms, "lend-lease" and "arsenal of democracy."

In making his assessments concerning Soviet Russia, FDR relied heavily on two of his senior advisers, Harry Hopkins and W. Averell Harriman. They had urged Roosevelt to bring in Russia under Lend-Lease. Meanwhile, it appears that FDR himself, or at least some in the War Department, may have felt hesitant at first about such assistance because of pessimistic analyses about the Red Army that lay on the desks of officials in that department as well as at the War Office in London. Pessimistic views were still heard for years, especially after the expensive and embarrassing virtual defeat of the Red Army in the two months-plus Winter War against Finland. Doubts were also fueled by Stalin's wholesale purge of his senior army staff and field officers in 1937 and beyond.

In July 1941, Roosevelt called on Hopkins, Ambassador Umansky, and Arthur Purvis (the British representative) to form an "intergovernmental committee," under White House control, that would be tasked to administer aid to Soviet Russia. At his own request, Hopkins was granted permission to fly to Russia, July 26, following a stop in London where he would first discuss the matter of aid to Russia with the Prime Minister there before flying on to the U.S.S.R.

When Hopkins met with Stalin, he was impressed by the Soviet leader. Stalin was anything but "paralyzed" or "demoralized" by the severe defeats the U.S.S.R. had suffered since June 22. Reflecting Harriman's and some others' opinions, Hopkins became convinced that the Soviets could survive the German attack and turn the war against the Germans. Following several meetings with Stalin. Hopkins cabled Washington from Moscow stating to the President his firm conviction that Russia would not collapse. Stalin had given Hopkins a wish list.

Then in early September of 1941, Roosevelt sent Averell Harriman—whose firm had been a large investor in the Soviet economy since 1918—to work out a temporary aid program with British representatives.

THE FIRST U.S.-SOVIET LEND-LEASE TALKS

Then on July 7, 1941, a Soviet delegation flew from Vladivostok to Nome, Alaska, and then on to Kodiak and Seattle, Washington, for secret talks with American officials. At the top of their list were the planned deliveries of, above all, *aircraft* to the U.S.S.R. via the relatively safer Pacific sea route. Other routes, as previously noted, were ruled out, especially the route to Tehran. Iran's notorious weather of blowing dust and sand could ruin aircraft engines.

From September 29 to October 1, 1941, representatives from Britain, the Soviet Union, and the United States attended an aid-related conference held in Moscow. These talks resulted in a detailed plan for making deliveries of armaments, equipment, and foodstuffs to the Soviet Union. On its part, the U.S.S.R. in its turn agreed to provide strategic raw materials for Britain and the United States. It was at this autumn 1941 conference that Harriman, for the first time, suggested delivery of U.S. combat aircraft to Russia via Alaska and Siberia using American air crews. Stalin, however, rejected this idea unconditionally, perhaps to avoid provoking Japan. Only the planes alone would be sent along, not with American crews but with instructors.

Despite political tensions at the Moscow conference, on October 30 Roosevelt gave his approval. Then on November 4, 1941, Stalin accepted $1 billion in aid to be repaid in ten years, interest free.

Although the Soviet government was pleased with the aid, as Stalin himself declared, they complained that no serious military action had been taken on the ground by the Allies against Germany. This was the first intimation that Stalin was going to raise the ticklish issue of the Western Allies' opening of a second front, a sore point that Stalin dwelt on several times in the months to follow. The Soviets resented, they said, the fact that the Soviet Union was bearing the brunt of the war virtually alone. The Russians suggested that the British and United States immediately open such a second front in France or in the Balkans, or send troops through Iran—which the Russians and British had jointly occupied in August in order to preclude German influence there—to attack Ukraine from the south.

In the ensuing months the Soviet government continued to insist that opening a second front in Europe would relieve pressure from enemy attacks on the eastern front. Opening of a second front became a diplomatic serious issue in East-West relations as well as an anti-West refrain of Soviet propaganda. It did not let up until the massive Allied crossing of the English Channel in June 1944. On their part, the Allies insisted that they could carry out such a plan prematurely. They simply lacked the forces necessary in order to open a second front in Europe. Too, they were involved in fighting a war in the Pacific and in the north African theaters.

Looking ahead as to territorial settlements in the aftermath of war, Churchill, Stalin, and Roosevelt understood that there was as yet no agreement on postwar peace aims. The Allies had made the commitment only to provide Lend-Lease support to Russia. Yet there was no thought of giving a green light to the large Soviet annexations of foreign territory in 1940 amid repressions and forced resettlements of native citizens—all clearly against the will of the peoples involved (namely, people of Estonia, Latvia, Lithuania, and in Poland and Romania).

December 1941 marked the signing of the first Lend-Lease "protocol" to providing aid to the Soviet Union for a period of a year. The U.S.S.R. accepted most of the Lend-Lease terms. Yet specific details had to be worked out.

PLANNING THE MAIN ROUTES

On May 29, 1942, Vyacheslav Molotov, commissar of foreign relations and deputy premier to Stalin, arrived in the United States to discuss the Lend-Lease matters. This was the first official visit of such a high Soviet official to American soil. Being cautious and uncertain in a formerly hostile country, he carried in his luggage some sausages, a piece of black bread, and a pistol—the latter, according to Eleanor Roosevelt, Molotov placed under his pillow in the White House Lincoln Bedroom.

During Molotov's visit, President Roosevelt suggested that (1) American aircraft be flown to the U.S.S.R. via Alaska and Siberia and (2) that Russian ships pick up Lend-Lease supplies from America's West Coast ports (namely, Seattle and San Francisco) for transport across the Pacific to Vladivostok as well as other Russian far east ports on the Pacific. This route was chosen, in addition to two other routes—the northern sea route to Murmansk and the southern Iran route—as proposed in July because of its relative safety. Liberty Ships (a major shipyard for these ships was located near San Francisco) would be assured of safe passage because they would fly Soviet colors from their masts (the U.S.S.R. and Japan had signed a mutually protective treaty with each other in April 1941).

In this way, Lend-Lease supplies could sooner and more safely reach the Soviet Ural Mountains industrial complex at Magnitogorsk and the warfronts to the west in European Russia by employing the Trans-Siberian Railway for hauling the valuable Lend-Lease cargoes.

After careful consideration of various proposals, the best route for planes seemed to be via Alaska and Siberia. Although great distances were involved and the worst possible weather conditions would be encountered, the planes would be delivered in flying condition, the possibility of enemy interference being remote. American support for the Alaska-Siberia route was also based on the hope that Siberia's air bases would be used eventually by U.S. forces eventually for bombing raids on Japan. (The U.S.S.R. did not agree to double-cross Japan by entering the war against her in the Pacific Theater until July 1945 as a result of the Potsdam summit.)

On their part, the Soviets, however, were hesitant to use this route. They thought that the Alaska-Siberia route was too dangerous and impractical, that Siberian cities were not prepared to accommodate the heavy air traffic, and that the presence of Americans in the Soviet far east would be unwanted. The Soviets were also afraid that the Pacific supply routes, and the Alaska-Siberia route in particular, would provoke Japanese military action against Russia. Nevertheless, with losses mounting on the sea run to Murmansk and the great distances involved in the Middle East, the Soviets finally agreed to open the Alaska-Siberia air route on August 3, 1942. The final Lend-Lease agreement was signed in Washington, D.C., on June 11, 1942, entitled "Agreement between Governments of the U.S.S.R. and United States on Principles Employed to the Mutual Assistance in Fighting the War Against the Aggressors."

The Alaska-Siberia delivery route finally became a reality in August 1942. The air route connected Great Falls, Montana, Edmonton and

Whitehorse, Canada, Fairbanks, Galena, and Nome, Alaska. A major field was built in Nome, the last stopping point for the planes before they left for Siberia. In Siberia airplanes continued their long trip from Uel'em through Markovo, Iakutsk, Kiernsk, Krasnoiarsk, and finally, to Novosibirsk. In the thirty-one months of the program, nearly eight thousand aircraft were sent through Great Falls for transfer to Russia.

"THE RUSSIANS ARE COMING"

On August 26, 1942, the first Soviet envoys, Colonel Piskunov and Alexis A. Anisimov, members of the Soviet Purchasing Commission, arrived in Nome. On September 4, 1942, the first Russian aircraft arrived in Alaska bringing more mission members to set up permanent command stations at Ladd Field, in Fairbanks, and in Nome. By the summer of 1943, there were many Russians stationed at Fairbanks, Nome, Galena, Edmonton, and Great Falls; at the height of the program there were anywhere from 150 to 600 Soviet pilots and other personnel at Ladd Field alone. Those Soviets who were assigned to work on American soil were ideologically drilled to maintain loyalty to their mother land and psychologically threatened about the possible consequences if they did not. Separate facilities were built in Fairbanks and Nome for Russian officers and other staff. The Russian government also preferred to use its own interpreters, predominantly women in uniform who had passed classified clearance procedures in the Soviet Union before coming to the United States.

Although the Russian airmen who were sent to Alaska to pick up the Lend-Lease aircraft were guests in Alaska and the Alaska mission was regarded as a rest from combat, they tended to remain aloof from the Americans. Sometimes Soviets socialized with Americans and expressed their ideological views, but reluctantly and with great caution. For the most part, the Soviets and Americans were cordial toward one another and some of them became good acquaintances afterwards, leaving a lasting mark of a good memory and compassion for each other. However, Soviet insistence that the planes be in perfect condition before being flown to Siberia caused constant delays and some antagonism between the two commands.

There were many crashes by both the Russian and American pilots, caused mainly by weather conditions but also by poor maintenance and overloading, lack of fuel, and incidentally, a large consumption of hard liquor by Russian pilots the day before a long and dangerous journey. Bill Schoeppe remembers that the winter of 1942–1943 was extremely cold in Alaska and planes had to be winterized before they could be flown out in very difficult conditions. From September 1942 to September 1945, 133 planes were lost to weather conditions or pilot error—only 1.6 percent of the 7,983 planes that were delivered to the Russians.

LEND-LEASE DETAILS

The Lend-Lease Act, passed by the U.S. Congress on March 11, 1941, was extended to cover the U.S.S.R. as early as on the third day after Germany's invasion of the Soviet Union.

What were the intervening events as that law, still a bone of contention among historians and politicians, came into in effect? Had the law been drafted primarily to pursue schemes championed by "outside observers" or to extend hands-on assistance to any countries invaded by the Axis aggressors? It was expected that the act would trigger debates among U.S. policy makers amid massive rallies supporting and protesting its newsworthiness. This went on for some time.

The Lend-Lease bill had been initiated by Roosevelt, who foresaw the inevitable risk of Germany and Japan attacking the United States. He sought, in fact, to improve the nation's defenses long before Pearl Harbor. For instance, in his December 1940 public address, Roosevelt indicated that Germany's Nazi rulers had most explicitly revealed their intentions to subjugate Europe and take advantage of the newly secured resources to achieve dominance over the rest of the globe.

Overall, the United States negotiated forty-two Lend-Lease agreements that varied greatly in scale from nation to nation. All reports and statements of the period emphasized the tremendous importance of Lend-Lease for the defense of the United States. Nevertheless, the Americans carefully kept track of the deliveries completed and their value in dollars. While the Act was in force, the overall Lend-Lease deliveries amounted to a total of $49,096 million or 14.9 percent of U.S. expenditures on the war. The U.S.S.R. had received armaments and goods valued at $11,141,470 or 25 percent of the entire Lend-Lease assistance, according to the Soviet Acquisition Commission.

Without going into the details of the intricacies and controversies of Lend-Lease deliveries, we shall merely touch upon the history of the American-built aircraft being ferried to Russia's fronts in the war against Nazi Germany. The aircraft and ground support equipment, transferred to the Red Army was valued at $1,556,000. That was 8 percent of the overall assets received by the U.S.S.R. under the Lend-Lease agreement.

The commitment to ship 400 aircraft to the U.S.S.R. each month, beginning in October 1941, that the allies formally made at the 1941 Moscow meeting is known to have been marred by quite a few difficulties. The difficulty was that the existing political problems were compounded by major technical challenges relating to the ferry of tactical aircraft over long distances to their destinations on the battlefield. In the course of 1941, the routes used to deliver American airplanes to the Soviet Union were obviously not very efficient. A sea route was charted from ports on the U.S. western seaboard via the Pacific and Indian Oceans, Arabian Sea, and Persian Gulf over to the sea port of Basra. On average, a convoy would be over two months in transit and that would inevitably be followed by aircraft assembly, test flights and delivery to the Soviet central Asia over the vast desert sands which were known to be death for aircraft engine.

The second sea route was just as long and even more hazardous. It ran from the U.S. eastern seaboard to Murmansk or Arkhangelsk in the Soviet Union. Ships taking this route crossed the upper-North Atlantic waters, passed via Icelandic sea ports and proceeded to the Barents Sea via the Northern and Norwegian Seas. The German Navy and Air Force based in occupied Norway actively and effectively countered the Allied convoys causing them to sustain heavy losses. Many of the deliveries never reached their destinations. The case of the British Lend-Lease convoy of thirty-five vessels is well known: Twenty-three of them were sunk by the Germans. As many as 210 aircraft were sent to the bottom of the sea, to say nothing of hundreds of tons of other types of military hardware.

Given that massive shipments of aircraft to the Soviet Union could not be made over the Iran and North Atlantic routes, new solutions needed to be found. So, on October 9, 1941, the State Committee for Defense passed a resolution on charting and establishing an Alaska-Eastern Siberia air route that could be used to ferry American-built aircraft to the frontline.

The team of aviators from the Civil Air Fleet, assigned to tackle the problem, did some research and came up with three USA-U.S.S.R. air route options. Eventually, the air route that went across Alaska and through the central part of north-eastern Siberia was approved, the segment from the Eskimo township of Uelkal to Krasnoyarsk being the most unfriendly leg in terms of weather conditions.

Meantime, the surveyors and developers discovered that this route not only solved the problem of aircraft delivery but also tremendously boosted the effort to tap the resources of Russia's north-eastern regions. The airfields, airport terminals, and air routes, developed in the years of WWII, came to be the U.S.S.R.'s best equipped facilities to support air transportation services in the first postwar decade.

Unprecedented conditions were created then to help ferry large numbers of combat aircraft over super long distances (up to 14,000 kilometers) across sparsely-populated areas with prohibitive ambient temperatures and permafrost. The Krasnoyarsk air route was fully ready for combat aircraft to be ferried to the frontline by October 1, 1942. The related facilities had been staffed with service, support, and managerial personnel, supplied with fuel, oils, and lubricants, and outfitted with communications and ground support equipment.

Since the ferry legs could not exceed 2,500 kilometers then, as many as twenty-three airfields and runways had additionally been constructed to help assure flight safety. The air route's readiness was checked by a dedicated team of experts from the Red Army's Air Force Inspectorate who proceeded to fly from Moscow to Fairbanks and back. Permission was granted for an American team of seven experts to get familiarized with the air route as well. The Air Force Inspectorate's team confirmed the operational readiness of the Krasnoyarsk route for ferry operations (the conclusion was confirmed by the American counterparts) and pointed out the high morale of the personnel in the assigned ferry regiments.

In assessing the cost of the Krasnoyarsk-Uelkal route, it should be noted that in the first place the effectiveness of the funds used by the state to provide for the ferry of tactical aircraft to the war fronts. The actual cost is reported to have been R536,329,000. That includes the cost of consumables, ground support equipment, and vehicles lost in transit. The per-vehicle ferry cost gradually went down: 1942 R1,920,000; 1943 R152,000; 1944 R60,000

Throughout the route's lifetime, the per-aircraft ferry cost averaged R110,000 In 1942, each ferried airplane was supported by approximately twenty servicemen, in 1943 1.4, and in 1944 1.08 personnel.

With only a few exceptions, the newly commissioned airfields, airport terminals, and runways built in areas with permafrost were kept functional throughout the year. Interestingly, many of those airport terminals are still operating to this day.

As new airfields came under construction in the faraway Siberia, the raising of the first Ferry Air Division commanded by the hero of the Soviet Union Ilya Mazuruk, a distinguished polar aviator, was in full swing in the city of Ivanovo (near Moscow). The division included one transport and five ferry regiments. By October 2, 1942, the division personnel had fully taken their stations at the specified locations and proceeded to ferry batches of tactical aircraft over the Fairbanks-Krasnoyarsk air route.

Given the weather extremes in Alaska, the American flyers had likewise grappled with tremendous challenges to assure delivery of Lend-Lease aircraft to Fairbanks where the vehicles were handed over to Soviet aviators. The Americans had constructed over twenty airfields and a trans-Alaskan highway to deliver supplies that ferry operations depended on. Incidentally, that highway has been kept in perfect repair to this day.

The first batch of twelve A-20 (Boston) aircraft led by Pavel Nedoskin left Fairbanks on October 7, 1942 and only arrived at Krasnoyarsk November 11, 1942—the trailblazing mission took over a month. The air route was quickly dubbed AlSib (Alaska-Siberia) in business correspondence. The newly commissioned American pilots would bring their A-20, P-39, and C-47 aircraft to Fairbanks and hand them over to their Russian counterparts who normally would be much older, more experienced, and steeled by their combat missions flown against the Germans. The Russian flyers would take their American-built aircraft to their limits. At times the P-39s were made to carry out such risky turns that the airframe would creak from the extreme loading conditions.

The aircraft were supposed to be flown to Nome in Alaska and then across the Bering Strait to Russia. At first, the fueling points in Alaska were merely dirt strips with a few tents to accommodate the technicians. Given the total lack of aircraft hangars, the mechanics could be seen fixing the aircraft right out in the open no matter if it was raining or snowing. One of the biggest problems was imperfect radio communications. As they flew from Great Falls to Fairbanks, a distance of 3,000 kilometers, the flyers had to depend on somebody who knew the route. The charts they used only showed the bigger streams and water basins. But lakes would often be mapped about a hundred kilometers away from their actual locations, and a hill indicated as 1,200 meters high could really be 1,500 meters Alaska's weather is known to be changeable to the extreme. Within a span of some twenty minutes you could see Nome air base rapidly lose its perfect visibility and wholly disappear from view. Whenever there was a cloud cover, the nebula would often come to be a few kilometers thick and there was a danger of icing throughout the year. Besides, it is generally warmer up high than closer to the ground for almost the complete duration of the Alaskan winter, with the ambient temperature patterns being most unpredictable. It could often be observed that $-59°$ C at ground level would rocket to $0°$ C at an altitude of 600 meters.

Ferry operations were maintained uninterrupted until the freezing cold set in. The 1942–1943 Alaskan winter happened to be the coldest in twenty-five years. During that winter, eleven American support personnel perished in the course of a single day. Some of them were aboard a transport plane that lost its bearings in the vast cloud cover hugging Canada. Local flyers conjectured that the airplane had hit some mountain peak causing the crew to get buried in a snow avalanche. The other victims were onboard a military plane that apparently tried to fly through a storm at night to reach Lake Watson. The crash killed both of the pilots and the two survivors were compelled to spend a fortnight near the bodies of their friends.

Eventually, they affixed skis to their injured legs, put their hands in galoshes, and crawled on all fours to safety. They were located four days later, still alive and struggling to survive in freezing temperatures of $59°$ C. They had only managed to cover six kilometers. The same day, a transport aircraft, heading for Fairbanks reached an altitude of 4,300 meters in an effort to circumnavigate bad weather and proceeded to fly across the entire Yukon territory at –71° C, with the heat exchanger malfunctioning all the way. One of the passengers warmed his feet with a blowtorch throughout the flight. These are just a few graphic instances of how tremendously difficult and dangerous the initial stage of the effort was, casualties, unfortunately, being unavoidable. Red Army flyers, engineers and technicians had to operate under the same, if not harsher, environments in those war years.

Under the cloak of total secrecy that had been maintained through 1944, the seventh ferry team and the Alaskan-based transport air detachment finally brought the mission to a close. By mid-1944, a total of more than 5,000 aircraft had been ferried to the Soviet Union via Canada and Alaska. They would set off by the hundreds and proceed to the specified bases following radio beacons and refueling their tanks at larger airfields with concrete runways and heated hangars. But in the first winter the operating conditions were truly terrible. One could even spot fur animals that had perished from the extreme cold. Many would suffer from overchilled lungs.

Not infrequently, all one had to do was take a breathe to have one's dental fillings sucked out. While Alaskans stayed close to their stoves and refused to leave home, teams of aircraft technicians had to do their jobs in the open. They would normally leave their highly-heated tents to do a twenty-minute shift outside. If you removed your mitten, your fingers would immediately be frozen stiff. But in mittens, a technician's movements were severely constrained and a regular plug replacement would often take as long as two hours. A freshly cut tree had to be warmed up with a blow torch to drive a nail into it. The gasoline spilled on your hands froze them just like liquid air under those extreme temperatures. People's toes would get frostbitten. And one captain unfortunately even had to have his lower lip cut away because of severe frostbite. Now and again, someone would get caught in a snow twister just a few steps off the runway, and could only be saved by rescue teams operating bulldozers to clear away the snowdrifts. The lubricating oil used to turn into a stony mass on the coldest days. High-grade fuels would refuse to ignite. The liquid coolant, developed for Allison aircraft engines, would often turn into a jelly.

Thanks to the selfless work of the flight crews and ground-support personnel operating the Krasnoyarsk air route, a total of 8,094 American-built aircraft were ferried to Krasnoyarsk and over 250 air regiments formed as a result of the effort. Incidentally, the Krasnoyarsk air route veterans are also known to have been directly involved in battles in the war against Japan and in mounting air landing operations in the rear of the Japanese Kwangtung army. Thirty of the pilots received government decorations for their heroism in battle. So, the aeronautical ferry venture was an unprecedented event in the history of aviation: large numbers of aircraft flew tremendous distances (more than 14,000 kilometers) over unpopulated areas and under extreme weather conditions (freezing temperatures at times dropping down to $-73°$ C). Only seventy-three aircraft (less than one percent of the total number dispatched) were reported lost on route in the course of the ferry operations.

Overall, the following number of tactical aircraft were delivered to the Soviet Union from different directions: 8,094 planes via the Krasnoyarsk air route, 3,868 through Iran, 1,232 by ship via Murmansk or Arkhangelsk, and 993 planes were flown across the Atlantic Ocean.

Soviet and American history books give slightly different figures for the number of Lend-Lease airplanes brought to Russian WWII fronts from the United States and Great Britain. It seems that the number which was reported by the concluding statement of the Soviet Acquisition Commission—14,828—appears to be correct. Since the American-released number of 14,833 vehicles only exceeds the Soviet figure by five units, the truth seems reflected by those statistics.

In October 1945, the first Red Banner Ferry Air Division stopped ferrying tactical and transport aircraft from the United States over to the Soviet bases, and in December 1945 it was deactivated. While the operations were underway, a large number of aviators were awarded government orders and medals.

The annual number of aircraft ferried over the newly established air route was as follows: 114 aircraft in 1942, 2,465 in 1943, 3,033 in 1944 and 2,482 in 1945 (9 months).

Later on, the Soviet Union's northeast received five air routes fully outfitted with ground support facilities:

- Krasnoyarsk-Uelkal air route stretching for 5,200 kilometers and including twenty-one airfields spaced 240–530 kilometers apart;
- Yakutsk-Khabarovsk route stretching 1,560 kilometers and including three en route airfields spaced 215–540 kilometers apart;
- Magadan-Uchur-Kirensk air route stretching 2,550 kilometers and including three intermediate airfields;
- Anadyr-Tanyurer-Magadan-Khabarovsk route stretching 3,500 kilometers connecting at the Tanyurer airfield in the upper north with the Krasnoyarsk-Uelkal route and at the Ekimchan airfield down south with the Yakutsk-Khabarovsk air route;
- Yakutsk-Tiksi air route stretching 1,200 kilometers.

The total length of the five air routes was 14,010 kilometers serviced by a total of thirty airfields. Twenty-six of them were constructed in the years of WWII. One time President Harry Truman admitted that the United States had been able to shift its economy to a war footing thanks to the heroic involvement of other countries in fighting against the common enemy.

In making his address to Congress and touching on the question of benefits gained by the United States from the Lend-Lease agreements, Truman underscored that the supreme benefit was the aggressors' defeat. To achieve an early victory and save American lives had obviously been the main motivation for the complex of Lend-Lease deals. Deliveries of American-made planes and equipment to the Soviet Union were carried out in keeping with the policy of providing mutual assistance in fighting the war against the aggressor. That strategy paid off handsomely and greatly contributed to achieving a victory over Hitler's Germany—our common enemy in WWII.

TRUSTING AND VERIFYING

In four years of war, the United States supplied nearly 15,000 aircraft to the Soviet Union. More than half were flown over the northwest route through Alaska. Looking back, some American military experts questioned whether the Russians needed all these aircraft. By 1943, the U.S.S.R. was building a great number of planes in factories in the Ural Mountains and already had technical military superiority over the enemy. In 1943, Soviet industry produced 35,000 airplanes and 24,000 tanks and self-propelled guns, compared to 25,000 airplanes and 18,000 tanks produced by Germany.

In sum, despite their smaller industrial capacity and a reduced base of strategic raw materials, the Soviet Union still produced more military equipment than Germany with a claimed total output during war of 137,000 aircraft, 104,000 tanks and self-propelled guns, and 488,000 artillery pieces.

According to some military analysts as well as some American participants in the program, the Soviet Union was stockpiling Lend-Lease equipment for postwar use. It may also have used the air route for espionage. For instance, American soldiers of the Korean War (1950–1953) were puzzled to see so much American equipment captured by American troops during that conflict. Evidently the Chinese and Soviets provided military aid to Korea using the very same supplies they had themselves received from the United States several years earlier. American analysts were not prepared to explain the extent and intention of Soviet secrecy during World War II—ranging from combat operations to agricultural production. Information would often have to come directly from Stalin. This led some officials to conclude that Stalin apparently was the only individual in the Soviet Union who had the authority to give out sensitive information.

Some American experts also argue that a quantity of uranium was shipped through Great Falls to the Soviet Union, that in May 1944, U.S. Treasury banknote plates had gone up the air route. Some deny any such Russian conspiracy.

Much else speaks of the helpful U.S. attitude toward the U.S.S.R. and vice versa during the war.

VITAL FOOD AID

Rations would often include *shchi*, a type of cabbage soup, and kasha, or boiled buckwheat. These are standard Russian peasant staples, prompting an old Russian saying, "*Shchi ee kasha, pisha nasha*"—that is, "shchi and kasha, that's our chow." Typical Lend-Lease additions would be tea or coffee, salt, bread, macaroni, salted fish, or canned meat.

It has been estimated that there was enough food sent to Russia via Lend-Lease to feed a 12,000,000-man army half pound of food per day for the duration of the war. Lend-Lease food didn't become be common until 1943. Yet many Lend-Lease staples were widespread for the rest of the war. Spam was invariably referred to as a "second fron." Powdered eggs was called "Roosevelt's eggs" (a half-joke since *yaitsa* is the Russian word both for "eggs" and "testicles"). Typical Lend-Lease foods were flour, dried peas and beans, sugar, canned meats, particularly Spam or a facsimile of *tushonka* (a kind of stewed pork product in gelatin), butter, vegetable shortening, oil and margarine, canned or dried milk, dried eggs, grits, and coffee. Although coffee was consumed when available, tea was the norm, the traditional drink, and samovars could often be seen glistening in the field. Bread and sausage were a common ration issued for troops during operations. They could be expected to last a few days without spoiling. Some of the troops, narrowing the "Stalingrad pocket" unintentionally killed some of their own liberated POWs by feeding the emaciated men bread and sausage from their own rations—the liberated men's aggravated digestive tracts couldn't handle it.

A little-known fact about Lend-Lease aid to Russia is that the military components of this aid constituted 20 percent of the assistance. Making up the rest were foodstuffs, nonferrous metals (particularly aluminum for aircraft production and for tank engines), chemical substances, petroleum products (particularly high-octane aviation fuel), and production-line equipment (factory machinery). The latter was crucial, Russian historians acknowledge, for maintaining adequate levels of Soviet defense production during the entire war.

From 1941 to 1945, about $12.5 billion in war materials and other supplies was shipped to the Soviet Union over the four major routes. In addition to military equipment, the U.S.S.R. received such nonmilitary items as cigarette cases, records, women's compacts, fishing tackle, dolls, playground equipment, cosmetics, foods, and even 13,328 sets of false teeth. Soviet requests for food focused on canned meat (*tushonka*), fats, dried peas and beans, potato chips, powdered soups and eggs, dehydrated fruits and vegetables, sugar, and other packaged food items.

Although dehydration had solved shipping problems to Russia, such requests resulted in the rapid expansion of American dehydration technology, which in turn like other wartime innovations eventually impacted on the U.S. domestic market itself and diet of the Americans after the war. Other by-products of the war included penicillin and sulfa drugs, radar, rocket and aircraft development, precision-bombing technology, long-range aerial navigation (Loran), psychoanalysis, the Internet, and many other innovations. To quote the proverb, "Necessity is the mother of invention."

Lend-Lease data show that in the last year alone of the war (1945), about 5.1 million tons of foodstuffs left for the Soviet Union from the United States. This compares, as Alexander Dolitsky points out, to the Soviets' own 1945 total agriculture output of approximately 53.5 million tons. If the twelve million-member Soviet Army received all of the foodstuffs that arrived in Russia through Lend-Lease from the United States, each man and woman would have been supplied with more than a half pound of concentrated food per day for the duration of the war.

Undoubtedly, therefore, Dolitsky concludes, Lend-Lease food proved vital to the maintenance of adequate nutrition levels for Soviets and other Lend-Lease beneficiaries. For example, as the author notes, 2 percent of the United States food supply in 1944 was exported to the Soviet Union; 4 percent went to the several other Lend-Lease recipients; 1 percent was in commercial export; and 13 percent went to the United States military.

"This aid was only possible," continues Dolitsky, "thanks to the sacrifices made by the American people and the enormous increase in American agricultural and industrial production—up by 280 percent by 1944 over the 1935–1939 average."

Although the Soviet government tried to minimize the importance of the Lend-Lease support by arguing that the United States supplies to Russia represented only 4 to 10 percent of the total Soviet production during the war, these aid items were essential for the survival of the Soviet Union. Many helped Soviet industrial processes themselves.[9] For example, while Soviet production of steel was about nine million tons in 1942, under Lend-Lease the Soviet Union received about three million tons of steel. The Soviet T-34 tank engine and Soviet aircraft made use of Lend-Lease aluminum. Copper shipments (about four million tons) equaled three-quarters of the entire Soviet copper production for the years 1941–1944. About 800,000 tons of nonferrous metals (e.g., magnesium, nickel, zinc, lead, tin), a million miles of field telegraph wire, 2,120 miles of marine cable, and 1,140 miles of submarine cable formed an impressive figure, especially when compared to Soviet production.

In addition to nonmilitary items, the Soviet Union also received under the Lend-Lease agreement 15,000 airplanes—equivalent to 12 percent of those produced in Soviet plants; 9,000 tanks and self-propelled guns, or 10 percent of Soviet production; 362,000 Lend-Lease trucks and 47,000 jeeps, compared to 130,000 trucks manufactured in the Soviet Union. All this equipment greatly contributed to the mobility and survival of the Red Army. Unfortunately, many of these materials deteriorated because they were poorly maintained or wastefully stockpiled due to Soviet carelessness and the inefficient state infrastructure. However, most of the materials were widely used and often admired by Red Army soldiers. In fact, the legendary Soviet air ace and three-time hero of the Soviet Union, Alexander Pokryshkin, used a Lend-Lease Airacobra to shoot down forty-eight of the fifty-nine Nazi planes credited to him.

Many nonmilitary and military items were funneled through Great Falls, Montana. The United States received payment from Russia for only a small fraction of these particular items. However, Bill Schoeppe, a resident of Juneau and then an airplane mechanic at Ladd Field, Fairbanks, as told by him to author Dolitsky, remembers two airplanes loaded with ten thousand pounds of gold—valued at about $5.6 million in 1943. They had traveled from Siberia to the continental U.S. in 1943. Yet up to now no written record has been found recording that transaction or, for that matter, of other transactions of a similar nature. The records of the Foreign Economic Administration's (FEA) Division of Soviet Supply (DSS) have long since disappeared. Nor does the National Archives have them or the U.S. Department of State, as noted by Dolitsky. In the early 1970s many of the FEA records were inadvertently shredded, and DSS records may have been among those that were destroyed.

SPASIBO ... BUT ...

Undoubtedly, the Alaska-Siberia Lend-Lease agreement was a major event in modern history. Many Alaskans worked together with Russians on the cooperative program. Although the two nations still faced possible invasion by the Japanese, the northwest route was a vehicle for hope. Just a few months after the tide of war turned in favor of the Allies, however, expectations of continued postwar cooperation shifted to mutual suspicion and antagonism.

The "Strange Alliance" Is Born

President Roosevelt was most instrumental in holding the Allies together against their enemies during the war and was responsible for implementation of the Lend-Lease program to the Soviet Union. As Alexander Dolitsky points out,

> Roosevelt gambled four times on strategic planning: He predicted Britain's survival and he won. He believed that Russia would withstand German attack and he won again. He was confident that Germany and Japan would eventually be defeated and he was right a third time. And he further speculated that by not attaching a dollar sign or political strings to Russian aid, he could secure their friendship and cooperation after the war. But this time he lost. He lost because he naively believed that sincerity and good intentions would change Communist objectives against capitalist countries. Roosevelt held the illusion that Lend-Lease was a channel of communication with the Soviet people that would eventually bring about democracy in the Soviet Union and cause partnership with the West to flourish. In reality it was only a channel of communication with one "Soviet"—Joseph Stalin. In fact, few Soviets knew much about the magnitude of American aid to Russia and the sacrifices on the American side connected with the program.

Relying as he was, Dolitsky continues, on unwritten rules of political reciprocity, Roosevelt was often puzzled that the Soviet government refused to permit Western allies to send military observers and technicians to the eastern front. Also baffling to the president was the Soviets' vigorous insistence on the opening of a second front in Europe early in the war, this when the United States was already involved in military activities in the Pacific and north African theaters, as well as with Lend-Lease convoys to Europe.

Yet, these Allied activities diverted significant enemy forces from the eastern front. Sometimes Roosevelt was irritated that the Soviets could not understand the complexity of the Lend-Lease delivery to the Soviet Union and its logistics; further, the U.S. Congress and 49 percent of the American people were consistently reluctant to support Soviet aid. The American administration often quarreled with the Soviets about delivery schedules. The Soviets even refused to open the Alaska-Siberia Lend-Lease route until August of 1942. "That was when they realized that they might not have other alternatives," Alexander Dolitsky writes "In addition, Soviet authorities insisted upon more rigid specifications for the war equipment than did, for instance, the war offices of Britain. As a result of all these complications and miscommunication, American officials were unable to adequately observe the use made of Western equipment. They had to rely largely on rather vague and general reports made by soviet authorities that great quantities of American equipment, for example, were being used in the 1945 offensive."

But what was most astonishing to American representatives was Soviet reluctance to acknowledge, either in the press or in public, the support they received from the United States. At the end of the war, the Soviet government regarded Lend-Lease as an insignificant 4 percent of the total industrial production of Soviet enterprises. The production of Soviet industry, of course, has always been exaggerated to demonstrate the accomplishments and advantages of the Soviet socialist state. On June 19, 1962, Soviet First Secretary Nikita S. Khrushchev asserted that " . . . during World War II American monopolists made billions of dollars on war deliveries. They fattened themselves on the blood of people lost during two world wars." The aid program was pictured by Soviet historians at that time as an effort to expand American imperialism and to use Soviet resistance for their own mobilization. Since the demise of the U.S.S.R., Russian historians have begun to revise this boilerplated, propagandistic line and to acknowledge the great contribution Lend-Lease aid made to the Soviet victory in the east. Today's admissions in this vein virtually depicts Lend-Lease as the "lifesaver" of Russia. At very least, the assistance shortened the length of the war thus saving countless lives—civilian and military.

In Dolitsky's view, the Soviet efforts to minimize the role of Lend-Lease may have been motivated by considerations of national prestige and image. Only recently have Soviet scholars been admitting that Lend-Lease actually contributed to the war effort. During the war, to be sure, the Soviet government gave decorations to a number of Westerners. Near the end of the Soviet period the government honored the seamen—foreign and Soviet—who had served on the Murmansk run. Yet, they still emphasized the putatively small size of Lend-Lease in relation to Soviet production (a distortion) and the heroism of the Soviet people in delivering the Lend-Lease supplies.

NOTES

1. Niblo, 106, from Robert E. Sherwood, *Roosevelt and Hopkins: An Intimate History*.

2. L. N. Nezhinskii, "*Dokumenty vneshnei politiki, 22 Iyunya 1941–Yanvarya 1942, Mezhdunarodniye otnosheniya* (Documents of Foreign Policy, June 22, 1941–January 1942 International Relations), Moscow, 2000, vol. 24, *Novaya noveishaya istoriya*, 216–17.

3. William H. Standley and Arthur A. Ageton, *Admiral Ambassador to Russia*, New York, Henry Regnery Company, 1955, 67–8.

4. Jones, 77.

5. Aleksandr Vislykh, "*Spasitel'nii Lend-Liz Ne nado preumenshivat' ego zacheniye v nashei pobede v Velikoi Otechestvennoi Voine*" ("Lifesaver Lend-Lease It Is Not Nec-

essary to Minimize Its Importance in Our Victory in the Great Patriotic War,") *Nezavisimoye obozreniye* (Independent Military Observer), Nov. 12, 2001, 5.

6. A. G. Khorkov, "Na yugo-zapadnom napravlenii" ("In the Southwestern Sector"), *Voyenno-istoricheskii zhurnal*, No. 6, 2002, 12.

7. The next several sections are derived from Alexander B. Dolitsky, Alaska-Siberia Research Center, Juneau, Alaska, "The Alaska-Siberia Lend-Lease Program during World War II," an offprint pamphlet from Proceedings of the International Congress on the History of the Arctic and Sub-Arctic Region, Reykjavik, June 12–18, 1998. Dolitsky is a leading U.S. authority on Lend-Lease who has helped organize memorial anniveraries tied to Lend-Lease events.

8. Suprun, 122.

9. A. Paperno, *Lend-Liz Tikhii Okean* (Lend-Lease Pacific Ocean), Moscow, Terra-Knizhnii Klub, 1998, 348–49.

8

Summation: Will the Debt Be Repaid?

You're studying management, right? Are there any people here from the History Department? I think the people from the History Department will probably support me in saying—in my saying the following: the World War II period and the Cold War period were but two of the most contrasting and sharpest examples of the evolution of our relations. But we can talk about a lot of different episodes in our cooperation. But it really began in the times of the Revolutionary War in the United States. At that time, the Crown of England appealed to Catherine the Great and asked for support in quelling the rebellion in the United States, and the Russian sovereign turned and said, that's not what we're all about, and declared a military neutrality vis-à-vis the war. And this neutrality played a significant role in allowing the United States to gain its independence and lay its foundations. And today I'm going to present to President George Bush two very interesting documents, two original documents having to do with the earliest days of our diplomatic correspondence between our two countries . . . The United States is a great and powerful power, and has an economy that is powerful enough to a great extent to determine world economics."

—President Vladimir Putin at the University of
St. Petersburg, Russia, May 25, 2002

Total Lend-Lease aid during the war years has been estimated to have been $42–50 billion. One-third of this was the Soviet share. In contemporary dollar values, the Soviet share would amount, roughly, to over $130 billion. Will this money ever be repaid?

Should it be repaid?

The background is this. President Roosevelt had supplemented bank loans to the Soviets with taxpayer-financed assistance. He arranged secret military transfers with the Soviets, to help defeat Adolf Hitler. In addition, the Lend-Lease program transferred industrial and military supplies to the Soviets on easy credit terms from 1941 to 1946. In 1944, Stalin noted that two-thirds of Soviet heavy industry had been built with U.S. help. Almost all the remaining one-third was imported from other Western nations. Massive transfer of equipment and skilled personnel from the occupied territories to the Soviet Union supplied further technical expertise.

SILVER BULLION TO STALIN

An addendum to the U.S. largesse to the U.S.S.R. was a shipment of 2,000 tons of silver bullion on the "Ghost Ship" *Barry* in 1944. However, this turned out to be one of the few missions to help the Soviets that never made it.

In 1944, Hitler's war against the Soviet Union in the east was reaching a climax. Meanwhile, in the west, the Allies had made their risky landings on the northern coast of France and were bogged down in intense fighting against the Wehrmacht on the Italian boot. For Hitler the nightmare of a two-front war—in the east and the west—had materialized. Yet, for the Allies the European phase of the war was by no means over.

Together with the western Allies Roosevelt was grateful to Stalin for the Soviet Army's brilliant successes in the east, for the way the tide was turning sharply against the German army in the U.S.S.R., particularly after the Soviet victory at Stalingrad in 1942–1943. FDR wanted to do all he could to keep the Red Army juggernaut rolling westward. Beyond Lend-Lease shipments, some way, he thought, must be found to make a stunning personal gesture to the Communist dictator himself. This could prove additionally useful in upcoming Big Three conferences between the United States, Britain, and the Soviet Union in which America, Roosevelt hoped, would play a key role.

FDR often used such expressions as "our gallant Soviet ally." In correspondence with Winston Churchill and others, Roosevelt spoke of Stalin jovially as "Uncle Joe." He was eager to demonstrate to Moscow how he personally felt about Stalin and the courageous Soviet armies, how he was ready to bypass, even upstage America's British allies in making a strong, unilateral gesture to Stalin, the British having begun to show a certain reticence about Stalin and Soviet communism and imperialism. Too, relations between the president and the prime minister at the time were sometimes tense. On his part, despite the three-year-long flow of Lend-Lease largesse to the Soviets, Stalin kept up a drumbeat of demands made on the Allies, often directly via Roosevelt, for more help. He expressed only reluctant gratitude for the "intentionally delayed" opening, as Moscow's propaganda worded it, of a second front in Europe in mid-1944. This only made Roosevelt more eager to placate the Soviet leader. The president also wished to play his assumed role of friendly "mediator" and "peacemaker" at the Big Three summits seeking to position himself (even physically, as shown in photographs) between the sometimes hard-line stance assumed by Churchill toward Moscow as a counterpoise to that of the hard-driving Stalin.

So, just after the Big Three's Tehran Conference in Iran, December 1943, and near the time of the Yalta Conference in the Crimea, February 1944, the decision was secretly made by the White House in Washington to send the Soviet leader personally a large shipment of American silver ingots weighing over 2,000 tons and their worth over $26 million, or $200 million in today's prices. This gift would be enough to buy the Soviets plenty of weapons. Above all, it was thought to be a gift generous enough to content if not "woo" Stalin. But, said the White House, the mission had to be carried out in extreme secrecy; not even London must know about it. As intelligence orders read, it was to be executed "under conditions of great secrecy." After all, it was not an American tradition to cater to dictators. In delivering the gift by sea aboard the specially assigned Liberty Ship *John Barry*, the presumably safer southern route to Russia via the Persian Gulf was chosen instead the famous northern route to Murmansk used by Allied convoys.

But *Barry* never made it to Abadan, Iran, at the head of the Gulf some 800 miles south of the Soviet border in the Caucasus. At a position in the Arabian Sea 127 miles southeast of Oman and the Strait of Hormuz, the German submarine U859 spotted the vessel in bright moonlight, having been alerted by the *Barry's* suspicious zigzag course. The U-boat trailed her, then with a torpedo fired into the *Barry* on August 28, 1944, sank her. Most of *Barry's* crew were saved but her valuable cargo was dispatched 8,500 feet beneath the waves to a deeper grave than that of the *Titanic*.

Meanwhile, it began to leak out that the *Barry* had held a valuable secret. Two war historians, Drs. John Gorley Bunker and Arthur Moore, had disclosed as much in two books published after the war. In the late 1980s, Navy pilot and salvager Capt. Brian Shoemaker, joined by a California restauranteur, Jay Fiondella, joined later by an inquiring young Arab-speaking British journalist, John Beasant, stationed in Oman and later the author of the 1995 volume, *Stalin's Silver,* collaborated with an enterprising group of deep-sea divers based in Key West, Florida to see what they could do to find the shipwreck and its treasure. Shoemaker and the others—with help of the governments of Oman and Yemen, and of the Germans and the surviving captain himself of the German U-boat—assembled all the charts and documents they could concerning the ill-fated voyage.

After several years of research and attempts to raise money—and despite stonewalling by a reticent officialdom in Washington—they launched an all-out effort to locate the wreck of the *John Barry*.

By 1994 the government of Yemen had agreed to donate financial assistance to the Ocean Group Consortium, as it is called, especially since the ship's papers showed that aboard the *Barry* were also 3,000 Saudi Arabian riyal silver coins worth £300,000, or over $1 million, in 1944 prices.

Using state-of-the-art equipment and defying various mishaps and less than good search conditions at sea, the consortium of salvagers managed to exactly pinpoint and reach the sunken hulk of *Barry* in fall 1994. Utilizing a unique fifty-ton remote-operated "grab" vehicle and other up-to-date equipment, they were able to make "forced entry" into the wreck—a first ever for any deep-sea salavage operation. After peeling back deck planking, they brought up a large share of the gleaming silver riyals, $1.4 million in coins (later auctioned off in Geneva, Switzerland) contained in hold #2. The ship had split in half and working on the stern portion, the salvagers had searched, much to their dismay, in the "wrong hold," the one containing the coins not the bullion. Still, the riyal find itself confirmed what had been previously learned about the ghost ship's cargo that, indeed, it bore treasure.

Meanwhile, the bullion, which had eluded them, is believed to be contained in the reinforced, starboard-side hold #3. The latter was sighted in the 1994 salvage dives along with a large specially constructed vault that is now suspected to contain the bullion. The consortium and author Beasant now believe that the bullion is lying in about a yard deep of seabed sand in the stern half of the wreck. Having gained inestimable knowledge the first time down, the consortium plans a second expedition for the very near future.

* * *

Here are the known details of the *John Barry*'s secret voyage as related by Beasant in *Stalin's Silver* and which is based upon several key documents and testimony reproduced in the book and its Appendices.[1]

In the summer of 1944, the *John Barry* had been diverted from her usual convoy duty in the North Atlantic. She abruptly was ordered by officials of the War Shipping Administration (WSA) in Washington—which provided no explanation for the diversion even to the ship's master and which had received its orders from still higher government authorites, including the FBI—to steam to Trinidad in the Caribbean Sea. It arrived there mid-June, her crew puzzled by the mysterious orders rendered preemptorily from above. *Barry* was then ordered to a port in Maine where her present cargo was discharged as new secret orders were given the captain to proceed south. *Barry* was ordered to sail to New York City, then to Philadelphia, and finally to Norfolk, her last call prior to the *Barry's* voyage into the South Atlantic, through Gibraltar and the Mediterranean, Suez Canal, and on to the Indian Ocean and Arabian Sea.

At Pier 38 in New York, the FBI oversaw the start of the hush-hush operation by providing, among other things, doctored sailing papers for the *Barry*. The Liberty Ship was loaded under a thick veil of secrecy with $26 million (in 1944 currency) in ingots of silver bullion secretly assigned by the U.S. Treasury. In Philadelphia, $500,000 in silver Saudi riyal coins, minted there, were put aboard. The *Barry* then set course with its crew of some fifty (including a squad of FBI agents) for Norfolk, Virginia. Arriving there in pitch darkness, the ghost ship's doctored manifest, as later examined by researchers, showed that hundreds of tons of cargo were unaccounted for. This was odd since the ship was officially reported, as most Liberty Ships were at the time, to be "overloaded." The manifest merely stated cryptically that the ship's ultimate destination was "a port in the Persian Gulf."

The FDR's and WSA's ghost ship put out into the Atlantic on July 19, 1944. The *Barry* veered south to take up its preordained course. The German submarine U859 had been tracking it for days when its elusive zigzag course raised suspicion that it was covering its tracks and apparently hiding onboard something critical. (Subs themselves were sometimes used as clandestine "transports" of smaller cargoes.) So, the German U-boat took a bead on the *Barry* on the night of August 28, 1944. At 10 P.M. under the command of Capt. Jan Jebsen, at a range of about 900 yards it fired its first torpedo, which struck the starboard side. As the ship filled with water, *Barry's* Capt. Joseph Ellerwald, after sending out an SOS (luckily responded to by a nearby Dutch transport), gave orders to stop engines and abandon ship. Having waited thirty minutes for the forty-four-man crew and twenty-seven U.S. Marines to clamber into four lifeboats and four square life rafts, Jebsen then fired a second torpedo, which broke the ship's back, splitting it in two just forward of the bridge. It sank quickly, according to testimony given by the U859's still-surviving First Engineer, Oberleutnant Horst Klast.

But the German U-boat itself was headed for the Deep Six. Three months later Klast's sub was trailed and destroyed by the British Royal Navy attack submarine, HMS Trenchant. Only nineteen of the U859's sixty-nine-man crew were saved, Klast being the only officer to survive. The

British sub surfaced and plucked him from the sea just before a Japanese warship loomed on the horizon.

* * *

Author Beasant notes that the U.S. Department of State and other officials in Washington "still refuse to confirm or deny the existence of the bullion. Surely [Washington] knows whether or not it loaded millions' worth of state silver into the holds of one of its own Liberty Ships during the Second World War, and if so, for whom it was intended." Under the Freedom of Information Act, he continues, American archives are open to inspection. "But," he complains, "there is a lot of information pertaining to the *John Barry* which has been withdrawn. So many parts of the jigsaw have been destroyed."

I likewise experienced frustration in independently tracking down information on the *Barry*. Numerous U.S. Navy and civilian trade books on U.S. ships omit any mention of the Liberty Ship *John Barry* with its gift to Stalin that wound up on the bottom of the Arabian Sea in late 1944. I found in naval archives that over the century, of the three ships named the *John Barry* (after the famous commodore in the American War of Independence), none were described as having served on a mission remotely resembling that of the doomed ghost ship. The latest of three vessels, some of which were military, some not, bearing that name as listed in the U.S. Navy Department's *Dictionary of Naval Fighting Ships*, Vol. I, published in 1959, was said to be a transport that had been converted from a destroyer in 1943. It was described as carrying troops in August 1944 as part of the Allied invasion of the Continent.

Meanwhile, however, the "other *John Barry*" was carrying out an extraordinary assignment that to this day remains clouded in secrecy.

SETTLING THE DEBT ISSUE

The silver bullion never made it to Stalin's coffers. But the bulk of Lend-Lease aid did. How was it to be paid for?

During the years following World War II, the U.S. government evolved a policy, with twists and turns, by which the bulk of the Lend-Lease debt came to be forgiven. In the first postwar years, Washington asked only for a $2.5 billion settlement to cover for civilian supplies. Then in 1960, the Soviet Union offered to settle all debts for $300 million. However, these negotiations were never concluded. As evidence of this, consider that in 1960 the American government offered to release the Soviet Union from its Lend-Lease debt to the United States of $11 billion if the Soviets would pay $300 million of it. Although the Soviets reportedly had $9 billion in gold in their national treasury in 1960, they refused. Without American taxpayer assistance, the Soviets would have been bankrupt.

The U.S. resumed negotiations in the Gorbachev period after 1985. Eventually the debt figure was whittled down to $800 million. Yet the Russians, claiming economic distress, refused in the end to agree to that amount. Finally, Moscow stated that Russia was willing to repay $300 million at 2 percent interest to be paid over thirty years.

So, it appears the Lend-Lease debt issue has been left at that and for all intents and purposes solved in the above fashion. Given the reasonably good relations obtaining between the R. F. and the United States in the post-Soviet period ("good," at least, as of late 2003), the debt issue is off any future agenda in American-Russian summits and talks.

As to attempts to sum up the importance of those four-year-long shipments of Lend-Lease for the Russian victory on the eastern front in World War II, the jury is still out—that is, in any definitive sense of establishing *exactly* how crucial this aid was. In any event that is clearly an impossible task. Suffice to say that the foregoing chapters, and the tables appended to this text, describe the quantity and many types of this aid. Described above have been the several post-Soviet, upward reevaluations of the importance of this aid as calculated by new Russian research of an unofficial sort. Marshal Georgy Zhukov, Russia's top soldier during the war, was the official perhaps best qualified within the Soviet leadership to sum up the importance of this aid, which was made in his remarks to Soviet war correspondent Konstantin Simonov. Speaking virtually confidentially long after the death of Stalin (who would have forbidden such candor or praise for Lend-Lease) Zhukov minced no words about how crucial this aid was for the Soviet victory (for Zhukov's statement, see opening of chapter 1, introduction).

The aid's crucial importance might be capsularized this way. In one outstanding example, the U.S. deliveries of high octane aviation fuel no doubt sustained Soviet air warfare, particularly against German tanks. Such shipments might even be described as making the Soviet air effort possible in its entirety. When it is recalled how desperate the Soviets were for such fuel in order to keep their Sturmoviks and other fighter aircraft in the air, this statement is seen as no exaggeration.

At the peak of this type of aid, U.S. shipments of aviation fuel totaled one-and-a-half times the Soviets' domestic production. Abetting the Soviet air war, of course, was the fact that as the war progressed, the Luftwaffe's planes and resources became seriously over-stretched. This resulted from the Germans' having to deploy aircraft to other fronts in the west—for example, to North Africa and, of course, to the German homeland as the Allies intensified their air war against German targets. Whether or not these diverted aircraft could have turned the tide at Stalingrad or Kursk in mid-1943 cannot be determined.

However, the fact that the Soviet Air Force could operate as efficiently as it did—thanks to the tons of shipped, U.S.-manufactured aviation gasoline—was unquestionably due to this vital Lend-Lease aid.

Another cardinal example are the Lend-Lease shipments of steel and aluminum. The western Allies (but mainly the U.S.) had supplied the Soviets with nearly 350,000 tons of aluminum. That represented double the amount of that key metal that was available to the German enemy. It composed the bulk of the aluminum that was used in the manufacture of Soviet aircraft at a time when aluminum production in the U.S.S.R. had fallen critically short of demand. Soviet statistics themselves show that without these shipments, Soviet aircraft production would have been less than one-half of what it was.[2] All told these and other combat-related vehicles (including 11,000 railroad freight cars) totaled a staggering 400,000 units.

Too, without Lend-Lease, the Soviet Union's diminished postinvasion economic base would not have been able to focus on producing weaponry rather than consumer goods, food, and machine tools.

THE "GRATITUDE FACTOR"

Soviet historians and reference books minimized the importance of Lend-Lease in the Soviet victories in the east. This plus Cold War tensions hardly contributed to a "healthy" attitude toward this assistance. On the American side, voices could be, and still can be heard that are adamant in demanding that the Russians make good on the debt.

Yet as time passes, the debt issue becomes more and more irrelevant. As U.S.-Russian friendship remains fairly strong, or at least does not appear likely in the foreseeable future to degenerate into Cold War–like frigidity, it is possible that at some future summit, the U.S. side will magnaminously forgive the debt altogether. A possible date for such a gesture, in fact, might be May 2005—the sixtieth anniversary of the end of the European phase of World War II (VE-Day), the month of the final Soviet victory over Nazi Germany on the eastern front. Most everyone now agrees that without that Soviet victory against Hitler in the east, the West's victory over the Axis would have been seriously delayed, or worse.

That said, and given the enormous sacrifices in lives and property suffered on the Russian side, it might seem reasonable one fine day to outright forgive the Soviet debt, and to suspend future payments on it on the schedules agreed to in previous years.

For this to happen, much will depend, of course, on the nature of U.S.-Russian relations in the years ahead.

NOTES

1. John Beasant, *Stalin's Silver*, London, Bloomsbury, 1995.
2. Burleigh, 737; B. V. Sokolov, throughout the present book.

Appendix

Mutual Aid Agreement between the United States and the Union of Soviet Socialist Republics: June 11, 1942[1]

Whereas the Governments of the United States of America and the Union of Soviet Socialist Republics declare that they are engaged in a cooperative undertaking, together with every other nation or people of like mind, to the end of laying the bases of a just and enduring world peace securing order under law to themselves and all nations;

And whereas the Governments of the United States of America and the Union of Soviet Socialist Republics, as signatories of the **Declaration by United Nations of Jan. 1, 1942**, have subscribed to a common program of purposes and principles embodied in the joint declaration, known as the **Atlantic Charter, made on Aug. 14, 1941**, by the President of the United States of America and the Prime Minister of the United Kingdom of Great Britain and Northern Ireland, the basic principles of which were adhered to by the Government of the Union of Soviet Socialist Republics on Sept. 24, 1941;

And whereas the President of the United States of America has determined, pursuant to the act of Congress of March 11, 1941, that the defense of the Union of Soviet Socialist Republics against aggression is vital to the defense of the United States of America;

And whereas the President of the United States of America has extended and is continuing to extend to the Union of Soviet Socialist Republics aid in resisting aggression;

AWAIT PROGRESS OF EVENTS

And whereas it is expedient that the final determination of the terms and conditions upon which the Government of the Union of Soviet Socialist

Republics receives such aid and of the benefits to be received by the United States of America in return therefore should be deferred until the extent of the defense aid is known and until the progress of events makes clearer the final terms and conditions and benefits which will be in the mutual interests of the United States of America and the Union of Soviet Socialist Republics and will promote the establishment and maintenance of world peace;

And whereas the Governments of the United States of America and the Union of Soviet Socialist Republics are mutually desirous of concluding now a preliminary agreement in regard to the provision of defense aid and in regard to certain considerations which shall be taken into account in determining such terms and conditions and the making of such an agreement has been in all respects duly authorized, and all acts, conditions and formalities which it may have been necessary to perform, fulfill or execute prior to the making of such an agreement in conformity with the laws either of the United States of America or of the Union of Soviet Socialist Republics have been performed, fulfilled, or executed as required;

The undersigned, being duly authorized by their respective governments for that purpose, have agreed as follows:

ARTICLE I

The Government of the United States of America will continue to supply the Government of the Union of Soviet Socialist Republics with such defense articles, defense services, and defense information as the President of the United States of America shall authorize to be transferred or provided.

ARTICLE II

The Government of the Union of Soviet Socialist Republics will continue to contribute to the defense of the United States of America and the strengthening thereof, and will provide such articles, services, facilities, or information as it may be in a position to supply.

ARTICLE III

The Government of the Union of Soviet Socialist Republics will not without the consent of the President of the United States of America transfer title to, or possession of, any defense article or defense information, transferred to it under the Act of March 11, 1941, of the Congress of the United States of America, or permit the use thereof by any one not an officer, employee, or agent of the Government of the Union of Soviet Socialist Republics.

ARTICLE IV

If, as a result of the transfer to the Government of the Union of Soviet Socialist Republics of any defense article or defense information it becomes necessary for that government to take any action or make any payment in order fully to protect any of the rights of a citizen of the United States of America who has patent rights in and to any such defense article or information, the Government of the Union of Soviet Socialist Republics will take such action or make such payment when requested to do so by the President of the United States of America.

ARTICLE V

The Government of the Union of Soviet Socialist Republics will return to the United States of America at the end of the present emergency, as determined by the President of the United States of America, such defense articles transferred under this agreement as shall not have been destroyed, lost, or consumed and as shall be determined by the President to be useful in the defense of the United States of America or of the Western Hemisphere or to be otherwise of use to the United States of America.

ARTICLE VI

In the final determination of the benefits to be provided to the United States of America by the Government of the Union of Soviet Socialist Republics full cognizance shall be taken of all property, services, information, facilities, or other benefits of considerations provided by the Government of the Union of Soviet Socialist Republics subsequent to March 11, 1941, and accepted or acknowledged by the President on behalf of the United States of America.

ARTICLE VII

In the final determination of the benefits to be provided to the United States of America by the Government of the Union of Soviet Socialist Republics in return for aid furnished under the Act of Congress of March 11, 1941, the terms and conditions thereof shall be such as not to burden commerce between the two countries, but to promote mutually advantageous economic relations between them and the betterment of world-wide economic relations. To that end, they shall include provision for agreed action by the United States of America and the Union of Soviet Socialist Republics, open to participation by all other countries of like mind, directed to the expansion, by appropriate international and domestic measures, of production, employment, and the exchange and consumption of goods, which are the material foundations of the liberty and welfare of all peoples; to the elimination of all forms of discriminatory treatment in international commerce, and to the reduction of tariffs and other trade barriers; and, in general, to the attainment of all the economic objectives set forth in the **joint declaration made on Aug. 14, 1941,** by the President of the United States of America and the Prime Minister of the United Kingdom, the basic principles of which were adhered to by the Government of the Union of Soviet Socialist Republics on Sept. 24, 1941.

At an early convenient date conversations shall be begun between the two governments with a view to determining, in the light of governing economic conditions, the best means of attaining the above-stated objectives by their own agreed action and of seeking the agreed action of other like-minded governments.

ARTICLE VIII

This agreement shall take effect as from this day's date. It shall continue in force until a date to be agreed upon by the two governments.

Signed and sealed at Washington in duplicate this eleventh day of June, 1942.

For the Government of the United States of America,

CORDELL HULL, Secretary of State of the United States of America.

For the Government of the Union of Soviet Socialist Republics,

MAXIM LITVINOV, Ambassador of the Union of Soviet Socialist Republics at Washington.

NOTE

1. Reprinted from the Avalon Project at Yale Law School.

Tables

Table I. Lend-Lease Shipments to the Soviet Union by Time Period, Cargo Type, Route, and Tonnage*

1. June 22, 1941–Sept. 30, 1941. Not shipped under Lend-Lease, but under $10,000,000 Treasury Department advance, the $50,000,000 Defense Supplies Corporation advance, and other arrangements.

Type of Cargo	Atlantic	Pacific	Total	Distribution of total tonnage, percentage
U.S. supplies				
R.R. transportation equip.	0	0	0	0
Trucks and other vehicles	1,561	14	1,575	1
Metals	1,251	3,404	4,655	3
Chemicals and explosives	1,033	3,693	4,726	3
Petroleum products	9,500	120,854	130,354	79
Machinery and equip.	280	15,575	15,855	10
Food	19	3,899	3,918	2
Other U.S. supplies	1,258	1,365	2,623	1
Canadian and British supplies	0	0	0	0
Other Sources	0	2,494	2,494	1
Total	14,902	151,298	166,200	100

2. Oct. 1, 1941–June 30, 1942, First Protocol period.

U.S. supplies				
R.R. transportation equip.	0	0	0	0
Trucks and other vehicles	214,148	16	214,164	15
Metals	411,619	12,906	424,525	30

(continued)

Table I. *(continued)*

Type of Cargo	Atlantic	Pacific	Total	Distribution of total tonnage, percentage
Chemicals and explosives	55,542	465	56,007	4
Petroleum products	132,459	35,536	167,995	12
Machinery and equip.	29,116	576	29,692	2
Food	129,999	175,038	305,037	22
Other U.S. supplies	74,281	1,943	76,224	5
Canadian and British supplies	137,841	8,770	146,611	10
Other sources	0	0	0	0
Total	1,185,005	235,250	1,420,255	100

3. July 1, 1942–June 30, 1943, Second Protocol period.

	Atlantic	Pacific	Total	%
U.S. Supplies				
R.R. transportation equip.	0	0	0	0
Trucks and other vehicles	308,919	139,569	448,488	15
Metals	460,874	289,016	749,890	24
Chemicals and explosives	70,697	110,669	181,366	6
Petroleum products	54,331	159,157	213,448	7
Machinery and equip.	28,604	139,864	168,468	5
Food	294,236	703,547	997,783	33
Other U.S. supplies	167,657	70,119	237,776	8
Canadian and British supplies	45,898	11,142	57,040	2
Other sources	0	0	0	0
Total	1,431,216	1,623,083	3,054,259	100

*Report on War Aid, 1–8; all tonnages are in long tons.

4. July 1, 1943–June 30, 1944, Third Protocol period.

	Atlantic	Pacific	Total	%
U.S. supplies				
R.R. transportation equip.	39,455	31,011	70,466	1
Trucks and other vehicles	641,618	100,719	742,337	13
Metals	699,971	312,430	1,012,401	18
Chemicals and explosives	288,848	219,301	448,149	8
Petroleum products[1]	45,272	401,434	446,706	8
Machinery and equip.	182,335	305,166	487,501	8
Food	936,541	798,260	1,734,801	30
Other U.S. supplies	350,517	122,451	472,968	8
Canadian and British supplies	31,741	298,652	330,393	6
Other sources	0	0	0	0
Total	3,156,298 [3,216,298][2]	2,589,424	5,745,722	100

Type of Cargo	Atlantic	Pacific	Total	Distribution of total tonnage, percentage
5. July 1, 1944–May 12, 1945,[3] Fourth Protocol period.				
U.S. supplies				
R.R. transportation equip.	146,901	208,838	355,739	6
Trucks and other vehicles	531,235	114,035	645,270	12
Metals	654,164	468,432	1,122,596	20
Chemicals and explosives	206,670	192,676	399,346	7
Petroleum products[4]	250,455	498,285	748,740	13
Machinery and equip.	232,585	243,060	475,645	9
Food	553,674	603,699	1,157,373	21
Other U.S. supplies	188,986	121,515	310,501	6
Canadian and British supplies	51,863	265,707	317,570	6
Other sources	0	0	0	0
Total	2,816,533	2,716,247	5,532,780	100
6. May 13, 1945–September 2, 1945, Operation Milepost period.				
U.S. supplies				
R.R. transportation equip.	9,067	32,313	41,380	3
Trucks and other vehicles	28,353	209,764	238,117	15
Metals	37,988	211,214	249,202	16
Chemicals and explosives	7,279	50,509	57,788	4
Petroleum products	34,496	371,670	406,166	26
Machinery and equip.	30,465	38,073	68,538	4
Food	22,594	235,607	258,201	17
Other U.S. supplies	13,972	103,235	117,207	8
Canadian and British supplies	7,613	97,487	105,100	7
Total	191,827	1,349,872	1,541,699	100

1. The United States sent 166,359 additional long tons from Abadan.
2. The apparent discrepancy in arithmetic appears in the tables in Report on War Aid. There is no way of knowing if these are actually errors or if an unknown factor was involved. The figure in brackets appears to be correct.
3. The German surrender on May 8 brought a new policy of aid on May 12, with the discontinuation of the European front. By May 12, 95 percent of the tonnage scheduled under the Fourth Protocol had already been exported.
4. The United States sent 388,843 additional long tons from Abadan.

(continued)

Table I. *(continued)*

Type of Cargo	Atlantic	Pacific	Total	Distribution of total tonnage, percentage
7. Sept. 3, 1945–Sept. 20, 1945, period of terminations.				
U.S. supplies				
R.R. transportation equip.	0	947	947	2
Trucks and other vehicles	0	879	879	2
Metals	2,801	9,014	11,815	30
Chemicals and explosives	39	343	382	1
Petroleum products	0	0	0	0
Machinery and equip.	819	1,330	2,149	5
Food	1,989	5,875	7,864	20
Other U.S. supplies	1,325	2,683	4,008	10
Canadian and British supplies	2,331	9,603	11,934	30
Other sources	0	0	0	0
Total	9,304	30,674	39,978	100

SUMMARY: 17,500,900 long tons shipped from the Western Hemisphere. 16,429,800 long tons (94 percent) shipped from the United States. Of the supplies sent to the Soviet Union from the Western Hemisphere from June 22, 1945, 98 per cent was of Lend-Lease origin. The total value of these shipments is reported at approximately $10,200,000,000. In addition, supply services such as ocean transport on American vessels, repairs to Soviet ships, ship supplies, bunkers, port dues, training of Soviet crews for Lend-Lease aircraft, and ships were valued at approximately $700,000,000.

Table II. Aircraft Deliveries to the Soviet Union (by Route)

June 22, 1941–September 20, 1945[1]

	ALSIB	S. Atlantic to Abadan	Water to N. Russia	Water to Abadan
Delivered to factories	8,058	1,055	1,543	4,142
Lost in the U.S.	74	17	0	0
Lost in Canada and Alaska	59	0	0	0
Departed N. America	7,925	1,038	1,543	4,142
Lost after departure	0	43	310	231
Arrived at destination	7,925	994	1,232	3,911
Delivered to U.S.S.R. at destination	7,925	993	1,232	3,868
Totals				
Delivered at factories:		14,798[2]		
Lost en route:		734		
Arrived at destination:		14,062		
Delivered to U.S.S.R. at destination:		14,018		

1. Report on War Aid, 18. This does not include deliveries destined for Britain but retransferred to the Soviet Union.
2. This does not include PBN and PBY patrol planes.

Table III.   Aircraft Deliveries to the Soviet Union (by Type and Route)

	June 22, 1941–September 20, 1945				
Type	ALSIB	Water To N. Russia	Water To Abadan	S. Atlantic To Abadan	Total
Pursuit					
P-40	48	910	1,090	0	2,048
P-39	999	49	300		349
	1,592	50	2,020	0	3,069
	27	30	961		2,583
P-47	3	28			55
P-63	2,312	4	188	0	195
	85				2,312
		3		0	85
					[88]
				Total	9,438
					[13,014]
Light bomber A-20	1,363	126	550	869	2,908
Medium bomber B-25	733	5	0	124	862
Heaver bomber	1	0	0	0	1
Ordnance Service Vehicles					
Field repair trucks	1,543	1,543	1,534	9	0
Tank recovery unit	130	130	130	0	0
Tank transporter	655	655	629	26	0
Total	2,328	2,328	2,293	35	0
Light tanks	1,682	1,682	1,239	443	0
Medium tanks	5,374	5,374	4,957	417	0
Self-propelled guns					
AT 75mm.	5	5	5	0	0
AT 57 mm.	650	650	650	0	0
AT 3 in.	52	52	52	0	0
AT 37 mm.	100	100	100	0	0
AA 50 cal.	1,000	1,000	1,000	0	0
Half-tracks	1,158	1,158	1,104	54	0
Armored scout cars	3,282	3,282	3,054	288	0
Total	13,303	13,303	12,161	1,142 [1,202]	

(*continued*)

Table III. (continued)

Type	ALSIB	Water To N. Russia	Water To Abadan	S. Atlantic To Abadan	Total
Motorcycles	35,170	35,170	32,200	1,870	1,100
Track-laying tractors	8,071	8,074	7,570	253	0
Engines for tractors	3,282	3,282	3,216	66	0
Railway Unit Steam					
Locomotives	1,911	1,911	1,900	11	0
Diesel-elec	70	70	66	4	0
Flat cars	10,000	10,000	9,920	80	0
Tank cars	120	120	120	0	0
Dump cars	1,000	1,000	1,000	0	0
Heavy Mach cars	35	35	35	0	0
Total	13,136	13,136	13,041	95	0
Cargo					
C-46	1	0	0	0	1
C-47	707	0	0	0	707
Observation					
O-52	0	19	0	0	19
Trainer					
AT6-C	0	8	20	0	28
AT6-F	54	0	0	0	54
				Total	4,580

PBN and PBY navy patrol: 185, some delivered from North Carolina, some from Kodiak, Alaska.

Table IV. Vehicles Delivered to the Soviet Union under the Lend-Lease Program

Items	Lend-Lease Export	Total Exports	Arrived	Lost En Route	Diverted
Trucks					
Jeeps					
½ ton 4×4	47,993	48,993	43,728	3,657	1,378
Amphibious	3,510	3,510	3,510	0	0
Trucks					
½ ton	25,240	25,240	24,564	78	598
1 ½ ton	153,415	159,494	148,664	6,660	1,826
2 ½ ton	190,952	193,603	182,938	4,300	1,130
2 ½ ton amphibious	589	589	586	3	0

Items	Lend-Lease Export	Total Exports	Arrived	Lost En Route	Diverted
5 ton and over	852	858	814	0	0
Special purpose	2,792	2,792	2,784	8	0
Truck tractor (w/o trailer)	1,941	1,960	1,938	6	0
Total	427,284	437,039	409,526	14,712	4,932
Trailers (w/o tractor)	102	105	105	0	0
Truck Engines	2,000	2,000	2,000	0	0

Table V. Random Exports to the Soviet Union under the Lend-Lease Program*

Items	Lend-Lease Export	Total Exports	Arrived	Lost En Route	Diverted
Weapons					
Guns					
AA 90 mm	270	270	241	9	0
AA 40mm	5,595	5,595	5,399	196	0
AA 37mm	424	424	340	16	0
AA 50 cal	1,925	1,925	1,925	0	0
AA 4.7 in.	4	4	4	0	0
AT 27 mm	63	63	35	28	0
Submachine guns, 45 cal.	131,633	135,633	112,293	23,340	0
Pistols and revolvers	13,000	13,000	11,500	1,500	0
Mortars	30	30	30	0	0
Smoke pots (1000 units)	1,423	1,423	1,423	0	0
Rocket launchers	3,000	3,000	3,000	0	0
Explosive (tons)					
Smokeless powder	140,531	140,531	129,667	4,909	0
Stick powder	2,210	2,210	2,210	0	0
Other powder	18	57	55	2	0
Cordite powder	927	1,027	1,027	0	0
TNT	136,335	136,335	129,138	3,848	250
TNT (from U.K. acc't.)	10,048	10,048	10,048	0	0

(continued)

Table V. *(continued)*

Items	Lend-Lease Export	Total Exports	Arrived	Lost En Route	Diverted
Dynamite	46,153	46,153	46,153	0	0
Picric acid	1,649	1,649	1,411	92	0
Colloyxlin (nitrocellulose in alcohol)	7,864	7,864	6,075	1,401	86
Radio					
Stations	35,941	36,871	35,800	966	32
Receivers	5,898	5,968	5,899	69	0
Locators	380	380	348	32	0
Direction finder	705	705	705	0	0
Altimeters	538	538	538	0	0
Beacons	63	63	63	0	0
Compasses	800	800	800	0	0
Parts, etc. ($1,000)	7,577	7,620	7,526	59	0
Construction					
Machinery (road, aircraft, railway, mixers, pavers) ($1000)	10,910	11,038	10,792	144	0
Foodstuffs (tons)					
Wheat	55,713	55,713	55,173	600	0
Wheat flour	659,051	659,051	638,796	8,827	5,062
Other flour	40,121	40,121	40,121	0	0
Other finished cereals & prod.	112,550	112,550	109,629	1,065	528
Dried peas & beans	270,514	270,514	239,429	7,905	23,138
Seeds	37,477	37,477	37,437	40	0
Sugar, U.S. stocks	532,845	532,845	502,195	18,285	12,364
Sugar, other sources	170,234	170,234	170,234	0	0
Canned dehyd. meat	14,942	14,942	14,942	0	0
Canned Tushonka	272,009	272,009	265,569	2,904	0
Other canned meat	485,181	485,181	452,084	17,497	15,422
Fatcuts	299,758	300,230	292,742	3,328	4,142
Butters	69,772	69,772	67,876	1,010	735
Lard	316,824	317,908	293,210	7,833	16,846
Veg. oil, short oleo, other oils	520,800	521,195	517,522	1,533	2,140
Canned milk	31,021	31,021	30,727	282	0

Items	Lend-Lease Export	Total Exports	Arrived	Lost En Route	Diverted
Dried milk	77,352	77,352	71,410	1,145	4,394
Dried eggs	121,144	121,144	110,651	4,949	5,296
Soya flour & grits	71,075	71,075	66,504	0	0
Coffee	10,581	10,910	10,350	0	560
Feed	33,631	33,631	28,417	5,214	0
Tools, machinery, and telephone equipment ($1,000)					
Generator sets, military, marine, & other	175,804	175,900	173,745	1,123	0
Machine tools	305,899	323,895	310,058	8,607	0
Secondary metal-forming machinery	59,215	68,738	66,567	995	27
Metal-cutting tools	34,736	34,936	34,878	55	0
Excavating & dredging mach.	33,443	34,241	31,050	2,036	1,005
Field telephones	19,272	19,552	16,968	1,850	26
Field phone units	415,426	422,426	380,135	39,238	0
Other telephone and telegraph equipment	14,324	14,572	14,419	59	0
Steel (tons)					
Hot-rolled aircraft steel	237,580	237,580	233,170	3,401	0
Cold-finish bars	171,555	171,555	160,248	7,407	671
Cold-rolled sheets	100,681	100,681	68,582	29,697	1,709
Tin plate	169,616	169,953	153,971	11,696	2,871
Rails & acces.	721,947	721,047	685,740	25,835	1,421
Hot-rolled sheets & plates	393,052	393,052	365,612	19,693	2,357
Steel pipe & tubing	244,096	244,096	222,107	17,320	1,654
Steel wire	123,975	123,975	115,555	6,289	673
Tool steel	43,396	43,609	40,766	1,640	48
High-speed tool steel	15,065	15,065	14,203	554	0
Bimetal	44,544	44,544	43,168	1,093	0
Stainless steel	13,156	13,156	12,822	98	0

(*continued*)

Table V. *(continued)*

Items	Lend-Lease Export	Total Exports	Arrived	Lost En Route	Diverted
Armor plate	8,950	8,950	5,786	2,897	267
Alloys (tons)					
Ferro-silicon	8,028	8,252	7,174	1,050	0
Ferro-chromium	4,197	4,197	3,703	494	0
Ferro-molybden.	2,906	2,906	2,906	0	0
Molybdenum concentrates	15,850	18,376	16,949	1,430	0
Cable and wire (miles)					
Marine cable	2,339	2,339	2,118	129	0
Submarine cable	1,186	1,186	1,136	50	0
Field telegraph wire	1,105,024	1,105,024	956,688	134,684	197
Metals (tons)					
Copper					
base alloys	356,523	358,494	359,599	17,510	0
tubes, etc.	35,751	35,751	34,168	1,193	36
electrolytic	17,944	17,944	17,944	0	0
Alum. ingots and bars	193,163	194,530	189,237	5,293	0
Fabricated aluminum	68,320	74,669	71,872	2,393	0
Zinc	57,148	57,149	54,826	2,323	0
Lead	20,145	20,145	20,139	0	0
Pig nickel	14,671	14,671	13,843	828	0
Magnesium	9,060	9,060	9,060	0	0
Petroleum prod. (tons)					
Gasoline blending agents	729,225	762,578	732,295	17,236	12,373
Aviation gasoline over 99 octane	602,949	628,134	590,434	0	37,650
Aviation gasoline, 87-99 octane	18,220	148,949	122,415	2,069	24,465
Aviation gasoline, 87 octane & under	19,269	19,690	19,690		
Automotive gas	207,222	278,770	267,088	0	11,682
Kerosene	16,864	16,870	16,870	0	0
Fuel oil	269,639	288,661	287,262	0	0
Lubricating oil & grease	104,841	114,919	111,676	1,678	0
Aviation gas over 99 octane from other accounts	572,979	572,979	572,979	0	0
Cloth, rubber, leather		106,895	102,673	2,662	0
Cotton cloth (1,000 yds)	106,893	62,748	60,138	1,258	0

Items	Lend-Lease Export	Total Exports	Arrived	Lost En Route	Diverted
Woolen cloth (1,000 yds)	62,485	58,257	53,803	2,427	0
Webbing (1,000 yds)	55,843	13,667	13,528	74	0
Tarpaulin (1,000 yds)	13,432	15,582	15,356	90	0
Cordage & twine (tons)	14,805	51,815	46,161	4,861	469
Leather (tons)	49,861				
Rubber (tons)					
crude	269	269	269	0	0
Vistanex	998	1,012	984	28	0
Other synth rubber	10,221	10,224	9,825	0	0
Tires (1,000 units)	3,775	3,786	3,606	110	61
Tubes (1,000 units)	3,813	3,824	3,640	111	63
Rubber hose ($1,000)	7,888	7,939	7,784	155	0
Other rubber items ($1,000)	21,114	21,118	20,843	174	0
Boots (1,000 pair)					
army	14,704	15,417	14,572	578	6
ski	225	225	221	0	0
Chemical products (tons)					
Causic soda	99,052	99,075	98,210	707	0
Ammonium nitrate	3,394	3,394	2,602	113	0
Acetone	12,977	12,977	12,264	654	0
Ethyl alcohol	388,449	388,449	379,742	159	0
Toluol	116,619	119,246	113,884	3,192	359
Phenol	40,453	40,901	38,549	1,732	171
Methanol	28,070	28,070	23,774	3,232	371
Paper					
Parchment (tons)	4,208	4,221	4,201	0	0
Map (tons)	9,277	9,280	8,835	265	0
Cigarette (tons)	1,055	1,055	987	68	0
Photo film ($1,000)	1,684	1,703	1,631	59	0
Miscellaneous ($1,000)					
Asbestos material	478	491	483	4	0
Buttons	1,647	1,647	1,598	49	0

*Random selection by the author from Report on War Aid, 19-26, 28. The total exports are sometimes greater than the total Lend-Lease exports because some items were shipped prior to Land-Lease or on Soviet purchase orders. There are some further discrepancies in the figures from this report. For example, total gun (AA go mm.) exports amount to 270, but the total found by adding arrivals + lost + diverted equals 250 (20 guns unaccountable). There is no way of knowing if these are actually errors or if an unknown factor was involved.

Table VI. Distribution of Tonnage by Ship Registry (Vessels Involved in the Transfer of Lend-Lease to the Soviet Union)

Category	Tonnage	Percentage
	June 22, 1941–September 20, 1945	
United States ships	8,199,000	46.8
United States ships transferred to Soviet registry	5,367,000	30.7
Soviet ships	3,401,000	19.4
Others	534,000	3.1

Table VII. Cargo Shipped from the Western Hemisphere to the Soviet Union

Route	Amount shipped (gross long tons)	Arrived %	Lost %	En route %
	June 22, 1941–September 20, 1945			
North Russia	3,964,000	93	7	0
Persian Gulf	4,160,000	96	4	0
Black Sea	681,000	99	0	1
Soviet Far East	8,244,000	99	0	1
Soviet Arctic	452,000	100	0	0

Totals
  Amount shipped: 17,501,000
  Arrived in Russia: 16,587,000 (83)
  Discharged in Britain: 343,000
  Lost: 488,000

The statistics in these tables use the following source:
Mikhail Suprun, Lend-Liz i severniye konvoi 1941–1945 (Lend-Lease and the Northern Convoys), Andreyevsky Flag, Moscow, 1997, which reproduces the statistical tables from RGAE (Rossiiskii Gosudarstvennii Arkhiv Ekonomii), the Russian State Economic Archive), Suprun, op. cit., pp. 357–59.

Bibliography

Afanas'iev, Yu. N, ed. *Drugaya voina* (The Other War). Moscow: Rossiiskii Gosudarstvennii Universitet, 1996.

Andrew, Christopher and Vasili Mitrokhin. *The Sword and the Shield: The Mitrokhin Archive and the Secret History of the KGB.* New York: Basic Books, 1999.

Antonov-Ovseyenko, A. *Portret tirana* (Portrait of a Tyrant). Moscow: Peidg, 1994.

———. *The Time of Stalin: Portrait of Tyranny.* New York: Harper & Row Publishers, 1980.

Berezhkov, Valentin M. *At Stalin's Side: His Interpreter's Memoirs from the October Revolution to the Fall of the Dictator's Empire.* New York: Birch Lane Press, 1994.

Beriya, Sergo. *Moi otets Lavrentii Beriya* (My Father, Lavrenty Beria). Moscow: Sovremennik, 1994.

Bezymenskii, Lev. *Gitler I Stalin pered shvatkoi* (Hitler and Stalin before the Fight). Moscow: Veche, 2000.

Brandt, M. Yu., et al. *Rossiya i mir Uchebnaya kniga po istorii* (Russia and the World Textbook on History). Moscow: Vlados, 1994.

Carley, Michael J. *1939: The Alliance that Never Was and the Coming of World War II.* Chicago: Ivan R. Dee, 1999.

Chamberlin, William Henry, ed. *Blueprint for World Conquest.* Chicago: Human Events, 1946.

Chaney, Otto P. *Zhukov.* Norman: University of Oklahoma Press, 1996.

Chubaryan, A. O. *V. I. Lenin I formirovaniye sovetskoi vneshnei politiki* (V. I. Lenin and the Formulation of Soviet Foreign Policy). Moscow: Nauka, 1972.

Churchill, Winston. *The Second World War*, vol. 1. New York: Houghton-Mifflin, 1948.

———. *The Grand Alliance.* Boston: Houghton-Mifflin, 1950.

Claasen, Adam A. *Hitler's Northern War: The Luftwaffe's Ill-Fated Campaign 1940–1945.* Lawrence: University Press of Kansas, 2001.

Colson, William R. and Robert Crowley, *The New KGB Engine of Soviet Power*. New York: William Morrow and Company, Inc., 1985.
Conquest, Robert. *The Great Terror: A Reassessment*. New York: Oxford University Press, 1990.
———. *Stalin: Breaker of Nations*. New York: Penguin Books, 1991.
Crocker, George N. *Roosevelt's Road to Russia*. New York: Da Capo Press, 1975.
Crozier, Brian. *The Rise and Fall of the Soviet Empire*. Rockland, Calif: Forum, 1999.
Dawson, Raymond H. *The Decision to Aid Russia 1941*. Chapel Hill: University of North Carolina Press, 1959.
Deane, John R. *The Strange Alliance: The Story of Our Efforts at Wartime Cooperation with Russia*. Bloomington: Indiana University Press, 1973.
Degras, Jane, ed. *The Communist International, 1919–1943*. London: Oxford University Press, 1956–1960, Vols. 1–2.
Deighton, Len. *Blood, Tears, and Folly: An Objective Look at World War II*. New York: Harper Collins, 1993.
Deriabin, Peter S. *Inside Stalin's Kremlin*. Washington, D.C.: Brassey's, 1998.
Djilas, Milovan. *Conversations with Stalin*, London: Harmondworth Publisher, 1969.
Doenecke, Justus. *The Battle against Intervention 1939–1941*. Malabar, Fla.: Krieger Publishing Co., 1997.
Donnelly, Christopher. *Red Banner: The Soviet Military System in Peace and War*. London: Jane's Information Group Ltd., 1988.
Dvoretsky, Lev. *Alien Wars: The Soviet Union's Aggressions against the West*. Novato, Calif.: Presidio Press, 1996.
Dyakov, Yuri and Tatyana Bushuyeva. *Red Army and the Wehrmacht: How the Soviet Militarized Germany, 1922–1933, and Paved the Way for Fascism*. Amherst, N.Y.: Prometheus Books, 1995.
Eissenstat, Bernard W. *Lenin and Leninism: State, Law and Society*. Lexington: Lexington Books, 1971.
Ericson, Edward E., III. *Feeding the German Eagle: Soviet Economic Aid to Nazi Germany, 1933–1941*. Westport, CN: Praeger Publishers, 1999.
Fest, Joachim. *Hitler*. New York: Random House, 1975.
Foreign Relations of the United States, Diplomatic Papers, 1941, vol. 1. General, the Soviet Union. Washington, D.C.: Government Printing Office, 1958.
Fugate, Bryan and Lev Dvoretsky. *Thunder on the Dnepr Zhukov—Stalin and the Defeat of Hitler's Blitzkrieg*. Novayto: Presidio Press, 2001.
Furet, Francois. *The Passing of an Illusion*. Chicago: University of Chicago Press, 1999.
Gaddis, John Lewis. *We Now Know: Rethinking Cold War History*. Oxford: Clarendon Press, 1997.
———. *Russia, the Soviet Union and the United States: An Interpretive History*. 2nd ed., New York: McGraw-Hill Publishing Co., 1990.
Gafencu, Grigore. *Prelude to the Russian Campaign*. Westport, CN: Hyperion Press, 1981.
Gareyev, M.A. *M. V. Frunze—Voyenniy teoretik* (M. V. Frunze—Military Theoretician). Moscow: Voyenizdat, 1986.
Glantz, David M. *Stumbling Colossus: The Red Army on the Eve of World War*. Lawrence: University Press of Kansas, 1998.

Glantz, David M. and Jonathan House. *When Titans Clash*. Lawrence: University Press of Kansas, 1995.

Goebbels, Joseph. *The Goebbels Diaries: The Journal of Joseph Goebbels from 1925–1926*. London: Weidenfeld and Nicolson.

———. *The Goebbels Diaries, 1939–1941*. New York: G. P. Putnam's Sons, 1982.

Goodman, Elliot R. *The Soviet Design for a World State*. New York: Columbia University Press, 1960.

Gor'kov, Yuri. *Kreml', Stavka, Genshtab* (Kremlin, High Command, General Staff). Tver, Russa: RIF LTD, 1999.

Gorodetsky, Gabriel. *Mif "Ledokola" Nakanunye voiny (The Myth of the "Ice-Breaker" on the Eve of War)*. Moscow: Progress Akademii, 1995.

———. ed. *Soviet Foreign Policy, 1917–1991: A Retrospective*. London: Frank Cass, 1994.

———. *Grand Delusion: Stalin and the German Invasion of Russia*. New Haven: Yale University Press, 1999.

Guglya, Yuri. *Dvukhmotorniye istrebiteli 1930–1945* (Twin-engined Fighters 1930–1945). Kiev: Arkhiv-Press, 2000.

Halder, Franz (Gen.). *The Halder Diaries, 1939–1942*. Novato, Calif.: Presidio Press, 1988.

Harrison, Mark. *Soviet Planning in Peace and War 1938–1945*. Cambridge: University Press, 1985.

Herring, George C. Jr. *Aid to Russia, 1941–1946: Strategy, Diplomacy, the Origins of the Cold War*. New York: Columbia University Press, 1973.

Heymann, Hans. *We Can Do Business with Russia*. New York: Ziff Davis, 1945.

Hillgruber, Andreas. *Germany and the Two World Wars*. Cambridge, Mass.: Harvard University Press, 1981.

Hitler, Adolph. *Hitler's Table Talk, 1941–1944*. New York: Enigma Books, 2000.

Hoffmann, Joachim. *Stalin's War of Extermination, 1941–1945*. Capshaw: Dissertations Press, 2001.

Hummel, Sebastian. *Die Sowjetische Nordwes- und Westfront Im Sommer 1941 (The Soviet Western and Northwestern Front, Summer 1941)*. Frankfurt am Main: Peter Lang, 2001.

Ivanov, Robert. *Stalin I soyuzniki 1941–1945 (Stalin and the Allies, 1941–1945)*. Smolensk: Rusich, 2000.

Johnson, Paul. *Modern Times from the Twenties to the Nineties*. New York: Harper Collins, 1991.

Jones, Robert Huhn. *The Roads to Russia: United States Lend-Lease to the Soviet Union*. Norman: University of Oklahoma Press, 1969.

Kahn, David. *Hitler's Spies and German Military Intelligence in World War II*. New York: Collier Books, 1978.

Kalugin, Oleg. *The First Directorate*. New York: St. Martin's Press, 1994.

Kinsella, William E. *Leadership in Isolation: FDR and the Origins of the Second World War*. Boston: G. K. Hall & Co., 1978.

Khrushchev, N. S. *The Crimes of the Stalin Era: Special Report to the 20th Congress of the Communist Party of the Soviet Union*. New York: New Leader Magazine, 1962.

———. *Khrushchev Remembers the Glasnost Tapes*. Boston: Little, Brown and Company, 1990.

Kokoshin, Andrei A. *Armiya I politika Sovetskaya voenno-politicheskayai voyenno-strategicheskaya mysl', 1918–1991 gody* (Army and Policy Soviet Military-Political and Military-Strategic Thought). Moscow: Mezhdunarodniye Otnosheniya, 1995.
———. *Soviet Strategic Thought, 1917–1991*. Cambridge, Mass.: MIT Press, 1995.
Krasnov, Valery. *Neizestnii Zhukov* (*The Unknown Zhukov*). Moscow: Olma, 2000.
Krivitsky, Walter. *In Stalin's Secret Service*. Westport, Conn.: Hyperion Press, Inc., 1939.
Langer, William L., and S. Everett Gleason. *The Undeclared War, 1940–1941*. New York: Harper & Brothers, 1953.
Laqueur, Walter. *Stalin Glasnost Revelations*. New York: Charles Scribner's Sons, 1990.
Lebedev, Igor. *Aviation: Lend Lease to Russia Historical Observations*. New York: Nova Science Publishers.
Lenin, V. I. *Sochineniya*.
Librach, Jan. *The Rise of the Soviet Empire: A Study of Soviet Foreign Policy*. New York: Praeger Publishers, 1964.
Loizam, Dmitry. *Attack of the Airacobras Soviet Aces American P-39s and the Air War against Germany*. Lawrence: University Press of Kansas, 2002.
Malenkov, Andrei, *O moem otse George Malenkove* (About My Father, Georgy Malenkov). Moscow: Tekhnoekos, 1992.
Manstei, Erich von. *Lost Victories*. Novato, Calif.: Presidio Press, 1994.
Mastny, Vojtech, *Russia's Road to the Cold War*. New York: Columbia University Press, 1979.
Medvedev, Zhores and Roi Medvedev. *Neizvestnii Stalin (The Unknown Stalin)*. Moscow: Prava Cheloveka, 2001.
Megenheimer, Heinz. *Hitler's War: Germany's Key Strategic Decisions, 1940–1945*. London: Cassell, 1997.
Mel'tyukohov, Mikhail I. *Upushchennii shans Stalina sovetskii soyuz i bor'ba za Yevropu 1939–1941* (Stalin's Lost Opportunity: The Soviet Union and the Battle for Europe, 1939–1941). Moscow: Veche, 2000.
Menaul, Stewart, and James E. Dornan, et al. *Russian Military Power*. New York: St. Martin's Press, Inc.,1980.
Molotov, V. M. *Molotov Remembers Conversations with Felix Chuyev*. Chicago: Ivan R. Dee, 1993.
Muller, Rolf-Dieter. *Ueberschaar: Gerd R. Hitler's War in the East 1941–1945*. Providence: Berghahn Books, 1997.
Nazi-Soviet Relations 1939–1941. Washington, D.C.: U.S. Department of State, 1948.
Nekrich, Aleksandr. *Pariahs, Predators, Partners: German-Soviet Relations 1922–1941*. New York: Columbia University Press, 1997.
Nevezhin, V. A. *Sindrom nastupatel'noi voiny (The Syndrome of Offensive War)*. Moscow: Seriya Pervaya Monografiya, Airo-XX, 1997.
Niblo, Peter B. *Influence: The Soviet "Task" Leading to Pearl Harbor, the Iron Curtain, and the Cold War*. Oakland, Oreg.: Elderberry Press, 2002.
Nisbet, Robert. *Roosevelt and Stalin: The Failed Courtship*. Washington, D.C. Regnery Gateway, 1988.
Ostrovskiy, V. P., and A. I. Utkin. *Istoriya Rossii XX vek* (A History of Russia in the 20th Century). Moscow: School textbook, Drofa, 1997.

Overy, Richard. *Russia's War: A History of the Soviet War Effort, 1941–1945.* New York: Penguin Books, 1997.
Page, Stanley. *The Geopolitics of Leninism.* New York: Columbia University Press, 1982.
Paperno, A. *Lend-Liz Tikhii Okean (Lend-Lease the Pacific Ocean).* Moscow: Terra-Knizhnii Klub, 1998.
Paperno, A. *Tainy istorii* (History's Secrets). Moscow: Terra-Knizhniy Klub, 1998.
Persico, Joseph E. *Roosevelt's Secret War: FDR and World War II Espionage.* New York: Random House, 2001.
Perlmutter, Amos. *FDR & Stalin: A Not So Grand Alliance 1943–1945.* Columbia: University of Missouri Press, 1993.
Pons, Silvio. *Stalin and the Inevitable War 1936–1941.* London: Frank Cass, 2002.
Possony, Stefan T. *Lenin, the Compulsive Revolutionary.* London: George Allen & Unwin Ltd, 1966.
Raack, R. C. *Stalin's Drive to the West.* Stanford: Stanford University Press, 1995.
Radzinsky, Edvard. *Stalin.* New York: Doubleday Publishing Co., 1996.
Ratkin, Semyon. *Tainy vtoroi mirovoi voiny* (Secrets of the Second World War). Minsk: Sovremennaya Literatura, 1995.
Rauschning, Hermann. *The Voice of Destruction.* New York: G. P. Putnam's Sons, 1949.
Raushning, German. *Govorit Gitler Zver' iz bezdni* (Hitler Speaks a Beast Out of the Abyss). Moscow: Mif, 1993.
Rees, Laurence. *War of the Century: When Hitler Fought Stalin.* New York: The New Press, 1999.
Ribbentrop, Joachim and Alan Bullock, eds. *The Ribbentrop Memoirs.* London: Weiderfeld & Nicolson, 1954.
Roberts, Geoffrey. *The Soviet Union and the Origins of the Second World War: Russo-German Relations and the Road to War, 1933–1941.* New York: St. Martin's Press, 1995.
Rommerstein, Herbert and Eric Breindel. *The Venona Secrets: Exposing Soviet Espionage and America's Traitors.* New York: Regnery Publishing, Inc., 2000.
Rossi, A. *The Russo-German Alliance, August 1939–June 1941.* Boston: Beacon Press, 1981.
Rudzinski, Aleksander. *Soviet Peace Offensives.* New York: Carnegie Endowment for International Peace., 1953.
Samuelson, Lennart. *Plans for Stalin's War Machine. Tukhachevsky and Military-Economic Planning, 1925–1941.* New York: St. Martin's Press, 2000.
Sarin, Oleg, and Lev Dvoretsk *Alien Wars: The Soviet Union's Aggressions Against the World, 1919–1939.* Novato: Presidio Press, 1996.
Savkin, V. Ye. *Osnovniye printsipy operativnogo iskusstva i taktiki* (Basic Principles of Operational Art and Tactics). Moscow: Voyennoye Izdatel'stvoi Ministerstva Oborony SSSR, 1972.
Schecter, Jerrold, and Leona Schecter. *Sacred Secrets: How Soviet Intelligence Operations Changed American History.* Washington, D.C.: Brassey's, Inc.
Schellenberg, Walter, and Alan Bullock, eds. *The Labyrith: Memoirs of Walter Schellenberg.* New York: Da Capo Press, 1984.
Sekrety Gitlera na stolye Stalina (Hitler's Secrets in Stalin's Desk). Moscow: Mostoarkhiv, 1995.

Sejna, Jan. *We Will Bury You*. London: Sidgwick & Jackson, 1982.
Shirer, William L. *The Rise and Fall of the Third Reich*. New York: Simon & Schuster, 1959.
Shturman, Dora. *Mertviye khavatayut zhivykh chitaya Lenina, Bukharina, i Trotskogo* (The Living Envy the Dead: Reading Lenin, Bukharin, and Trotsky). London: Overseas Publications Interchange, Ltd., 1982.
Smith, Blake W. *Warplanes to Alaska*. Blaine, Wash.: Hancock House Publishers, 1998.
Sokolov, Boris. *Okhota na Stalina Okhota na Gitlera* (The Hunt for Stalin: The Hunt for Hitler). Moscow: Veche, 2000.
———. *Pravda o Velikoi Otechestvennoi Voiny* (The Truth about the Great Patriotic War). Sankt Petersburg: Aleteiya, 1998.
Soroko-Tsyupi, O. S., et al. *Mir v XX veke* (The World in the 20th Century), Russian history textbook for the 10th–11th grades. Moscow: Proveshcheniye, 1997. *Soviet Diplomacy and Negotiating Behavior*, Committee on Foreign Affairs, 98th Congress, vol. 1, Government Printing Office, 1979.
Spahr, William J. *Stalin's Lieutenants: A Study of Command under Duress*. Novato, Calif.: Presidio Press, 1997.
Stalin, J. V. *Sochineniya*.
Stalin., J. *On the Great Patriotic War of the Soviet Union*. Calcutta: Suren Dutt, 1975.
Standley, William H. and Arthur A. Ageton. *Admiral Ambassador to Russia*. New York: Henry Regnery Company, 1955.
Stevenson, William. *A Man Called Intrepid*. New York: Harcourt Brace Jovanovich, 1976.
Sudoplatov, Pavel, and Anatoli Sudoplatov. *Special Tasks*. New York: Little, Brown & Company, 1994.
———. *Razniye dni tanoi voiny I diplomatii 1941 god* (During Various Days in the Secret War and Diplomacy of the 1941). Moscow: Olma, 2003.
Sul'yanov, Anatoli. *Arestovat' v Kremlye O zhizne I smerti Marshala Berii (Arrested in the Kremlin: On the Life and Death of Marshal Beriya)*. Minsk: MP Slavyanye, 1993.
Suprun, Mikhail. *Lend-Liz i severniye konvoi 1941–1945 (Lend-Lease and the Northern Convoys, 1941–1945)*. Moscow: Andreyesvskii Flag, 1997.
Sutton, Anthony C. *National Suicide Military Aid to the Soviet Union*. New Rochelle: Arlington House, 1973.
Suvorov, Viktor. *Ledokol* (Ice-breaker). Moscow: ACT, 1997.
———. *Den' "M"* (M-Day). Moscow: ACT, 1997.
Tanenhaus, Sam. *Whittaker Chambers: A Biography*. New York: The Modern Library, 1997.
Taubman, William. *Stalin's American Policy from Entente to Détente to Cold War*. New York: W. W. Norton & Co., 1982.
Tokaev, G. A. *Stalin's War*, London: George Weidenfeld & Nicolson Ltd, 1951.
Tolstoy, Nikolai. *Stalin's Secret War*. New York: Holt, Rinehart, and Winston, 1981.
Topitsch, Ernst. *Stalin's War: A Radical New Theory on the Origins of the Second World War*. New York: St. Martin's Press, 1987.

Tucker, Robert C. *Stalin in Power: The Revolution from Above, 1928–1941*. New York: W. W. Norton & Co., 1990.

U.S.S.R. Government Documents and Materials Relating to the Eve of the Second World War. New York: International Publishers, 1954.

Utkin, A. I. *Rossiya i zapad (Russia and the West)*. School textbook. Moscow: Gadariki, 2000.

Vigor, P. J. *The Soviet View of War, Peace and Neutrality*. London: Routledge & Kegan Paul, 1975.

Vikhavainen, Timo. *Stalin i Finni* (Stalin and the Finns). Sankt Peterburg: Zhurnal Neva, 2000.

Vishlov, O. *Hakanunye 22 Iyuniya 1941 god. Dokumental'niye Ocherki* (On the Eve of June 22, 1941. Documentary Studies). Moscow: Nauka, 2001.

Volkogonov, Dmitri. *Stalin and Tragedy*. Rocklin, Calif.: Prima Publishing, 1991.

———. *Autopsy for an Empire: The Seven Leaders Who Built the Soviet Regime*. New York: The Free Press, 1998.

———. *Lenin: A New Biography*. New York: The Free Press, 1994.

Volkov, V. K., and L. Ya Gibanskii, eds. *Vostochnaya Yevropa mezhdu Gitlerom I Stalinym 1939–1941 (Eastern Europe between Hitler and Stalin, 1939–1941)*. Moscow: Izdatel'stvo Indrik, 1999.

Vyshinksy, Andrei A. *The Law of the Soviet State*. New York: MacMillan Company, 1948.

Walker, Martin. *The Cold War: A History*. New York: Henry Holt and Company, 1993.

Weeks, Albert L. *The Other Side of Coexistence: An Analysis of Russian Foreign Policy*. New York: Pitman, 1970.

———. *Soviet and Communist Quotations*. New York: Pergamon-Brassey's, 1987.

———. *Stalin's Other War: Soviet Grand Strategy, 1939–1941*. Lanham, Md.: Rowman & Littlefield, 2002.

Weinberg, Gerhard L. *A World at Arms*. Camridge: Cambridge University Press, 1994.

———. *Germany and the Soviet Union 1939–1941*. Leiden: E. J. Brill, 1954.

Weinstein, Allen, and Alexander Vassiliev. *The Haunted Wood: Soviet Espionage in America—The Stalin Era*. New York: The Modern Library, 2000.

Whymant, Robert. *Stalin's Spy: Richard Sorge and the Tokyo Espionage Ring*. New York: St. Martin's Press, 1998.

Wills, Matthew B. *Wartime Missions of Harry Hopkins*. Raleigh: Pentland Press, Inc. 1996.

Yakovlev, A. N., ed. *1941 god Dokumenty v 2-kh knigakh* (The Year 1941: Documents in Two Books), First-Second Books. Moscow: Mezhdunarodniy Fond "Demokratiya," 1998.

———. *Omut pamyati (Swarm of Memories)*. Moscow: Vagrius, 2000.

———. *Sumerki* (Nightfall). Moscow: Mterik, 2003.

Zhilin, P. A. *Istoriya voyennogo iskusstva* (History of Military Art), Officer's Library Series. Moscow: Voyenizdat, 1986.

Zhukov, Georgi K. *Reminiscences and Reflections*. Moscow: Progress Publishers, 1970.

———. *Dokumenty* (Documents). Moscow: Rossiya XX vek, 2001.

Zhukov, Yu. N. *Tainy Kremlya Stalin, Molotov, Beriya, i Malenkov* (Stalin, Molotov, Beria, and Malenkov). Moscow: Terra-Knizhniy Klub, 2000.

ARTICLES

Artemov, V. A. *"Germanskoye napadeniye na Sovetskyi Soyuz v 1941"* ("The German Attack on the Soviet Union in 1941"), book review of *Der deutsche Angriff auf die Sowjetunion 1941. Die Kontroverse um Preventifkriegsthese* (The German Attack on the Soviet Union in 1941. Controversy Concerning the Thesis of a Preventive War), Darmstadt, 1998, *Voprosy istorii*, No. 8, 2001, 166–69.

Batayeva, T. V. *"Uchebnik po istorii: orientiry i adresati"* ("Textbook on History: Guides and Addressees"), *Prepodavaniye istorii v shkole*, No. 4, 1998, 46–56.

Bezymenskii, Lev A. *"Sovetskaya razvedka pered voinoi"* ("Soviet Intelligence Before the War"), *Voprosy istorii*, No. 9, 1996.

Bobylev, Pavel N. *"Tochku v diskussii stavit' rano. K voprosu o planirovanii v general'nom shtabe RKKA vozmozhnoi voiny s Germaniyei v 1940–1941 godakh"* ("Calling an Early Halt to the Discussion About the Problem in the General Staff of the RKKA on Planning a Possible War with Germany from the Years 1940–1941"), *Otechesvennaya istoriya*, No. 1, 2000, 41–64.

Borichevskii, Capt. Oleg. *"Rashen, Pliz–Poluchite Lend-Liz"* ("Russians: Please Accept Lend-Lease"), *Soldat otechestva* (Soldier of the Fatherland), Sept. 5, 2000.

Bushuyev, T. S. *Proklinaya—poprobuite ponyat'* ("Curse It but Try to Understand"), book review of two books by Viktor Suvorov, *Novyi mir*, No. 12, 1994, 230–37.

Chernyak, Aleksandr. *"O nashei velikoi pobede"* ("About Our Great Victory"), *Pravda*, April 12, 1995.

Chernyavsky, G. I. *"Dnevniki G. M. Dimitrova"* ("The Diaries of G. M. Dimitrov"), *Novaya i noveishaya istoriya*, No. 5, 2001, 47–58.

Dimitriev, V. *"Diplomatiya i voyennaya strategiya"* ("Diplomacy and Military Strategy"), *Voyennaya mysl'*, No. 7, July 1971, 51.

Dolitsky, Alexander B. "The Alaska-Siberia Lend-Lease Program During World War II." Proceedings of the International Congress on the History of the Arctic and Sub-Arctic Region, Reykjavik, June 12–18, 1998, Reyjavik, 2000.

Firsov, F. I. *"Arkhivy kominterna i vneshnynya politika SSSR v 1939–1941"* ("Archives of the Communist International and the Foreign Policy of the USSR 1939–1941"), *Novaya i noveishaya istoriya*, No. 6, 1992, 18–19.

Gareyev, M. A. *"Voyennaya nauka i voyennoye iskusstvo v velikoi otechestvennoi voine"* ("Military Science and Military Art in the Great Fatherland War"), *Voyennaya mysl'*, No. 3, May–June 2000, 42–49.

Gilensen, V. M. *"Fatal'naya oshibka"* ("The Fatal Mistake"), *Voyenno-istoricheskii zhurnal*, No. 4, 25–35, 1998.

Goffman, Joakhim (Hoffman, Joachim). *"Podgotovka sovetskovo soyuza k nastupatel'noi voine"* ("Preparation by the Soviet Union for Offensive War"), *Otechestvennaya istoriya*, No. 47, 1993, 19–31.

Gor'kov, Yu. A. *"Gotovil li Stalin uprezhdayushchii udar protiv Gitlera v 1941 g.?"* ("Did Stalin Plan a Preemptive Strike Against Hitler in 1941?"), *Novaya i noveishaya istoriya*, 1993, No. 3, 29–45.

Gurkin, V. V., and M. I. Golovnin, *"K voprosu o strategicheskikh operatsiyakh velikoi otechestvennoi voine 1941–1945 gg."* ("About the Problem of Strategic Operations During the Great Fatherland War 1941–1945"), *Voyenno-istoricheskii zhurnal*, No. 10, 1985, 10–33.

Historicus. "Stalin on Revolution," *Foreign Affairs*, January 1949, 175–214.
Kells, Robert E. Capt. U.S. Army, "Intelligence, Doctrine and Decision-making," *Military Intelligence*, July–September 1985.
Karpov, Ye. A., and G. A. Mokhorov, V. A. Rodin. *"Uroki velikoi otechestvennoi voini i voyennaya doktrina Rossiiskoi Federatsii"* ("Lessons of the Great Fatherland War and the Military Doctrine of the Russian Federation"), *Voyenna mysl'*, No. 3, May–June 2000, 34–41.
Khachaturyan, A. O. *"Polkovodcheskaya deyatel'nost' G. K. Zhukova kak Komanduyushchego voiskami frontov"* ("G. K. Zhukov's Military Leadership as Commander of Military Fronts"), *Voyennaya mysl'*, No. 3, May–June 2000, 72–75.
Khorkov, A. G. *"Na yugo-zapadnom napravlenii"* ("In the Southwestern Sector"), *Voyenno-istoricheskii zhurnal*, No. 6, 2002, 10–12.
Korotkov, I. "The Military-Theoretical Legacy of Lenin," *Soviet Military Review*, April 1968, 2–6.
Kostin, A. A. *"Pozitsiya SShA v otnoshenii Yugoslavii v yanvarye-marte 1941 goda"* ("The Position of the USA in Its Relations with Yugoslavia January–March 1941"), *Voprosy istorii*, No. 1, 2002, 107–15.
Kuleshov, N. Yu. *"Voyenno-doktrinal'niye ustanovki stalinskogo rukovodstva i repressii v Krasnoi Armii kontsa 1930-kh godov"* ("Military-Doctrinal Principles of the Stalin Leadership and Repression Against the Red Army at the End of the 1930s"), *Otechestvennaya istoriya*, No. 2, 2001, 61–72.
———. *"'Bol'shoi den'' gryadushchaya voina v literature 1930-kh godo"* ('The Big Day': The Coming War in Literature of the 1930's"), *Otechestvennaya istoriya*, No. 1, 2002, 183–190.
Kumanev, G. A. *"Voina glazami nachal'nika genshtaba. K stoletiyu so Dnya pozhdeniya A. M. Vasilevskovo"* ("The War Through the Eyes of the Chief of the General Staff. On the 100th Anniversary of the Birth of A. M. Vasilievsky"), *Pravda*, Sept. 28, 1995.
Kunitskii, P. T. Maj.-Gen. *"Dostizheniye vnezapnosti po opytu velikoi otechestvennoi voiny"* ("Achievement of Surprise Based on the Experience of the Great Fatherland War"), *Voyenno-istoricheskyi zhurnal*, No. 10, 1985, pp. 24–30.
Lenin, V. I. *"Ya proshu zapisyvat' menshe; eto ne dol'zhno popadat' v pechat'"* (I Propose Writing Less and Not Reproducing This in the Press), *Istoricheskyi arkhiv*, No. 1, 1992, 12–30.
Lukashev, V. K. *"O cheloveke kotoriy propustil 'cherez svoi ruki' ves' Lend-Liz"* ("About the Man Through Whose Hands Passed All of Lend-Lease"), *Izvestiya*, June 17, 1992.
Lyulechnik, V. *"A k voine my gotovilis' i byli gotovy"* ("We Prepared and Were Prepared for War"), *Panorama*, May 8–14, 1996.
———. *"Nakanune i v gody voiny"* ("On the Eve and During the Years of the War"), *Panorama*, June 18–24, 1997.
Mar'ina, Valentin B. *"Dnevnik G. Dimitrova"* (G. Dimitrov's Diary), *Voprosy istorii*, No. 7, 2000, 32–54.
Markoff, Alexei (Gen.). "Stalin's War Plans," *Saturday Evening Post*, Sept. 20, 1952.
Medvedev, R. A. *"I. V. Stalin v perviye dni voiny"* ("J. V. Stalin During the First Days of the War"), *Voyenno-istoricheskii zhurnal*, No. 6, 2002, 4–9.
Mel'tyukhov, Mikhail I. *"Narashchivaniye sovetskovo voyennovo prisutstviya v pribaltike v 1939–1941 godakh"* ("The Growing Soviet Military Presence in the Baltic Region in the Years 1939–1941"), *Otechestvennaya istoriya*, No. 4, 1999, 46–70.

Mirenkov, A. I. Gen.-Maj. *"Obespecheniye deystvuyushchei armii Vooruzheniyem, boyevoi tekhnikoi, matertial'nymi Sredstvamoi v 1941–1943 gg"* ("Supplying the Combat With Military Equipment and Materiel in 1941–1943,") *Voyenno-isporicheskiy zhurnal*, No. 5, 2002, 24–29.

Nevezhin, V. A. *"1941 god: v 2 kn. Sost. L. Ye. Reshin Pod red. V. P. Naumova; vstupit. St. Akad. A. N. Yakovleva."* Mezhdunarodnii Fond "Demokratiya," Moscow, 1998 ("The Year 1941. In 2 volumes compiled by L. Ye. Reshin under the editorship of V. P. Naumov; Introduction by A. N. Yakovlev. International Fund, Moscow, 1998"), Book review in *Otechestvennaya istoriya*, No. 4, 1999, 212–15.

Nezhinskii, L. N. *"Dokumenty vneshnei politiki, 22 Ilyunya 1941–Yanvarya 1942, Mezhdunarodniye otnosheniya, Moscow, 2000," t. XXIV, Rezentsii*, ("Documents in Foreign Policy, June 22, 1941–January 1942," Vol. 24), *Novaya noveishaya istoriya* 216–17.

"Nauchniye konferentsii v svyazi c 60-letnem nachala velikoi otechestvennoi voiny" ("Scientific Conferences in Connection with the 60th Anniversary of the Start of the Great Fatherland War"), *Novaya i noveishaya istoriya*, No. 6, 2001, 204–12.

Ogarkov, N. V. "History Teaches Vigilance," Foreign Broadcast Information Service, Aug. 30, 1985.

———. "The Defense of Socialism: Experience of History and the Contemporary World," *Red Star*, May 9, 1984.

Ostroumov, N. N. *"Geroi sovetskogo soyuza Glavnyi Marshal Aviatsii K. A. Vershinin (k 100-letiyu so dnya rozhdeniya)"* ("Hero The Soviet Union Chief Marshal of Aviation, K. A. Vershinin [On the 100th Anniversary of His Birth"], *Voyennaya mysl'*, No. 3, May–June 2000, 76–79.

Plimak, Yevgenii, and Vadim Antonov *"Stalin znal, shto delal"* ("Stalin Knew What He Was Doing"), *Moskovskiye novosti*, Mar. 10–17, 1996.

Pozdeyeva, L. V. *"Dnevnik I. M. Maiskogo. iz zapisei o britanskoi politike 1938–41"* ("The Diary of I. M. Maisky. From Notes on British Policy 1938–41"), *Novaya noveishaya istoriya*, No. 3, 2001, 46–63.

Raack, R. C. "Stalin's Plans for World War II," *Journal of Contemporary History*, No. 26, 1991, 215–27.

———. "Stalin's role in the Coming of World War II," *World Affairs*, Spring 1996, Washington, D. C., 1996, 1–18.

Rabiner, Boris. *"Samiy perviy den' voiny"* ("The Very First Day of the War"), Panorama, June 12–18, 1996.

Sakharov, A. N. *"Voina I Sovetskaya Diplomatiya"* ("War and Soviet Diplomacy"), *Voprosy istorii*, No. 7, 1995.

Schwarz, Benjamin. "Rethinking Negotiation with Hitler," *The New York Times*, Nov. 25, 2000.

Shevelev, Lev. "Stalin and the Nuremberg Trial," Interview with Historian Natalya Lebedeva, *Moscow News*, No. 11, Mar. 24–30, 1995.

"60 let so dnya nachala velikoi otechestvennoi voiny voyenno-istoricheskaya konferentsiya 1941–2001 spetsial'nyi vypusk" ("60 Years Since the Start of the Great Fatherland War Military-Historical Conference Special Edition"), *Voyennyi istoricheskyi zhurnal*, 2002.

Sluch, Sergei Z. *"Sovetsko-Germanskiye otnosheniya v sentyabre-dekyabre 1939 goda I vopros o vystupolenii SSSR vo vtoruyu mirovuyu voinu"* ("Soviet-German Relations in September 1939 and the Question of the Entry of the U.S.S.R. into the Second World War"), Two parts, *Otechestvennaya istoriya*, Nos. 5 and 6, 2000, 46–58.

Sokolov, B. V. "The Role of Lend-Lease in Soviet Military Efforts, 1941–1945," *Journal of Slavic Military Studies*, Vol. 7, No. 3, (September 1994), 567–586.

Sokolov, B. V. "*I. M. Maiskyi mezhdu I. V. Stalinym i U. Churchillem v perviye mesyatsi voiny*" ("I. M. Maisky Between I. V. Stalin and W. Churchill During the First Months of the War"), *Novaya i noveishaya istoriya*, No. 6, 2001, 18–40.

Stanyshnev, Boris. "*Stalin, Gitler i Suvorov*" ("Stalin, Hitler, and Suvorov"), *Argumenty i fakty*, No. 15, 1995.

Suprun, M. H. "*Prodovol'stvenniye postavki v SSSR po Lend-Lizu v godi vtoroi mirovoi voiny*" ("Shipments of Foodstuffs to the U.S.S.R. During the Second World War"), *Otechestvennaya istoriya*, No. 3, 1996.

Vislykh, Aleksandr. "*Spasitel'nii Lend-Liz Ne nado preumenshivat' ego zacheniye v nashei pobede v Velikoi Otechestvennoi Voine*" ("Lifesaving Lend-Lease It Is Not Necessary to Minimize Its Importance in Our Victory in the Great Patriotic War"), *Nezavisimoye obozreniye* (Military Observer), Nov. 12, 2001, 5.

Voin Rossii (Russian Soldier). "*Tochka Zreniya: Pravda o Lend-Lize*" (Point of View: The Truth About Lend-Lease, May 19, 1999.

Volkogonov, Dmitri. "*Mir–eto tsel', kotoraya dostigayetsya lish' soobshcha*" ("Peace Was a Goal Achieved Only Jointly"), *Rossiiskiye vesti*, Jan. 12, 1995.

Vorob'iev, I. N. "*Evolyutsiya roli i mesta taktiki v voyennom iskusstve*" ("Evolution of the Role and Function of Tactics in Military Art,") *Voyenna mysl'*. No. 1, 2002, 46–51.

Weeks, Albert L. "The Garthoff-Pipes Debate on Soviet Doctrine: Another Perspective," *Strategic Review*, Winter 1983, 57–64.

———. "The Soviet View Toward Prognostication," *Military Review*, September 1983, 49–57.

———. "Soviet Military Doctrine," *Global Affairs*, Winter, 1988, 170–87.

———. "The Soviet Defense Council," *Defense & Diplomacy*, May 1990, 42–47.

———. "Russia Unfurls Its New/Old Military Doctrine," *The Officer, ROA National Security Report*, January 1994, 30, 35.

———. "Was General Andrei Vlasov, Leader of the Russian Liberation Army, a True Russian Patriot or a Traitor?" *World War II*, November 1997.

X. "The Sources of Soviet Conduct," *Foreign Affairs*, January 1949, 566–82.

Yakovlev, A. N. "*Bol'shevizmu ne uiti ot otvetstvennnosti*" ("Bolshevism Cannot Evade Responsibility"), *Rossiiskiye vesti*, November 29, 1995, 1.

PERIODICALS

Argumenty i Fakty

Voprosy Istorii

Journal of Contemporary History

Kommunist Vooruzhennikh Sil

Krasnaya Zvezda

Novaya Noveishaya Istoriya

Otechestvennaya Istoriya

Panorama

Pravda

Prepodavaniye Istorii v Shkolye

Reason

Rossiiskiye Vesti

SShA Ekonomika Politika Ideologiya

Survey (U.K.)

Voennaya Mysl'

Voennyi Istoricheskyi Zhurnal

Voprosy Istorii

GOVERNMENT DOCUMENTS

Nazi-Soviet Relations 1939–1941, U. S. Department of State, 1948.

Russian archive material from, among other sources: the State Archive of the Russian Federation (GARF); Russian State Archive of Socio-Political History (RGACPI); Russian State Military Archive (RGVA); Russian State Archive on the Economy (RGAE); Center for the Collection of Contemporary Documents (TsKhSD).

Soviet Diplomacy and Negotiating Behavior, Committee on Foreign Relations, U.S. House of Representatives, 96th Congress, Vol. 1, 1979.

Soviet Political Agreements and Results, Staff Study, Committee on the Judiciary, U.S. Senate, 86th Congress, 1959.

Index

Adams, John Quincy, 56, 57, 59
Afghanistan, 16
agents of influence, 7, 12, 41–49
agricultural technology, 70–71, 74–76
aid programs, 48. *See also* American Relief Administration; Lend-Lease; technological assistance
air bases, 113–14, 117–18
aircraft, 8, 26, 109; aviation fuel, 8, 122, 134–35, 150; casualties, 114–15, 118–19, 120; deliveries, 111, 113, 115–16, 144–46; equipment losses, 118–19, 120; types, 117–18, 124, 145
Air Force Inspectorate (Red Army), 117
air routes, 112–14, 116–21
Alaska, 1–2, 58–59, 63–64, 71
Alaska-Siberia (Alsib) routes, 2, 26, 113–14, 116–18
Alaska-Siberia Lend-Lease Program (ASLLP), 1–2
Aleutian Islands, 58
Alexander Foundry, 70
Alexander I, 56–58, 59
Alexander II, 61
Alexander III, 71
Alexander III Canal, 79

Alexander Nevsky (ship), 61–62
Allies. *See* Britain; United States
American Expeditionary Force, 54
American Federation of Labor, 24
American Relief Administration (ARA), 48, 51n18, 66–67
American Revolution, 55–56
Anglo-American Atlantic Charter, 13
Anisimov, Alexis A., 114
anti-Communism, 14, 24
ARA. *See* American Relief Administration
archive material, 7, 98
army staff talks, U.S.-U.K., 13
arsenal of democracy, as term, 11, 110
atomic fission, 42
aviation fuel, 8, 122, 134–35, 150
Axis, 6, 14; Quadpartite Alliance, 20, 93; Soviet propaganda on, 16–17, 20. *See also* Germany; Italy; Japan

Balkans, 93–94, 97–98
Baltic States, 109
Barker, Wharton, 79
Basistov, Yu. B., 41
Bates, Linden W., 79
Battle of the Atlantic, 3–4

Beasant, John, 130–31, 133
Belorussia, 109
Beria, Lavrenty, 37, 41, 99, 104
Beria, Sergo, 41–42
Bering, Vitus Jonassen, 58
Bering Strait, 58
Big Three summits, 15, 35, 43, 46, 129, 130
Black Sea ports, 75
blitzkrieg, 5, 88
Bolsheviks, 14, 53, 65, 77, 78
Brain Trust, 14, 23
Brest-Litovsk territorial deal, 89
Brezhnev, Leonid, 16
bridge building, 69
Britain, 13, 40, 96; American Civil War and, 60–61; convoys and, 3–4; Lend-Lease aid to, 6, 22, 29n8, 100, 103–4; nineteenth-century relations with Russia, 55–57; repayment agreement, 23; Soviet espionage and, 44, 103–4; Stalin's suspicion of, 43–44, 90
British Admiralty, 3–4
Buchanan, James, 60, 63
Bulgaria, 93
Bullitt, William C., 46
Bunge, N. K., 71
Bunker, John Gorley, 130
businessmen, U.S., 82–83

Cabinet, 40
California, 58
Cambridge Five, 44
Canada, transatlantic convoys, 3–4
capitalism, success of, 21–22
Castro, Fidel, 47
Catherine the Great, 55–56, 63
Caucasus, 44
Chadayev, Ya. Ye., 94
Chamberlain Cabinet, 12
Chase Bank, 66
chemical substances, 122, 151
China, Lend-Lease aid to, 25, 29n8, 95
China, Nationalist, 95
Chinese Eastern Railway, 73
Churchill, Winston, 3, 15, 23, 43, 52, 97; flexible attitude toward Soviet Union, 104–5; view of Stalin, 5, 33, 41
Civil Air Fleet, 116
Civil War, American, 59–63, 71
Clay, Cassius Marcellus, 61
Cold War, 54, 135
Collins, Perry, 72
Commissariat of Foreign Affairs, 43, 104
Commission of Railway Experts to Russia, 77
Communist Party of the USA (CPUSA), 19, 40, 85n2, 92
concentration camps, 91
Congress, 5, 22, 110, 125
Constantine, Grand Duke, 79
consumer goods, American, 20–21
Convention as to the Pacific Ocean and Northwest Coast of North America, 59
Convention as to the Rights of Neutrals on the Sea, 60
convoys, 3–4, 13, 26–27, 116
Cossacks, 59
Council of People's Commissars, 94
Crimea, 109
Crimean War, 55, 60, 63
Cuba, 58
Currie, Laughlin, 45
Czechoslovak Army, 78
Czechoslovakia, 16, 92, 95

Dana, Francis, 56, 67, 83
Declaration of Independence, 55
Declaration of the United Nations, 13
decryptions, 27, 97, 100–101
defense plants, Communist sabotage of, 92
defense production, U.S., 2–3, 21–22
defensiveness, Soviet ideology of, 16–17
dehydration technology, 123
demarche, 103–5
democracies, Stalin's view of, 41–42
Dictionary of Naval Fighting Ships, 133
Dimitrov, Georgy, 94

disarmament, 47
Division of Soviet Supply (DSS), 124
Doenitz, Admiral, 27
Dolgoruky, Sergius, 79
Dolitsky, Alexander, 2, 123–26
draft, U.S., 13
Dulles, Foster Rhea, 61

Eden, Anthony, 5–6, 24
Egnatashvili, G. A., 96
Eighteenth Party Congress, 17
Ellerwald, Joseph, 132
Emerson, George, 77
Engels, Friedrich, 88
engineering schools, Russian, 83
Enigma decryptions, 27, 97, 100–101
Epstein, Jay, 49
Estonia, 109
European economy, 21
exports, Soviet, 100

Fairbanks, Alaska, 1–2
fairs and exhibitions, 76
Fascists, 88, 95
Fatherland War, 57
Federal Bureau of Investigation (FBI), 132
Fedorenko, Ya. N., 108
Festung Europa, 6
Finland, 34, 93, 108; Soviet aggression against, 14, 16, 24, 44, 102; Winter War, 39, 110–11
Fiondella, Jay, 130
First Protocol, 13
Five-Year Plans, 14, 66, 74, 82–85
food aid, 9, 122–24, 148–49; ARA, 48, 51n18, 66–67
Ford, Alexander Hume, 73–75
Foreign Economic Administration (FEA), 124
France, 73, 90, 92 American Civil War and, 60–61; nineteenth-century relations with Russia, 56–57
Francis, David R., 77, 79–80
Freedom of Information Act, 133
Friedman, Elisha, 83
fueling points, 118

Funds for Purchase of Implements and Agricultural Machinery to the Peasants, 75

Gaddis, John Lewis, 99, 100
Gallatin, Albert, 57
garages, 9
gas chambers, 91
gas wagon, 90–91
geopolitical factors, 45, 54–55, 94, 98
German-Soviet Commercial Agreement, 91
Germany: agricultural machinery and, 74–75; defense development, 4, 8, 42; fears of American involvement, 14, 21–22, 42–43, 96; June 22, 1941 attack on Soviet Union, 3, 5, 16, 18, 43, 99, 101, 104, 108–9; Lebensraum policy, 97; Stalin's ambivalence toward, 87–89; submarines, 3, 13, 25, 27–28, 130; tensions in Soviet relations, 93–94; trade with Soviet Union, 90–91, 102; war against Poland, 6, 91
Gestapo, 90
Gleason, Everett, 102
Goddard, Robert, 3
Goebbels, Joseph, 27, 96
Gorchakov, Alexander, 61
Graves, William S., 78
Great Depression, 21
Great Patriotic War (Eastern Front), 9, 107–9; June 22, 1941 attack on Soviet Union, 3, 5, 16, 18, 43, 87, 99, 101, 104, 108–9. *See also* World War II
Greece, 41, 98
Greenland, 13
Groza, 17
GRU (military intelligence), 14, 40
Gulags, 91
Gwin, William M., 63

Hammer, Armand, 49–50
Harriman, Averell, 110, 111
Harrison, Mark, 29
Haushofer, Karl, 42

Hiss, Alger, 45
historians, Russian, ix–x, 7–9, 28, 93, 98;
History of the National Economy of Russia (Lyashchenko), 72
Hitler, Adolf, 2, 6, 14, 35–37; fear of American involvement, 21–22, 42–43; *Mein Kampf,* 95; Stalin's view of, 12, 88, 92–93, 104; U-boats and, 27–28
Hoover, Herbert, 66
Hopkins, Harry L., 9, 13, 23, 45–46, 49, 107, 110
House of Representatives, 66
Hull, Cordell, 48
human capital, 69–70, 83–84
Hungary, 108

Iceland, 13, 25, 116
"imperialists," Soviet view of, 15–16, 18, 53, 82
intelligence, Stalin's control of, 121–122
interwar period, 53–54
Iran, 111
Italy, 25, 47, 88
Ivanov, Robert, 31–32, 44–45, 50n2, 93, 94

Japan, 2, 6, 25, 44–45, 47, 95
Japanese-Soviet treaty of 1941, 1, 25, 101, 103, 113
Jebsen, Jan, 132
Jefferson, Thomas, 56, 63
Jews, 44
John Barry (ship), 129–33
Johnson, Andrew, 64
Johnston, Eric, 85
Jones, Robert H., 8, 29

Kaiser, Henry, 4
Karelia, 109
Kennan, George, 89
Khrushchev, Nikita S., 31, 86, 126
Klast, Horst, 132
Knowles, Tony, 2
Kolchak, Admiral, 78

Korean War, 16, 34, 121

Ladd Field, 114
Langer, William L., 102
Latvia, 109
League of Nations, 34
Lebensraum, 97
Ledyard, Jonathan, 63
Lend-Lease air routes, 112–14, 116–21 sea routes, 2, 4, 25–28, 113, 116, 120
Lend-Lease: agreements, 29n8, 115; aviation fuel, 8, 122, 134–35; to Britain, 4, 6, 22, 29n8, 100, 103–4; casualties, 26–27, 114–15, 118–19, 120; to China, 25, 29n8, 95; commemoration of, 1–2; deliveries, 25, 111, 113, 115–16; details, 115–21; early 1941 talks, 111–12; equipment losses, 27, 116, 118–19, 120; expenditures, 22–23, 25, 128; food aid, 9, 122–24, 148–49; items supplied, 9, 84–85, 107, 122–24; as life-saver, 7–9; mutual suspicion and, 124–26; negotiations, 34–36, 41, 46, 111; nineteenth-century roots, 52–64; origins of, 22–25; passage of, 13, 101, 115; planning routes, 112–14; political challenges, 4–6; random exports, 123, 147–51; repayment negotiations, 133–34; repayment of, 124, 128–29, 133–36; Roosevelt's order, 103; shipments by time period, cargo type, route, and tonnage, 141–44; Soviet propaganda, 28–29, 123, 126; Soviet stockpiling of, 121, 124; Stalin's decision-making procedures, 36–37; Stalin's gratitude for, 101–2, 107–8; as term, 110; trust and verification, 121–22; underway, 25–28. *See also* aircraft
Lenin, V. I., 18, 34, 37, 45, 47–48, 53; on America, 31, 52; view of Germany, 88, 89
Leningrad, 109
Liaison Committee, 13
Liberty Ships, 4, 113

Lincoln, Abraham, 60
Lithuania, 109
Litvinoff, Maxim, 31–32, 39, 43–44
London Disarmament Conference, 47
Lozovsky, S. A., 43–44, 104
Ludendorff, Chancellor, 88
Luftwaffe, 134–35
Lyashchenko, Peter I., 72

machinery, 9, 84–85, 122, 148, 149; agricultural, 70–71, 74–75. *See also* railroads
Madison, James, 57–58
Magenheimer, Heinz, 42, 90
Maisky, Ivan M., 44, 92, 97
Malenkov, Georgy, 37
Marcy, William L., 63
mariners, fatalities, 26–27
Marshall Plan, 48
Marx, Karl, 88
Marxist-Leninist ideology, 32, 33, 54
Matsuoka, Yasuke, 101
Maxwell, John S., 69
Mazuruk, Ilya, 117
McRoberts, Samuel, 79
Mein Kampf (Hitler), 95
memorials, 26–27
merchant ships, 13
Merkulov, V. N., 22
metals, 9, 84–85, 122–24, 149–50
military preparedness, 2–3
Ministry of Ways and Communications, 77
Moldavia, 109
Molotov, Vyacheslav, 96, 100, 103, 104; Berlin talks, 93–95; visit to U.S., 112–13
Molotov-Ribbentrop Non-Aggression and Friendship Pact. *See* Nazi-Soviet Pact of Nonaggression (1939)
Momp (Mid-Ocean Meeting Place), 4
Monroe, James, 57
Monroe Doctrine, 58, 59
Moore, Arthur, 130
moral embargo, 13
Moscow, 109
Munich Conference of 1938, 16, 17

Napoleon, 34, 35, 56, 57
National Archives, 124
national emergency, 13, 24–25
naval patrols, 13
Nazi-Soviet alliance, 12, 18, 87–92
Nazi-Soviet Pact of Nonaggression (1939), 14, 20, 24, 87–88, 90, 92, 97, 104
Nedoskin, Pavel, 117
neutrality, Soviet claims of, 17
neutrality, Soviet-Japanese agreement, 1, 25, 101, 103, 113
Neutrality Act, 6, 12, 24, 49
neutrality patrol, 3
New Order, 53
Niblo, Peter, 1, 49–50
Nicholas I, 60, 68–69
Nicholas II, 79
Nicolayevsky Railroad, 68–69
Niles' Register, 57–58
Nizhni-Novgorod fair, 76
NKVD-NKGB (civilian intelligence), 14, 19, 40, 90, 101; Silvermaster spy ring, 22, 23
North Atlantic Treaty Organization (NATO), 55

Ocean Group Consortium, 131
Office of Lend-Lease Administration, 23
Office of Strategic Services (OSS), 13
Oman, 131
Operation Barbarossa, 5, 97, 98, 105, 108–9
Operation Snow, 23
ordnance, 9
Ottoman empire, 60

Pacific and Baltic fleets (Russia), 61
Pacific Fleet, 2
Paine, Thomas, 55
Paul I, 59
Pearl Harbor, 2, 3, 12
peasants, 62, 71, 75–76
Peter the Great, 68
petroleum products, 122
Piskunov, Col., 114

"plutocrats," 18
Pokryshkin, Alexander, 124
Poland, 60–61, 91
Politburo, 36, 37
ports, 25, 79, 92. *See also* air routes; sea routes
Potsdam summit, 113
Pravda, 99, 103
Pravda o Velikoi Otechestvennoi Voine (Sokolov), 8–9
Pravitel'stvennii Vestnik, 72–73, 75, 76
prisoners of War, 109
proxy wars, 54
public opinion, United States, 24, 42, 61–63, 110, 125
Putin, Vladimir, 2, 128

Quadpartite Alliance, 20, 93
Quadrille of Europe, 55, 57

radar, 27
Radek, Karl, 88
radio communications, 118
Raeder, Admiral, 27
railroads, 9, 68–74, 91; Railway Advisory Commission, 77–78; Root Commission, 76–77; Trans-Siberian Railway, 73, 78, 113
Railway Advisory Commission, 77–78
Randolph, John, 60
Raymond, Ellsworth, 67
Red Army, 87, 109; pessimistic views of, 5–6, 110–11; Stalin's 1941 reception speech, 87, 96–97, 105–6n21
Ribbentrop, Joachim von, 11, 24, 103
Romania, 95, 108
Roosevelt, Eleanor, 45
Roosevelt, Franklin D., 3–4, 90, 105; announcement of aid to Soviet Union, 110; anti-Soviet statements, 14, 24, 102; on arsenal of democracy, 11, 110; authority of, 40–41; December 1940 public address, 115; positive view of Soviet Union, 5, 46, 90; quarantine speech, 12; Stalin and, 39–41; Stalin's view of, 15, 31, 43, 52; State of the Union address, 110; view of Soviet army, 5–6, 110–11; view of Stalin, 5, 15, 46, 129
Roosevelt Administration, 4, 90; preparations for war, 12–14; recognition of U.S.S.R. as state, 32, 47, 54, 67, 82. *See also* United States
Roosevelt and Hopkins (Sherwood), 47
Root Commission, 76–77
Royal Canadian Navy, 3–4
Russia: financial reforms, 71–72; goal of economic self-sufficiency, 65–66; nineteenth-century relations with America, 55–58; nineteenth-century relations with Britain, 55–57; peasants, 62, 71, 75–76. *See also* Soviet Union; U.S.-Russian relations
Russia in Transition: A Businessman's Appraisal (Friedman), 83
Russian American Company, 59, 63
Russian Railway Service Corp, 78
Russo-American Black Sea Steamship Line, 75
Russo-American Treaty of Commerce and Navigation, 60
Russo-Japanese War, 57

Sacred Secrets: How Soviet Intelligence Operations Changed American History (Schechter and Schechter), 103–4
Schechter, Jerrold, 103
Schechter, Leona, 103
Schellenberg, Walter, 52
Schoeppe, Bill, 114, 124
sea routes, 2, 4, 25–28, 113, 116, 120
Secrets of the Second World War (Sokolov), 28–29
September 11 terrorist attacks, 2
serfs, 62, 71
Seward, William H., 61, 63–64
Seward's Folly, 59, 63–64
Sherwood, Robert, 47
Shoemaker, Brian, 130–31
Siberia, air bases, 113
silver bouillon, 129–33

Silvermaster spy ring, 22, 23
Simonov, Konstantin, 134
SLOCs, 2
Small Soviet Encyclopedia, 66
Sokolov, Boris Vadimovich, 8–9, 28–29, 29n1
Soviet Acquisition Commission, 115, 120
Soviet foreign policy: chess analogy, 33–35, 46–47; diplomacy, 32–34, 38–39, 95; world domination plans, 19, 32–34, 36, 39, 53–55
Soviet-German talks (1940), 20
Soviet-Japanese neutrality agreement, 1, 25, 101, 103, 113
Soviet propaganda, 8–9, 66, 80; anti-Stalin, 19; on Axis, 16–17, 20; defensiveness, 16–17; against "imperialism," 15–16, 18, 53, 82; on Lend-Lease, 13, 28–29, 126; on Western states, 16–18
Soviet Purchasing Commission, 114
Soviet Union: agents of influence, 7, 41–49; America as distant from, 89–90; Americans as factor for, 14–15; demarche toward West, 103–5; espionage in Britain, 44, 103–4; German attack on, June 22, 1941, 3, 5, 16, 18, 43, 87, 99, 101, 104, 108–9; industrialization, 14, 20–21, 48, 65–66, 68; Marxist-Leninist ideology, 32, 33, 54; positive view of America, 38, 43, 94–95, 99; Roosevelt's view of, 5–6; Russian-American economic ties, 65–66; secrecy, 121–22, 125; tensions with Germany, 93–94; trade with Germany, 90–91, 102; warnings of attack on, 97–101. *See also* Russia; Soviet foreign policy; Stalin, Joseph; U.S.-Russian relations; Western-Soviet relations
soyuz, 19–20
Stalin, Joseph, 9; 1941 Red Army reception speech, 87, 96–97, 105–6n21; admiration for Hopkins, 45, 46; ambivalence toward Germany, 87–89; brutality of, 37, 46; burglar analogy for, 33, 41; chess analogy for, 33–35, 46–47; Churchill's view of, 5, 33, 41; conflicting views of America, 15–18, 40–41, 85n2; contradictory behavior, 15–18, 33–35; control of intelligence, 121–22; curiosity about foreign countries, 35–36; decision-making procedures, 36–37; on defensive strategy, 16–17; diplomacy and, 33, 38–39, 95; gratitude for Lend-Lease aid, 101–2, 107–8; ignores warnings of attack, 97, 98–99; memory, 31, 36, 47; nationalism of, 48–49; post-invasion speech (1941), 19–20, 95; realism of, 31–32, 36; on Roosevelt, 31, 52; Roosevelt and, 39–41; Roosevelt's view of, 5, 15, 46, 129; shift toward West, 14–15, 46, 94–95, 102; suspicion of Britain, 43–44, 90; suspiciousness, 37, 43–44, 92–93, 99, 101, 104; on technological assistance, 81–82; two-pronged approach, 18–20; view of democratic countries, 41–42; view of Hitler, 12, 88, 92–93, 104; view of "imperialists," 15–16, 18; view of Roosevelt, 15, 31, 43, 43; view of U.S.-Soviet alliance, 14–15, 19–20; withdraws from public view, 19, 87; work ethic, 37–38. *See also* Soviet Union
Stalin i Soyuzniki 1941–1945 (Ivanov), 94
Stalin's Silver (Beasant), 130–131
State Committee for Defense, 116
State Department, 5, 124
Stavka, 36
Steinhardt, Lawrence A., 43, 100, 104
Stettinius, Edward R., Jr., 23
Stevens, John F., 77, 78
Stoeckl, Edward von, 63
submarines, 3, 13, 25, 27–28, 130
subversion, 32, 53
Sudoplatov, Pavel, 34, 45, 87
Supreme Court, 41

Taubman, William, 31
technological assistance: agricultural machinery, 70–71, 74–76; earliest period, 68–71; human capital, 69–70, 83–84; miscellaneous aid, 78–80; nineteenth and twentieth centuries, 71–80; official Soviet figures, 84; quotations from Soviet sources, 80–82; during Soviet period, 80–85; Stalin on, 81–82; U.S. businessmen and, 82–83. *See also* railroads
technology, 123
Tehran Conference, 130
"They and We" (Ilf and Petrov), 83
Third Communist International (Comintern), 19, 53, 92
tonnage, 25–28, 152
Topitsch, Ernst, 93
Trans-Siberian Railway, 73, 78, 113
Treasury Department, 7
Trenchant, HMS, 132–33
Tripartite Pact, 103
Truman, Harry S., 5, 43–44, 121
Turkey, 60, 93
Turkish Straits, 94, 98

U-boats. *See* submarines
Uita decryption process, 97
Ukraine, 48, 109
"Ultra," 97
Umansky, Konstantin, 99–103
United States: anti-Communism, 14, 24; defense production, 2–3, 21–22; economic ties with Russia, 48, 65–68; economy, 15, 20–22; interwar period, 53–54; isolationism, 2, 12, 24, 31, 47, 53–54, 89, 110; national emergency, 13, 24–25; Northwest, 58–59; preparations for war, 12–14; presidential system, 40–41; public opinion, 24, 42, 61–63, 110, 125; Soviet sympathies toward, 38, 43, 94–95, 99. *See also* Roosevelt, Franklin D.; Roosevelt Administration

UNRRA, 48
uranium shipment, 122
U.S. Advisory Commission for the Council of National Defense, 13
U.S.-Russian relations: American Civil War and, 59–63; American Northwest and, 58–59; geopolitical factors, 54–55; history of, 48–49; nineteenth century, 55–58; pre-June 1941, 44–45, 50n2; repayment of Lend-Lease, 134–36; Russian-American economic ties, 65–68; slavery-serfdom comparison, 62, 71; technological assistance, 67–76; traditional ties, 54–55; warming of in late 1940, 92–93; Welles-Umansky talks, 99–103. *See also* railroads; technological assistance; United States
Ushakov, Yuri, 2

vehicles, 8–9, 146–47
Venona Papers, 23, 45
Versailles Treaty, 88
Vladivostok, 77–78

Wall Street crash of 1929, 47, 53
War Department, 5, 77, 110
War of 1812, 57–58
War Office (Britain), 110
Warsaw Pact, 55
War Shipping Administration (WSA), 131
weather conditions, 116–19
Weeks, Albert L., 10n1, 29n5, 50nn3, 4, 64n1, 85n1, 105n7
Wehrmacht, 5, 108
Welles, Sumner, 99–103
Welles-Umansky talks, 99–103
Wells, H. G., 15
Western-Soviet relations, 86–87; demarche, 103–5; Nazi-Soviet alliance and, 90–92; pre-invasion détente trend, 96–98; Stalin's ambivalence toward Germany, 87–89; Stalin's shift toward West,

14–15, 92–95; tensions with Germany, 92–93; warnings of attack and, 97–101
Westomp (Western Ocean Meeting Place), 4
Wheeler, Burton K., 22
Whistler, George Washington, 69–70
White, Harry Dexter, 23, 45
Wilson, Woodrow, 77
Winter War, 39, 110–11
Witte, Sergius, 71–72
wolf packs, 4
World War I, 21, 54, 77, 89
World War II: Battle of the Atlantic, 3–4; Eastern Front, 5–6, 9, 107–9, 129; June 22, 1941 attack on Soviet Union, 3, 5, 16, 18, 43, 87, 99, 101, 104, 108–9; Operation Barbarossa, 5, 97, 98, 105, 108–9; Pearl Harbor, 2, 3, 12; Western Front, 129; Winter War, 39, 110–11

Yalta Conference, 35, 49, 130
Yeltsin, Boris, 59
Yemen, 131
Yugoslavia, 41, 98

Zhukov, Georgy, 86, 134; on Lend-Lease importance to the U.S.S.R, x, 1

About the Author

Dr. Albert L. Weeks, professor emeritus of New York University, is the author of several books on Russia and international affairs. His latest, *Stalin's Other War: Soviet Grand Strategy, 1939–1941*, was published by Rowman & Littlefield in 2002. In his present study on Lend-Lease aid, Weeks, who is fluent in Russian, has used the latest statistics on this wartime assistance as well Russian archive material. Revised assessments of the importance of this aid to Russia, as found in Weeks's book, is based on new findings by post-Soviet Russian historians. Himself a lieutenant in the USAF in World War II, the author flew in some of the aircraft sent to the U.S.S.R. under Lend-Lease during the war.